THE LAW OF TREASON IN ENGLAND
IN THE LATER MIDDLE AGES

CAMBRIDGE STUDIES
IN ENGLISH LEGAL HISTORY

Edited by
D. E. C. YALE
Fellow of Christ's College, Cambridge,
and Reader in English Legal History;
Barrister-at-Law, Inner Temple

THE LAW OF TREASON
IN ENGLAND
IN THE
LATER MIDDLE AGES

BY

J. G. BELLAMY

Associate Professor of History
Carleton University, Ottawa

CAMBRIDGE
AT THE UNIVERSITY PRESS
1970

Published by the Syndics of the Cambridge University Press
Bentley House, 200 Euston Road, London, N.W.1
American Branch: 32 East 57th Street, New York, N.Y. 10022

Library of Congress Catalogue Card Number: 70–111123

Standard Book Number: 521 07830 X

Printed in Great Britain
at the University Press, Aberdeen

CONTENTS

EDITOR'S PREFACE

'Treason', wrote Maitland,[1] 'has a history all of its own.' Nevertheless that history has not previously received connected and comprehensive study in the literature of legal history, and it is therefore with the greatest pleasure that my first duty as general editor of this series of studies is to commend to all those interested Professor Bellamy's survey of the subject at large over the span of the thirteenth, fourteenth and fifteenth centuries.

The history of the law of treason has diverse origins and its story many turning points. One of the most critical occurred in the period with which this book is concerned, that is, the Statute of Treasons of 1352. As Plucknett[2] has remarked, 'the history of treason in the middle ages is as distinctive as the nature of the offence. It is one of the very few crimes which were defined by statute during this period; and it is one of the equally few crimes whose scope was extended by "construction". Unlike treason, the medieval felony was (generally speaking) neither statutory nor constructive'.

But the clear difference between treason and felony is the outcome of time and of refinement by lawgivers and lawyers. The further back in time we go, the less distinct do the lines of difference appear and indeed in the feudal dawn they vanish away. Originally the idea of felony included much of what later became separate categories of treason, for in origin felony denoted a breach of feudal faith or fidelity on account of which the vassal's fee or tenement escheated to his lord. As the notion of felony was extended to the more serious kinds of crime, so the incidence of escheat multiplied; or we may with equal plausibility regard the widening of the incidence of escheat as extending the scope of felony beyond its earliest feudal context. Indeed if as a matter of historical development the legal effect dictated the classification, it is possible to see the points of definition as so many attempts to reach grounds of compromise between the conflicting claims of feudal escheat and royal forfeiture. Thus if the statute of 1352 can be regarded as 'a rude compromise',[3] then it bears some

---

[1] Pollock and Maitland, *History of English Law*, II, 502.

[2] *Concise History of the Common Law*, p. 443.

[3] Such was Maitland's view. Pollock and Maitland, II, 508. But Professor Bellamy, pp. 21–2, sees less force in the economic considerations of forfeiture.

resemblance to the concession made by King John in his Great Charter[1] where he promised that he would not retain the lands of those 'qui convicti fuerint de felonia nisi per unum annum et unum diem, et tunc reddantur terre dominis feodorum'. Here then, as Maitland believed, was one peculiarly strong incentive to formulate a law of treason, 'for if there was any crime which would give the offender's land not to his lord but to the king, that crime could not be a mere *felonia*'. So treason was felony but more than felony, and long after the categories had become divided, the lawyers moved by unconscious instincts of the past wrote both words, treason and felony, into their indictments. As late as the eighteenth century Blackstone,[2] after noticing that the words of the statute of 1352 provide that parliament may declare of future dubious crimes 'whether they be treason or *other* felony', remarks that 'all treasons therefore, strictly speaking, are felonies, though all felonies are not treason'.

It is clear that the general idea of treason and the particular understanding of the 1352 Act must 'accommodate what came to be known as petty treason'.[3] The Act specified as 'another sort' of treason the killing of a husband by a wife, of a master by his servant, and the killing of a prelate by his subject, secular or religious. But there was no inclusion of the killing of a feudal lord by his vassal or tenant. The omission has often been remarked. 'Perhaps', suggests Professor Milsom,[4] 'the original sense of felony was too well remembered'. Certainly royal forfeiture never reached into the last enclaves of the feudal world, the unfree or customary lands within the lord's manor, and this sanctuary of feudal society remained untouched, for as Hale[5] wrote long after feudal principles had been shut into the closed community of each manor, 'an attainder of treason or felony of a copyholder gives the king no forfeiture, but regularly it belongs to the lord unless special custom be to the contrary'. And that was, it seems, a general rule applicable to all treasons, greater or lesser. Now the lesser treasons set out in the Act gave escheat to the lord, not forfeiture to the king,[6] and as Professor Bellamy[7] reminds us, 'the

[1] Ch. 32.   [2] Comm. IV. 94–5.
[3] Milsom, *Historical Foundations of the Common Law*, p. 370.
[4] *Ibid.*   [5] *Pleas of the Crown*, I, 360.
[6] Other differences included the difference that petty treason was clergyable till 1497. High treason lost that privilege much earlier. Pollock and Maitland, I, 446: 'It is probable that already in the thirteenth century a clerk charged with

process of trial in cases of petty treason was like that for any other felony'. The difference lay in the mode of capital punishment. Thus in the account of a trial of a servant indicted for wounding and robbing his master as related in *Placita Corone*[1] at the end of the thirteenth century, the judge dwells on the treasonable nature of the offence, yet 'the prisoner is sentenced merely to be hanged, which he deserved for the theft alone, whereas had the case been regarded as one of completed petit treason, we should have expected some sort of additional punishment, such as drawing'. If the servant had killed his master, doubtless he would have suffered a traitor's death. But he did not; nevertheless the judge insists on his treason.

But these difficulties are of our own making. Treason later became a category of crime, or after the Act the lawyers came to think of two categories of treason, and there is a gap fixed between felonies and treasons. These categories however are the product of time and change. The idea of treason as a type of crime was only formed by degrees and the further one goes behind the Act so the entity fades and the list collected in the Act and in earlier texts becomes dispersed, and those parts which are attributable to feudal origins lose their identity in the original felony. The 'petty' traitor is guilty of aggravated felony. The homicides which are collected in the Act (apart from those striking at regal government) are merely those forms of aggravated or atrocious treachery to which the name of treason is attached for the sake of the severer

high treason, at all events with one of the worst forms of high treason, such as imagining the king's death or levying war against him, would in vain have relied on the liberties of the church'. In this connexion it is worth noticing that when Thomas Merks, bishop of Carlisle and courageous adherent of Richard II, claimed in 1401 (KB. Roll, no. 559, m.4, crown) that he was an anointed bishop and should not be arraigned before royal justices, the reply was: 'super quo dictum est ei per eosdem iusticiarios quod premissa in indictamento predicto contenta tangunt mortem domini regis et destruccionem totius regni Anglie et consequenter ecclesie anglicane, per quem se clamat privilegiari, depressionem et subversionem manifestam, que omnia et singula alta et maxima proditio sunt et crimen lese majestatis, nec debet quisquam de iure legis auxilium petere nec habere qui in ea peccatum committit seu intendit committere . . .'. The justices may not have had in mind the phrase of D. 48.4.1.pr: 'Proximum sacrilegio crimen est quod majestatis dicitur', but the idea behind the concluding words has an interesting history in civilian and canonist literature. See (1969) 85 *Law Quarterly Review*, 472.

[7] Appendix II, p. 230.

---

[1] Selden Society, supplementary series, 4, 21–2, and Mr Kaye's comments at pp. xxxvi–xxxvii.

punishment, at the same time ensuring that they shall not be within the reach of royal forfeiture.

The Act of 1352 defined treasons and yet left open the limits of definition.[1] Into the statutory definitions went many different ingredients, both feudal and imperial. But the statutory definition was a legal and not a political definition. To borrow Professor Bellamy's words,[2] 'in England during the later middle ages there existed not one but two doctrines of treason side by side. One doctrine was the one which has been the concern of this volume, the law of treason as seen through the eyes of the king and his legal advisers. The other was the theory of treason of the barons and to a lesser extent of the people'. This other doctrine was founded on a notion of the unity of the nation, *rex* set against *regnum*, the king against the crown, and with this notion went the charges of accroaching royal power. But it was a doctrine only emerging in times of turmoil. *'Seditio regni'*, to borrow the phrase in Glanvill,[3] is not in the Act of 1352, and the later lawyers repudiated with all their vigour 'the seditious doctrine of the Despencers' that 'homage and the oath of allegiance are more in respect of the crown than in respect of the king's person and are more closely related to the crown than the king's person; and this is evident because before the right to the crown has descended to the person, no allegiance is due to him'.[4] The lawyers who developed the doctrine of double capacities in the fifteenth century and further developed in the sixteenth century that doctrine with quasi-theological fervour[5] rejected its application to the law of treason.[6]

---

[1] The reserved power to declare new forms of treasons is one source of the parliamentary attainders of the fifteenth century, as Professor Bellamy demonstrates in Ch. 7. More generally, the reservation to parliament accounts largely for the later developments being legislative rather than judicial in character.

[2] Pp. 209–10.

[3] I. 2, also XIV. 1: 'Crimen quod in legibus dicitur lese maiestas, ut de nece vel seditione persone domini regis vel regni vel exercitus.'

[4] The opening words of the 'alleged' articles against Gavaston in 1308. The text is now set out in Richardson and Sayles, *The Governance of Medieval England*, Appendix VII, at pp. 467 and 469. For the authors' view on the authenticity of the text, *ibid.* p. 15. But whatever its authenticity, there can be no doubt as to its later influence and importance.

[5] E. H. Kantorowicz, *The King's Two Bodies, a Study in Medieval Political Theology*, explores the medieval background. A further study is in Richardson and Sayles, *The Medieval Governance of England*, Ch. VII, 'The Undying King'.

[6] The extremes to which such 'seditious doctrine' could lead can be seen in

The metaphysical reasoning of Coke in *Calvin's case*[1] that treason, being to 'intend or compass *mortem et destruccionem domini regis*, (which must needs be understood of his natural body, for his politic body is immortal, and not subject to death)' reflects in figurative language[2] the much more down to earth attitude of the medieval lawyers. As Maitland[3] wrote, 'the medieval king was every inch a king, but just for that reason he was every inch a man and you did not talk nonsense about him. You did not ascribe to him immortality or ubiquity or such powers as no mortal can wield. If you said that he was Christ's vicar, you meant what you said, and you might add that he would become the servant of the devil if he declined towards tyranny. And there was little cause for ascribing to him more than one capacity.' The medieval lawyers found some causes for contrasting the office of king and the office-holder, but practically none in the field of treason.[4] Still less did they indulge in artificial jurisprudence to the degree of raising the crown to the status of a corporation sole, though the king might be a part, the head, of a truly collective

the parliamentary justification for waging war against Charles I and indeed the theory upon which the king was accused of treason in 1649.

---

[1] 7 Co. Rep. at p. 10 b. And Coke adds, since the indictment concludes *contra ligeantiae suae debitum*, therefore 'the ligeance is due to the natural body'.

[2] The Elizabethan judges used metaphorical language of some extravagance. *Willion v. Berkley* (1561) Plowden 238, and the *Case of the Duchy of Lancaster* (1561) Plowden 212 reveal most clearly what Kantorowicz calls the 'monophysitic' leanings of the Elizabethan judiciary.

[3] *The Crown as Corporation*, Collected Papers, III at p. 246.

[4] Stephen, *History of the Criminal Law of England*, II, 254, n.2, says of the statute 11 Hen. 7, c. 1 that 'this statute may perhaps be regarded as the earliest recognition to be found in English law of a possible difference between the person and the office of the king, though nothing can be more vague and indirect than the way in which the distinction is hinted at by the words "king and sovereign lord of this land for the time being".' For a thorough review and reinterpretation of the purpose of this statute, see A. M. Honoré, 'Allegiance and the usurper', (1967) *Cambridge Law Journal*, p. 214. The author is surely correct in believing that the statute's phrase "king for the time being" does not mean a king *de facto*, but simply means the person who is king at any given time. But the author's view that Henry and his parliament contemplated within that description a future king whose title (on Henry's view) would be illegitimate, and who would therefore be a usurper, is very hard to accept. For reasons which cannot here be developed it seems more likely that the statute was thoroughly 'lancastrian' in intention and purpose, and that Henry meant by "king for the time being" himself and his successors whose titles were (from his own dynastic standpoint) legitimate. Coke and other lawyers reading the text in later ages interpreted it in a manner which turned allegiance in this context into 'a shifting sand'.

body, a corporation in aggregate. As Fineux C. J. said in 1522,[1] 'the parliament of the king and the lords and the commons are a corporation'. As was a lord or a commoner, so also was the feudal king a man, and while 'the practical application of the feudal theory of kingship in England . . . accounted for the development of representation', so on a more theoretical level, ideas of royal theocracy were kept in check as long as the king remained in any real sense a feudal overlord. 'The feudal side of the king made him, as it were, human. . . .'[2]

But if the feudal idea of kingship left indelible marks on the medieval law of treason, it cannot satisfactorily and fully account for the nature of treason as a crime. Feudal allegiance was essentially conditional and might be withdrawn by renunciation. And similarly a seizure by a feudal lord might be conditional upon a return to allegiance. When after the loss of Normandy King John seized the English lands of his Norman nobles who had adhered to the king of France, those seizures were conditional sequestrations, 'donec terrae fuerint communes', until the Normans shall have returned to their allegiance. It was only after long lapse of time and the loss grew permanent, that they hardened into full and irretrievable forfeitures.[3] Yet from the earliest times the Norman kings had endeavoured to impose allegiance without restriction to the feudal relationships of tenure. Homage or the act of commendation was not allowed to stand in the way, and even before liege homage had become owed to the king alone, the oaths of fidelity or allegiance had been exacted from all men.[4] The idea of ligeancy was at the core of the matter, as the lawyers recognized when every indictment for treason charged a breach of the duty of allegiance, *contra ligeantiae suae debitum*. So as a matter of public law and duty, homage became something of an irrelevance. 'Homage did not bind men closer to their lord or

[1] YB. Mich. 14 H. VIII, f. 3, pl. 2.
[2] W. Ullmann, *A History of Political Thought in the Middle Ages*, Ch. 5 (III), 'Kingship in England and Constitutionalism', pp. 145–58.
[3] The apocryphal statute *De Prerogativa Regis* c. 14, speaks of forfeiture. For this change and its significance, see Pollock and Maitland, I, 461–4, II, 501–2.
[4] Ganshof, *Feudalism*, pp. 165–6, writes that 'the idea behind these oaths was subsequently influenced by the idea of ligeancy, and one came to term all those who had taken them the liegemen of the king. In the reign of Henry I the crown insisted that a reservation of fealty should form part of the ordinary oath of vassalage'.

introduce a new concept of fidelity. Men followed their lord to the
death—or betrayed him—after the Conquest as they had done
before. Liege homage to the king stands apart; but with or without
the ceremony of homage the duty of the subject would remain.'[1]
The relationship of king and subject prevailed over that of lord and
man, and the growth of the duty of allegiance both instilled and
distilled the nascent ideas of nationality and alienage.

   Professor Bellamy in summing up the sources of the medieval
concept of treason concludes[2] that 'the English law of treason of
the later middle ages was founded on a Germanic base but contained also much that was derived either from the law of classical
Rome or from contemporary European practice'. The idea of
treachery and betrayal was certainly at the centre, or at one of the
centres,[3] but the further question arises, who or what is betrayed
or is the object of treason. The answer of the medieval lawyers
was, the king or regal government, but as this book truly shows,
the answer however it was formulated in law reflected a political
position, not merely a theory of kingship nor always the policies
of particular kings, but the constant practical need to produce
public order. The law of treason in the later middle ages was
necessarily created as the feudal organization of society decayed
and as the feudal state was replaced by sovereignty.

D. E. C. YALE

[1] Richardson and Sayles, *The Governance of Medieval England*, p. 112.
[2] P. 14.
[3] Maitland's geometrical figure which Professor Bellamy chooses as his
opening words.

PREFACE

My interest in the history of medieval treason dates back ten years or more and sprang, I believe, from my early postgraduate training under Professor J. S. Roskell. I began serious investigation in 1961 and continued thereafter whenever the exigencies of teaching and academic administration allowed. Much of the present book was offered as a thesis for the degree of Ph.D. of the University of Nottingham. This work was supervised by Dr R. L. Storey, who gladly undertook the task of guidance in a field that was at first unfamiliar to him and did so in a manner which was encouraging, stimulating and most effective. His deep knowledge of the Public Records was an immense boon and his criticism, ever friendly, not less so.

My gratitude is also extended to Professor S. F. C. Milsom, whose valuable advice has saved me from more than one serious error, to the General Editor of this Series, Mr D. E. C. Yale, who pointed out certain omissions, and to my wife, for her continuous encouragement.

Although I have felt it necessary to go back as far as the laws of classical Rome by way of introduction, this book is concerned in essence with the period from the middle of the thirteenth century to the end of the fifteenth, the prelude to the great treason statute of 1352 and the aftermath. I feel no obligation to justify the importance of the theme. No one studying the constitutional, the legal, or the political history of later medieval England can fail to be impressed by the vital role of treason in the development of concepts and institutions in this period. Whether I have been able to do the subject justice is another matter.

Transcripts and translations of Crown-copyright records in the Public Record Office appear by permission of the Controller of H.M. Stationery Office.

Carleton University, Ottawa   J. G. B.
June 1969

ABBREVIATIONS

Bracton	*Henrici de Bracton de Legibus et Consuetudinibus Angliae.* References are to the edition of G. E. Woodbine (New Haven, 1915–42), unless stated otherwise.
Britton	*Britton.* Ed. F. M. Nichols (Oxford, 1865).
Cal. Chanc. Rolls	*Calendar of . . . Various Chancery Rolls.*
Cal. Close Rolls	*Calendar of . . . Close Rolls.*
Cal. Docs. Scot.	*Calendar of Documents relating to Scotland.* Ed. J. Bain (Edinburgh, 1881–4).
Cal. Pat. Rolls	*Calendar of . . . Patent Rolls.*
Camden Soc.	Camden Society.
Coke	E. Coke, *The Third Part of the Institutes of the Laws of England* (London, 1797).
Eng. Hist. Rev.	*English Historical Review.*
Fleta	*Fleta, II, Prologue, Bk. I, Bk. II.* Ed. H. G. Richardson and G. O. Sayles (Seld. Soc., 1953).
Hale	M. Hale, *Historia Placitorum Coronae: the History of the Pleas of the Crown.* Ed. Sollom Emlyn (London). The edition of 1778 has been used unless stated otherwise.
K.B. 9	King's Bench, Ancient Indictments (in the P.R.O.).
K.B. 27	King's Bench, Coram Rege Rolls (in the P.R.O.).
Mirror	*The Mirror of Justices.* Ed. W. J. Whittaker (Seld. Soc., 1895).
Pollock and Maitland	F. Pollock and F. W. Maitland, *The History of English Law before the time of Edward I* (Cambridge, 1895).
P.R.O.	Public Record Office, London.
Procs. and Ords.	*Proceedings and Ordinances of the Privy Council.* Ed. N. H. Nicolas (Rec. Comm., 1834–7).
Rec. Comm.	Record Commission.
Rot. Parl.	*Rotuli Parliamentorum.* Ed. J. Strachey and others (London, 1767).
R.S.	Rolls Series.
Seld. Soc.	Selden Society.
Stat. Realm	*Statutes of the Realm* (Rec. Comm., 1810–28).
Stow	J. Stow, *Annales or a Generall Chronicle of England.* Ed. E. Howes (London, 1631).

Trans. Roy. Hist. Soc.	*Transactions of the Royal Historical Society.*
Year Books	*Les Reports del Cases en Ley.* References are to the edition of Sawbridge, Rawlins and Roycroft (London, 1678–9), unless stated otherwise.
Year Books, Liver des Assises	*Le Liver des assises et plees del Corone* within the same edition of *Les Reports del Cases en Ley.*

I

THE MEDIEVAL CONCEPT OF TREASON

'TREASON', said Maitland, 'is a crime which has a vague circumference and more than one centre'.[1] The law of treason which operated in England in the later middle ages had two major centres or elements, the Germanic and the Roman. This was also true of the treason laws of continental Europe, where the relative importance of the two components varied from state to state and even from province to province. The Germanic element was founded on the idea of betrayal or breach of trust [*treubruch*] by a man against his lord, while the Roman stemmed from the notion of *maiestas*, insult to those with public authority. *Seditio* is the word often associated in medieval writings with the Germanic concept, *laesa maiestatis* with the Roman. From the time of the collapse of the Roman Empire in the west in the fifth century, the Germanic idea of breach of trust was in retreat before the intellectually more advanced although partially conflicting notion of loss of majesty. As the invading peoples established primitive states they absorbed the atmosphere of *Romanitas* and their rulers assumed the dignities which they felt were suited to the successors of the Roman Emperors. To emulate Roman imperial style, as was often the aim, meant also to adopt in some degree the ideas of Roman law.

The laws of the Anglo-Saxons were affected by this process more slowly than those of most other Germanic peoples. What Roman influence there was may have been conveyed to England through the medium of the church. But even among the Anglo-Saxons pure Germanic treason, wherein loyalty to the lord was all and there were no special sanctions against hostility directed towards the king, can hardly ever have existed. The earliest of Anglo-Saxon law collections admitted the notion that it was a crime to violate the king's peace and by the time of the laws of Ine the idea had arisen that such crimes were unamendable and should be dealt with by the king because they were in contempt of him.[2] The first recognizable reference to treason itself was in the laws of Alfred, which separated

[1] Pollock and Maitland, II, 503.
[2] W. S. Holdsworth, *History of English Law* (3rd edn, London, 1923), II, 48–9.

plotting against the life of the lord from plotting against the life of the king: perhaps the earliest mention of what were later called high and petty treason. The same laws showed a definite Roman influence by their mention not only of open act of treason but also of the plotting of such a deed, a conception which figured in the law of *maiestas*.[1] The laws of later Saxon kings, those of Athelstan and Edgar, referred to plotting against lords in general rather than specifically against the king. Exceptional were the laws of Ethelred and Cnut, which clearly set out the procedure to be followed in rebutting charges of high treason, that is to say against the monarch.[2] Important for the later history of treason was also the law of Ethelred which allocated for the crime of false moneying the same processes and penalties as undergone by traitors.[3]

Obviously the Anglo-Saxons, like the other Germanic peoples, although not perhaps to the same degree, were influenced by the ideas of Roman law, and their notions of treason were affected by the concept of *maiestas*. This offence was created in the third century before Christ as a protection against the impugning of the authority of plebeian officials by insult or personal injury.[4] The crime was an amalgam of a number of different ideas. There was the misdeed of *perduellio*, that is to say an act often military in character which was hostile to the state: for example, deserting it or comforting or aiding the enemy. There were acts contrary to the constitution of the state, acts of maladministration by magistrates, the violation of civic duties both secular and religious, and personal injury done to magistrates. There was also a category of *maiestas* which included all types of insult to the emperor, for example by wearing the imperial purple, destroying a statue of the emperor, committing adultery with a princess of the imperial family, using divination, soothsayers or horoscopes to discover the future in matters of state or concerning the imperial family, and counterfeiting the emperor's image on coins.[5] Nearly all of these

---

[1] *The Laws of the Earliest English Kings*, ed. F. L. Attenborough (Cambridge, 1922), pp. 64–7.

[2] F. S. Lear, *Treason in Roman and Germanic Law* (Austin, 1965), pp. 188–9; *Laws of the Earliest English Kings*, ed. Attenborough, pp. 130–1; *The Laws of the Kings of England from Edmund to Henry I*, ed. A. J. Robertson (Cambridge, 1925), pp. 26–7, 86–7, 206–7.

[3] Lear, *Treason*, pp. 189–90; *Laws of the Kings of England*, ed. Robertson, pp. 68–9.

[4] Lear, *Treason*, pp. 11–12.

[5] *Ibid.*, pp. 26–9.

Roman ideas were to reappear in the laws of the European states of the later middle ages, as were details of interpretation, such as the blurring of the distinction between intent and actual deed, details of procedure, such as trial of the accused even after death, and details of penalty, like the damnation of the traitor's memory, the confiscation of his property, the denial to his heirs of their inheritance and the treating of failure to reveal traitorous plots as actual complicity. These laws of treason of classical Rome were confirmed by Justinian in the severer form which they had assumed in the later years of the Roman Empire in the west, and through his *Corpus Juris Civilis* were readily available to the lawyers of later centuries.

From the sixth to the eleventh centuries in Europe, as in England, the Roman theory of *maiestas* influenced codes which were basically Germanic but it never succeeded in supplanting the more primitive ideas of treason. The medieval mind was hardly mature enough to understand and apply the concepts of Rome and the unsophisticated nature of government did not suggest much need for Roman public law. The law collections which showed greatest debt to Roman law in general and to Roman treason in particular were probably the Visigothic *Breviary*, the Burgundian *Papian*, the *Leges Alammanorum* and the *Leges Baiuvariorum*. The lesemajesty of Rome, despite a fleeting appearance in the capitularies of Charlemagne,[1] did not figure significantly in law again until the revival of classical learning in the twelfth century. This heralded the renewed study of Roman law, which was a prime requisite for the development of new concepts of treason.

From the time of Archbishop Theobald, perhaps even before, Englishmen went abroad to study Roman law. Bologna was especially favoured and some, like John of Tilbury and Richard de Morins, were probably good enough to teach there. Nearly all of them returned later on to their own country and it must have been partly on their account that the teaching of Roman law began to flourish at Oxford, Northampton and other centres.[2] By the later twelfth century many ecclesiastical libraries were provided with a good number of books on Roman law, although rather on the

---

[1] *Monumenta Germaniae Historica* (*Legum, Sectio II, tomus i*), ed. A. Boretius (Hanover, 1883), p. 205.

[2] H. G. Richardson and G. O. Sayles, *Law and Legislation from Aethelberht to Magna Carta* (Edinburgh, 1966), pp. 71–3.

medieval than the classical variety.[1] A demand for the purer text of Justinian was first noticed towards the end of the reign of Henry II: it must have arisen from study in greater depth. From about 1160 there was some competition among prominent ecclesiastics to acquire the services of those skilled in the Roman law, the *jurisperiti*, but in fact outside the jurisdiction of the church courts there were to be few opportunities for the civilian in England. There was nothing approaching a twelfth-century reception of Roman law. The influence exerted on the common law was not decisive. For a time technical terms from the laws of Justinian were applied to English law, but then the limitations on the use of words which were not the precise equivalent of the original English were discovered, and the move towards conversion ceased.[2] How far the thoughts of English common lawyers engaged on a particular problem were influenced by a knowledge of Roman law, either that of Justinian or of their own age, there is no way of telling.

Those who wrote treatises on legal matters were more likely than most to be affected by Roman law. The author known as Glanvill was patently influenced by Roman manuals of procedure, the *ordines judiciarii*, although in arrangement rather than content, where there was little direct borrowing. Always he bore in mind the practices of the king's courts and, unlike Bracton later on, he did not insert whole passages from civilian and canon law. When he came to deal with treason he showed clearly that the civilian crime of lese-majesty was in his mind. He referred to the crime 'quod in legibus dicitur lese maiestatis':[3] the 'leges' must have been the Roman laws. Two elements of the offence were the killing or the sedition, that is the betrayal, of the king. For these an Anglo-Saxon origin seems very likely. The betrayal of the realm and of the army, which follow, are not so easily explained. The treason *seditio regni* was not one commonly mentioned by subsequent writers. It appeared in the works of only two of the English thirteenth-century legal treatises, in *Fleta* and in the *Summae* of Ralph Hengham.[4] Whence it derived is difficult to decide. Perhaps

---

[1] *Royal Writs in England from the Conquest to Glanvill*, ed. R. C. Van Caeneghem (Seld. Soc., 1959), pp. 367–70.

[2] Richardson and Sayles, *Law and Legislation*, pp. 72–3, 80–2.

[3] Glanvill, *De Legibus et Consuetudinibus Regni Angliae*, ed. G. E. Woodbine (New Haven, 1922), p. 42.

[4] *Radulphi de Hengham Summae*, ed. W. H. Dunham (Cambridge, 1932), p. 5: 'Constat quod placita de crimine lese maiestatis, ut de nece vel seditione persone domini regis vel regni vel exercitus . . . '; *Fleta*, p. 57.

it came from the old Germanic crime of *landesverrat*, which was treason against land and folk, that is, attempts on the life of the organized group whether family, community or state. It may have derived from the works of the continental canonists or decretists or even the glossators of the Roman law, each of whom laid some emphasis on love of the fatherland [*patria*]. The glossators even suggested it might be treason to fight against the fatherland.[1] Perhaps this speculation is too fanciful and the answer is more simple. *Seditio regni* might merely have been an early example of the extension of the aura of majesty from the king's person to his country. There are other comparable examples of the use of the word *regnum* in a treason context but they are rare before the fourteenth century.[2] It may have been that the word *regnum* was being used, as it was in the later period, as a synonym for 'crown', a juristic expression of the unity of the king and his subjects. *Seditio regni* did not find a place in the treason act of 1352 unless perhaps it was concealed within the offence of adhering to the king's enemies.

Like Glanvill, Bracton and *Fleta* after him both included in their definition of treason the crime *seditio* (or *seductio*) *exercitus*, although like *seditio regni* it did not appear in the act of 1352.[3] Special penalties of the type associated with the gravest of offences were awarded by the Anglo-Saxons against those who left the army without permission when the king was present. This was in the dooms of Ethelred.[4] There were similar rules in continental Germanic laws, such as those of the Lombards and Franks. However, since the fomenting of sedition and riots among the soldiers was considered *laesa maiestas* under the Roman Empire, Glanvill may equally well have been drawing on a Roman source. One other type of treason to which this author referred was the crime of forgery or falsifying. It was not the making of false coin or of false measures which he specifically distinguished as lese-majesty, though they were each given separate mention, but the making of a false royal charter in contrast with forging a private charter.[5] The Anglo-Saxons were wont to punish false moneyers

[1] G. Post, 'Two Notes on Nationalism in the Middle Ages', *Traditio*, IX (1953), 281–96.
[2] Below, chapter 8.
[3] Bracton, II, 334; *Fleta*, p. 56.
[4] *Laws of the Kings of England*, ed. Robertson, pp. 86–7.
[5] Glanvill, *De Legibus*, ed. Woodbine, p. 179.

with the same penalties and by the same processes as were used in cases of high treason, but reference to the forgery of royal charters is lacking, as is the case in the other less sophisticated Germanic laws. Thus a Roman origin for Glanvill's forgery is the more likely, bearing in mind that the crime of *maiestas* included counterfeiting, destroying or desecrating or displaying lack of respect for the image of the emperor divine through making a fraudulent likeness,[1] and that some alteration or forging of a seal was likely to have been employed.

For Glanvill therefore the law of treason was a mixture of Roman and Germanic ideas, but he should not be regarded as the chief cause of the fusion. Well before the lifetime of this author, even in the sixth century, Roman and Germanic concepts of treason were joining together in Europe and even the Anglo-Saxon kings appropriated Roman ideas useful to their laws. Glanvill very probably wrote down the rules which judges in his day had come to accept. The concise formula 'the killing of the king or the betrayal of the realm or the army' has the ring and appearance of a neat and pliable contemporary legal maxim. How it was applied in each case was doubtless for the judges to decide.

The history of the influence of Roman law in thirteenth-century England is more complex. Its new-found popularity as an important study for lawyers was no longer maintained: indeed it suffered some notable defeats. Crucial no doubt were the principles of government obtaining. The later Angevins displayed a tendency to ignore due process of law and act how they wished. They were tempted to override established customs and rights although they rarely did so openly.[2] What pleased the king might indeed have had the vigour of law, but even the Angevins found it politic to clothe their acts with a legal fabric. In their case the law so used was often Roman and their servants had to have knowledge of it. Unfortunately for later kings the royal power was decisively curbed by Magna Carta, the feudal pact by which the king's aspirations to a theocratic capacity were greatly reduced.[3] Nonetheless, Roman law did not lose its foothold in England for about a century. It could be learned at Oxford, and there was no shortage

[1] Lear, *Treason*, p. 119.
[2] W. Ullmann, *The Principles of Government and Politics in the Middle Ages* (London, 1961), p. 157; J. E. A. Jolliffe, *Angevin Kingship* (London, 1955), pp. 60 n, 61 n.
[3] Ullmann, *Principles of Government*, pp. 160–74.

of popular textbooks on the subject, which had been translated into French. Most important was the fact that the king's justices were often clerics who knew something of the civil law as a result of their study of canon law. Not until the end of the reign of Edward I was the judiciary laicized. One particular use which was found for Roman law in the thirteenth century was to fill gaps in the young system of English common law. Thus there was probably some copying of civilian and canonical practice in cases of novel disseisin, even if there is more doubt about the Roman ancestry of the idea of damages and the actions of trespass and *cessavit*. The great influence in this field, however, was the writings of Bracton, who had very definite views of how the Roman law should be used to combat the weaknesses of the common law. His great treatise contained not a cross section of cases before the courts but those cases which were significant to his own point of view, which was that the confused English system of pleas and writs needed the assistance of the legal thought of Rome.[1] Propaganda or not, the treatise influenced lawyers greatly for the next half-century, persuading them to make use of a number of Roman legal terms and concepts.

How far was Bracton's definition of treason a derivation of Roman ideas? He started the relevant chapter by using a few words from the *Institutes* and later on utilized Tancred's *Ordo Judiciarius* and Glanvill.[2] Like Glanvill he called high treason *laesa maiestas*, a term which was used by his copiers and by monastic chroniclers but which was only accepted by the English chancery clerks in the reign of Edward IV, and in fact never did find a place in the plea rolls. There *traditio, seditio* or *seductio* and ultimately *proditio* were preferred. Going beyond Glanvill, Bracton stated that the crime exceeded in turpitude all other crimes. When he listed the various categories of *laesa maiestas* Bracton followed Glanvill by regarding sedition done to the king and his army (but not the realm) as the central offence. In making as criminal as the actual committing of treason the misdeeds of procuring treason to be done or giving aid or consent to those who were plotting treason, even if the plans were not carried out, Bracton advanced the English doctrine

[1] T. F. T. Plucknett, 'The Relations between Roman Law and English Common Law down to the Sixteenth Century', *University of Toronto Law Journal*, III (1939), 37–43.

[2] H. G. Richardson, *Bracton. The Problem of his Text* (Seld. Soc., 1965), pp. 122–5.

of treason a great deal.[1] There can be little doubt that his ideas influenced the makers of the statute of 1352. Plotting treason, forming part of a conspiracy against a member of the imperial council and consistory or the senate, or against any other person in imperial service, or the emperor by implication, was defined as lese-majesty in the *Lex Quisquis* of Justinian. Treasonable conspiracy may have been borrowed by Bracton from Roman sources but, as we have seen, plotting against the king's life was emphasized at the expense of actual killing in the laws of King Alfred and in the Edict of Rothar (A.D. 643) where cogitating (*cogitaverit contra animam regis*) was high treason.[2] Another crime which was lese-majesty to Bracton was forgery. This included fabricating base coin, debasing or clipping good coin and counterfeiting the king's seal on charters or writs: it was an extension of Glanvill's category which seems to have contained only the latter.[3] Bracton, like Glanvill, probably drew on Romanesque sources here, perhaps the chapter 'De Falsa Moneta' in Justinian's *Codex*. Thus, in defining treason Bracton added to Glanvill rather than contradicted him, and his aim seems to have been to provide a reasonably comprehensive law of treason by drawing on his knowledge of Roman law either in its contemporary continental or its more ancient form.

In the matter of procedure to be employed in cases of treason, Bracton again supplemented Glanvill. He may have done so not by reference to the customs of Rome but by utilizing professional opinions based on actual cases in the English courts. When he wrote about conspiracy of treason and the danger in waiting for treasonable plots to become public knowledge, he was probably bearing in mind a particular case. He argued that any man who possessed information about such a conspiracy should inform the king immediately without delaying for two nights in any one place, on peril of being held a manifest traitor.[4] Yet even in this sphere a Roman influence can be argued, if with less certainty. In the later Roman Empire failure to reveal treasonable conspiracy was punished as complicity, and informers [*delatores*], those who told of an offence without making a formal accusation, were encouraged.[5] The punishment of traitors had hardly been mentioned by Glanvill. It depended, so he said, on royal clemency, as

---

[1] Bracton, II, 334–7.   [2] Lear, *Treason*, pp. 44, 185, 236–7.
[3] Bracton, II, 337–8.   [4] *Ibid.*, II, 335.   [5] Lear, *Treason*, p. 33.

with felonies. However, the goods and chattels of a convicted traitor were to be confiscated [*confiscandis*] and his heirs disinherited for ever.[1] This provision Bracton embellished. The convicted man was to suffer the last punishment with an aggravation of corporeal pain. He was to lose all his goods, and his heirs were to be perpetually disinherited, as in Glanvill, but then Bracton added that it was scarcely permissible for the heirs to live, perhaps thinking of the penalties of infamy, confiscation of property and incapacity to inherit imposed on traitors' sons in the later Roman Empire.[2] The increased concern with which late medieval society, when provided with some notion of Roman ideas, viewed attacks on the king, showed itself in the devising of particularly gruesome modes of execution.

Concepts of treason never flourish in a vacuum. They depend greatly on the prevailing thesis of government. Throughout the later middle ages there was a tendency for European kings to seek, even if they did not readily gain, the power of absolutism. This has been attributed in part to the rediscovery of Aristotle's *Politics* in the thirteenth century, but there were two other causes which were more important. The concept of obedience, much favoured by ecclesiastical writers early in the eleventh century, although more in regard to the pope than to kings, was overshadowed later on by Gregory VII's extreme measures against the emperor, involving deposition and the freeing of his subjects from their duty of obedience. In the twelfth century the German ecclesiastical princes assumed the right to judge the ruler whom they had crowned and there was one writer, John of Salisbury, who actually advocated tyrannicide. The argument in favour of right of resistance to the monarch seems to have called forth the antithesis of divine right of kings, which emphasized the duty of passive obedience on the part of the subject as well as the divine consecration of the ruler.[3] It was then that the medieval monarchs, searching for legal arguments to bolster their political position, discovered the arsenal of Roman law. Whereas in Germanic thought the king lived and ruled under the law of his people, Roman Emperors had been regarded as vicars of God and as such above the law.

[1] *Tractatus de Legibus et Consuetudinibus Regni Angliae qui Glanvilla vocatur*, ed. G. D. G. Hall (London, 1965), p. 173.
[2] Bracton, II, 335; Lear, *Treason*, pp. 35–6.
[3] F. Kern, *Kingship and Law in the Middle Ages* (Oxford, 1939), pp. 97–117.

It was to this theocratic station that most late medieval monarchs aspired. Each saw himself as God's vicegerent, transformed by the oil with which he was anointed at his coronation. Despite the existence of the Holy Roman Emperor, who claimed sole secular sovereignty, there were from the end of the twelfth century kings who demonstrated both by deed and word that they admitted no lay superior and claimed to be themselves sovereign. In 1202 King John equated the kingdom of England with an empire and in the same year in the decretal *Per Venerabilem*, Innocent III mentioned that Philip Augustus of France recognized no superior in temporal matters.[1] Soon after 1200 some canonists were willing to grant *de facto* recognition to the sovereignty of kings, for example Vincentus Hispanus, Alanus and Guido de Baysio, a glossator on the *Decretum*, who suggested that despite the general jurisdiction of the emperor each king had similar power within his dominions.[2] But in general the claim was closely disputed throughout the thirteenth century. The opposition derived, as we might expect, largely from the lawyers of the emperor, who quibbled about sovereignty *de facto* and *de iure*. Not until the beginning of the fourteenth century did the march of events decide the issue of the battle, and the formula of Guido de Baysio that every king was emperor within his own kingdom become generally accepted.

The acknowledgement of the king as sovereign had an effect on the treason laws of many European states. Most noticeable was the alteration in attitudes towards rebellion. In the earlier middle ages, as Kern pointed out, the subject owed his ruler fealty rather than obedience. Fealty was reciprocal and was owed only as long as the other party kept faith. Neither king nor subject was a free agent: both were bound by the law of the kingdom. Thus when in the later middle ages the king claimed to be *lege solutus* the old balance was upset. Before the thirteenth century many a ruler recognized a subject had the right to disobey him: tacitly this understanding was included in every act of homage. It was even argued that a man wronged by his king had a duty, after offering formal defiance [*diffidatio*], to seek justice through rebellion. Who was in the right would be decided by judgement of God as revealed by victory in pitched battle. By no accident did the baronial rebels in England

---

[1] F. Schultz, 'Bracton on Kingship', *Eng. Hist. Rev.*, LX (1945), 149–51.
[2] W. Ullmann, 'The Development of the Medieval Idea of Sovereignty', *Eng. Hist. Rev.* LXIV (1949), 4, 9.

in 1215 call themselves the 'army of God'.[1] In one important aspect England was different from most other European states. Formal defiance of the king on the part of rebels was rarely held to excuse some form of judicial penalty if the insurrection failed. Nonetheless, before the reign of Edward I weighty retribution rarely occurred. In France the change from a generous to a severe royal policy on rebellion came at about the middle of the thirteenth century. In their legal treatises Guilelmus Durandus and Jean de Blanot both suggested that a baron who rose against the king was committing lese-majesty and in 1259 the jurisconsults decided the king could be the object of the same crime. As a result a baron who committed such an offence might forfeit his privileged position by royal decree.[2] Maitland, writing about treason in England, stated that only after 1340, when he had renounced his homage to the king of France and was therefore sovereign, did the English king adopt a severer policy towards those of his subjects guilty of insurrection. He was thinking apparently of the rubric about levying war against the king within the realm, which appeared in the treason statute of 1352.[3] The argument is unsound. For levying war against the king men had been convicted of treason during the two preceding reigns. Kings assumed the guise and the rights of sovereign princes some considerable time before they were universally recognized as such.

The full Roman law doctrine of lese-majesty was never accepted in England. Magna Carta and later on baronial cohesion effectively prevented the English kings becoming theocratic monarchs, although they made several attempts in that direction through the use of such instruments as the privy council, the privy seal, the royal household, the wardrobe and the chamber. In France, in contrast, because of a system of administration which was staffed by jurists trained in Roman law, because of the nature of the judicial process and the lack of baronial cohesion and articulateness, theocratic kingship flourished properly. The French king's avowed aim was a high level of public order, but this turned into the removal of all forces which opposed him. In criminal law one most important change which occurred in the thirteenth century was the substitution for the old method of accusation, much like the

---

[1] Kern, *Kingship*, pp. 85–92.
[2] Ullmann, *Eng. Hist. Rev.*, LXIV (1949), 10–11.
[3] Pollock and Maitland, II, 505–6.

English appeal, of inquisitorial procedure. This was official prosecution based on the model of Roman and canon law.[1] Another important introduction was of a new wide category of offence which involved in some way the violation of royal dignity. Such crimes were called *cas royaux* and originated at the time when cases of lese-majesty first began to occur. The king was never obliged to give them careful definition or to list them exhaustively, and they tended to multiply in number through the instrumentality of royal officials keen to extend royal authority.[2] Cases of lese-majesty were a central element in the collection of *cas royaux* and like them were never given precise definition. In the thirteenth century lese-majesty was held to include all attempts on the person or the honour of the king, but by the end of the middle ages it embraced, as well as the obvious crimes of attempts no the life of the king or his family or levying war against him, the offences of highway robbery, abduction of women, saying that the king needed his subjects' consent to their taxation, selling a fortress or refusing the king entry to it, having dealings with the king's enemies or with infidels, or speaking badly about the king by, for example, saying he was not worthy to live. Bouteiller referred to a crime he called 'combination' as lese-majesty: this seems to have been an urban offence, probably conspiracy, for purposes of revolt, including the taking of a common oath. The making of false coin, unlike the English practice, was not generally held as lese-majesty, although Bouteiller regarded it as such.[3] The scope of lese-majesty in France was in practice very similar to that of high treason in England. There are in fact one or two pieces of evidence, rather vague, which point to the French definition of lese-majesty influencing the English directly,[4] but the similarities between the two are really to be discovered in a common debt to the law of Rome.

In contrast with England, where men were usually tried for treason according to the same procedures as they would have been for any other crime, those accused of lese-majesty in France were

[1] Ullmann, *Principles of Government*, pp. 195–200.
[2] J. Brissaud, *Manuel d'histoire du droit Français* (Paris, 1898), p. 671.
[3] C. L. Von Bar, *History of Continental Criminal Law* (London, 1916), pp. 163–4, 173, 183; C. E. Dumont, *Justice Criminelle des Duchés de Lorraine et de Bar, du Bassigny et des Trois Évêchés* (Nancy, 1848), pp. 113–17; Brissaud, *Manuel d'histoire*, p. 925; F. Aubert, *Parlement de Paris de l'origine à François I, 1250–1515* (Paris, 1894), I, 266.
[4] Below, p. 74, n. 1. Perhaps also in the Gerberge, Litel and Beche cases.

tried in the king's courts by special process. It was not one peculiar to treason, but was operable for other serious crimes, especially those which were denied and had been committed secretly. It was called the 'extraordinary procedure'. Since there could be no death penalty without a confession from the accused, torture was the normal method by which the judges attempted to discover the truth: they might even inflict it on the accuser. Almost without exception the depositions of witnesses were hidden from the accused. As in England, conspirators were held equally guilty with those who committed overt treasonable acts. He who had knowledge of any traitorous design was expected to reveal it immediately, on pain of sharing in the guilt:[1] this was the same rule as in Bracton. The punishment meted out to traitors was more severe than that inflicted on other convicted criminals. In France they might be flayed alive or hanged and quartered, first being dragged, as in England, to execution at the horse's tail. All their goods were forfeited, usually to the king, and their fiefs went to their feudal lords. General confiscation such as this was limited in France to lese-majesty and heresy: even for these crimes it did not prevail in every province. Punishment did not necessarily cease with the traitor's death and the forfeiture of his possessions. His children might also lose their lives. The argument was that the crime of treason was so horrible that the traitor's offspring were contaminated by his misdeed and ought to be destroyed with him. If in fact the lives of the children were spared they might still suffer civil death. The severity of the punishment was only moderated in regard to daughters: they were supposed to be allowed a quarter of the property of their mother.[2] Some details of emphasis were slightly different, but in general the punishment of traitors, like the scope of high treason, was similar all over Europe at this time. The Golden Bull of the Emperor Charles IV (1356), giving the protection of the laws of lese-majesty to the German electors, ordered the confiscation of traitors' possessions in very similar terms.[3]

[1] A. Esmein, *History of Continental Criminal Procedure* (London, 1914), pp. 128 ff.; Von Bar, *Continental Criminal Law*, pp. 163–4.

[2] Von Bar, *Continental Criminal Law*, pp. 189, 192; P. C. Timbal, 'La Confiscation dans le Droit Français des XIIIe et XIVe siècles', *Revue Historique de Droit Français*, XIX–XXI (1940–2), 44–61.

[3] E. F. Henderson, *Historical Documents of the Middle Ages* (London, 1896), pp. 252–4.

Thus the English law of treason of the later middle ages was founded on a Germanic base but contained also much that was derived either from the law of classical Rome or from contemporary European practice. From about the mid-thirteenth century there was considerable, but not continuous, resistance to the introduction of Romanist notions, although the kings tried repeatedly to make them. Two of the more successful were Edward I and Henry V. Edward introduced the treason of levying war against the king, doubtless being influenced by the Roman theory that the right of levying war belonged only to princes without a secular superior, while Henry utilized elements of the laws of war, which were closely based on Roman doctrines, in his statutes (2 Henry V st. 1, c. 6 and 4 Henry V st. 2, c. 7) about truces and their preservation and marque. The finding of mere words as treason in the fifteenth century had parallels on the continent which may have had an influence on English thought. Edward III attempted to turn highway robbery and abduction of women into treason, as they were in France, but was unsuccessful. During the first half of the fourteenth century the crime of accroaching or usurping the royal power made several appearances, figuring both in accusations by the king and by the baronial opposition. This class of offence approximated quite closely to the category of *cas royaux* in France, both being concerned with infringement of the royal dignity. It never took proper root, for in the definition of treason contained in the great statute of 1352 accroaching was deliberately omitted. This was partly because the king feared its use against himself or his ministers by the baronial opposition, but mostly because the magnates disliked the use he had made of the formula in the 1340s to extend the law of treason as it then stood. This abandonment meant the loss of an important means of extending royal power and contributed greatly to the continuance of the feudal state. It is worth noting that the king was prompted to introduce Roman notions into the treason laws not so much to increase his own powers *per se* as to maintain a reasonable level of public order. The extension of the penalties for treason to lesser crimes both at this time and in the fifteenth century was intended to remedy complaints about lack of governance, which was a perennial grievance in the England of the later middle ages.

2

THE TREATISE WRITERS AND THE ENGLISH
LAW OF TREASON AT THE END OF THE
THIRTEENTH CENTURY

BRACTON'S definition of treason in his *De Legibus et Consuetudinibus Angliae*[1] or rather that definition as refined by the later
writers *Fleta*[2] and *Britton*[3] was the *terminus a quo* for all later
declaration of law in that field. The works of *Fleta* and *Britton*
were compiled at least a generation after Bracton's *De Legibus* and
were based largely upon it. They do however help to establish
more precisely how the law of treason stood at the time of Edward I.
Bracton, *Fleta* and *Britton* each included the killing of the king or
plotting to kill the king and Bracton and *Fleta* appended the mere
giving of assent to such a scheme.[4] *Britton* held it was treason to
disinherit the king of his kingdom as it was to kill the king's
father, mother, consort or children.[5] Only Bracton included the
concealment of a knowledge of a traitorous plot in as many words.[6]
Unlike the other two writers *Britton* distinguished between great
and little treason. These were not the same as the crimes referred
to in the 1352 act as high and petty treason. Great treason was not
only to procure the death of the king but also to kill one's own
lord or to violate his wife or daughters. One treason on which all
the three writers were in agreement was forgery. This was held to
include the counterfeiting of false coin, the clipping of good coin
and the falsifying of the king's seal. The *Mirror of Justices*,
written about 1290 and attributed to Andrew Horn, chamberlain of
London, seems to have owed less to Bracton than did *Fleta* and
Britton. Nonetheless it defined treason in similar terms: killing
the king, betraying his army, disinheriting him of his kingdom
or compassing to do any of the three. A small but noteworthy addition to the definitions of the other treatises was the classifying
as a traitor he who should defile the king's wife or his eldest

[1] Bracton, II, 334–7.   [2] *Fleta*, pp. 56–9.
[3] *Britton*, I, 40–1, 99.   [4] Bracton, II, 334; *Fleta*, p. 56; *Britton*, I, 40.
[5] *Britton*, I, 40, 99.
[6] Bracton, II, 335.

3

legitimate daughter before her marriage or the nurse suckling the heir of the king.[1]

In addition to the crimes listed in treatises there were other types of offences which had been shown to be treason during the course of the thirteenth century. Maitland referred to two cases which occurred in the reign of King John where the offence was predicting the death of the king.[2] Peter of Wakefield predicted John would not be king on the following Ascension Day and another accused man was convicted for declaring there was no king's peace as the king was among his Welsh enemies and would never return.[3] Going back further, in a case of Henry II's reign Robert de Montfort appealed of treason and by battle convicted Henry of Essex for having cried aloud that the king had been slain.[4] All three crimes might be widely construed as compassing the king's death but there were no similar cases in the fourteenth century. Not until the fifteenth did predicting the death of the monarch reappear as a treasonable offence.[5] The legal treatises make no reference to adhering to the king's enemies, a crime which occurred with great frequency in the fourteenth century, both before and after the great statute of treason. Nevertheless there were several good examples at the end of the thirteenth century. In 1285 Master Nicholas de Wantham was accused of seditiously allying himself with Guy and Aymer Montfort and Llewelyn of Wales, the king's enemies, and coming to King Edward's court to spy out his secrets.[6] The crimes committed by Sir Thomas Turberville in 1295, it has been suggested, also amounted to adhering to the king's enemies by spying, a crime which was 'already recognised as treasonable'.[7]

[1] *Mirror*, p. 15.
[2] Pollock and Maitland, II, 507.
[3] Matthew Paris, *Chronica Majora*, ed. H. R. Luard (R.S., 1872–83), II, 535, 547; *Select Pleas of the Crown*, ed. F. W. Maitland (Seld. Soc., 1888), pp. 67–75.
[4] Montfort also claimed that Henry of Essex 'in expedicione belli apud Waliam in difficili transitu de Coleshelle vexillum domini regis fraudulenter abiecisse': *Chronicle of Jocelin of Brakelond*, ed. H. E. Butler (London, 1949), p. 70.
[5] Below, chapter 5: for example, the cases involving Eleanor, duchess of Gloucester, in 1441 and Thomas Burdet in 1477.
[6] *Oxford City Documents*, ed. J. E. Thorold Rogers (Oxford Historical Society, 1891), pp. 204–5: 'et inde constare fecit seditiose ut seductor et parti ipsorum adhaesit et se eis confoederavit, et eorum consiliarius devenit contra fidelitatem suam et contra Dominum Regem . . .'
[7] J. G. Edwards, 'The Treason of Thomas Turberville, 1295', in *Studies in Medieval History presented to F. M. Powicke*, ed. R. W. Hunt, W. A. Pantin and R. W. Southern (Oxford, 1948), p. 307.

At the end of the century when Edward I was engaged in the suppression of the Scottish rebellion any Englishman who fought on the Scots' side was likely to find his lands forfeited to the king for his adherence: there is no doubt that the crown considered the offence treasonable.[1] In that the enemies of the king ultimately intended his death, to adhere to them was obviously akin to assenting to a plot for his destruction. Thus quite possibly the crime of adhering to the king's enemies was a late thirteenth-century construction on the definitions of treason current earlier in that century. There was no need for the introduction of statute law before derivation of this type could commence. One crime which Bracton said was the equivalent of treason it may be possible to trace back to a single historical event. As we have seen he wrote that if a man knew that treason had been committed he should immediately inform the king. If the man dissembled and kept the secret for a time he would be held 'a manifest seductor' of the crown.[2] In a case which occurred in 1225 Viel del Engaine, Ralph de Bray and William FitzEly were appealed of the crime of treason by a knight named Richard FitzNigel. They were arrested and imprisoned in the Tower of London. But because FitzNigel was of ill-fame and had once broken out of Oxford gaol and because he had not reported the crime for some six months after it had come to his knowledge, the appeal was not allowed and the accuser was drawn and hanged, the penalty for treason.[3] As with the crime of predicting the king's death there are no other examples of the concealment of treason being held as treason before the fifteenth century.[4]

A category of treason clearly delineated in the legal writings of the late thirteenth century was the counterfeiting or clipping of coin or the forging of the king's seal. However, the theories of the writers and the practices of the king's judges were sometimes at odds. The most notable contemporary coinage offence resulted in the drawing and hanging of 293 Jews and three Christians in London in 1279.[5] They had been found guilty of the clipping of

[1] For example, see *Cal. Pat. Rolls, 1292–1301*, p. 407. [2] Bracton, II, 335.
[3] *Annales Monastici*, ed. H. R. Luard (R.S., 1866), III, 97; *Curia Regis Rolls, 1225–7*, no. 1055.
[4] The first subsequent example concerned Henry, Lord Scrope of Masham, and occurred in 1415; see *Rot. Parl.* IV, 65–6.
[5] *Chronicles of the Reigns of Edward I and Edward II*, ed. W. Stubbs (R.S., 1882–3), I, 88; *Wilhelmi Rishanger, Chronica et Annales*, ed. H. T. Riley (R.S.,

coins. To draw a man to the gallows for execution had always been the hall-mark of treason but the crimes of the accused were referred to in the chancery rolls merely as trespasses.[1] They were not called felonies or treasons as was to be the practice in the fourteenth century. The introduction of counterfeit or clipped coin into England was a problem which first demanded government legislation in the last decade of the thirteenth century. Edward I found it necessary to ordain that those foreign or native merchants who offended in this way should suffer forfeiture of the body and all their goods for the third offence.[2] Whether the crime rated as treason at that time is not clear but it was made definite treason if committed by Englishmen by the statute of 1352. The position of a man who was found merely to be in possession of counterfeit coin was equally obscure. In 1320 the sheriff of Norfolk was ordered to send for trial in the king's bench a man who had been discovered to possess forged money and had been indicted for that offence. The royal writ stated that the matter was forgery which was a special form of treason [sedicionem].[3] Unfortunately how the judges construed the misdeed is unknown. There was no mention of this crime as treason in the 1352 act. Another matter which required further definition concerned royal seals. The thirteenth-century treatise writers refer to the treason of forging the king's seal but do not specify which seal.[4] There is no reference in the thirteenth century to trial on accusation of forging the privy seal but there did occur one such case in 1312. John of Reading, a clerk, accused Sir Edmund de Maule 'super falsatione parvi sigilli regis'. The accuser must have been a man whose word was not

---

1865), p. 92; *The Chronicle of Walter of Guisborough, previously edited as the chronicle of Walter of Hemingford or Hemingburgh*, ed. Harry Rothwell (Camden Soc., 1957), p. 216.

[1] *Calendar of Fine Rolls, 1272–1307*, pp. 113–15.

[2] *Cal. Close Rolls, 1288–96*, p. 203.

[3] P.R.O., K.B. 27/242, Rex m. 21 (printed in *Select Cases in the Court of the King's Bench*, ed. G. O. Sayles (Seld. Soc., 1955), p. 102): 'Cum Petrus Munke pro falsacione monete nostre unde rettatus est cum quadam summa monete false captus sit . . . idem Petrus super falsacione predicta que sedicionem nobis et populo regni nostri factam specialiter tangit alibi quam coram nobis vel iusticiariis nostris . . . iusticiari . . . non poterit.' The exact nature of the charge was obscured by a certain Bertram le Munk testifying during the trial, on the king's behalf, that Peter was wont to make such forged money. The accused man put himself on the country claiming he was in no way guilty of the forgery and wrongdoing [*falsitate et malicia*]: he was acquitted.

[4] Bracton, II, 337–8; *Fleta*, p. 58; *Britton*, I, 40–1. The act of 1352 was specific.

trusted since before the king's judges at Westminster Maule was allowed to purge himself. Then the clerk was convicted of the crime and eventually drawn and hanged.[1] He who appealed another of treason and failed to secure a conviction could still be executed himself for the same crime. The most interesting legal writer on the matter of forging seals was *Britton*. He seems to distinguish between two degrees of offence. He said that if the falsifying of a seal be of small consequence the guilty party should be sentenced to judgement of pillory only or to lose an ear: but if the act was heinous and touched on disherison or caused lasting damage the sentence should be death.[2] Whether he based this distinction on actual English criminal practice is impossible to tell.

Those who wrote legal commentaries at the end of the thirteenth century and who discussed treason were as much interested in judicial process as in the definition of the crime. All were agreed that the king or his ministers ought to receive information about a treasonable crime not by the presentment of a jury but by the immediate communication of the discoverer. Bracton states that a man who acquires knowledge of treason should not delay in one place for two nights or for two days together nor attend to his own business before seeing the king.[3] According to *Britton* any person ought to be admitted to make such an accusation: even a serf or a minor below age, adds Bracton.[4] They really meant people of unblemished character 'quia criminosi ab omni accusatione repelluntur, ut si accusans fuerit latro cognitus vel utlagatus, vel aliquo genere feloniae convictus vel convicendus'.[5] Also excluded were conspirators in the same plot and any man who, although not taking an active part, had consented to the crime.[6] No doubt because of the enormity of the offence of treason it was felt that an accuser should be admitted without finding pledges for prosecuting. If there was no accuser yet the crime was notoriously known to men of good repute, the suspect should be arrested and remain under arrest until he had his trial.[7] In the trial, so Bracton argued, judgement should not be by the king or his judges otherwise he would be the plaintiff and judge in his own cause. His own answer was that a court of peers should give judgement and the crown act as

---

[1] *Chronicles of Edward I and Edward II*, I, 272.
[2] *Britton*, I, 40–1.   [3] Bracton, II, 335.
[4] *Britton*, I, 99; Bracton, II, 334.
[5] Bracton, II, 335.   [6] *Fleta*, p. 56.
[7] *Ibid*.

plaintiff.[1] The author of the *Mirror of Justices* implied that in cases of treason which were notorious there was no need for a proper trial at all and that the suspected parties should be judged without respite.[2] Presumably this meant the notoriety of their offence should work an immediate conviction. All the writers assumed that judicial process against a suspected traitor would be by way of individual appeal and paid considerable attention to the actual form which the appeal should take. The accuser had to have been present at the committing of the crime and to have seen and heard it with his own eyes and ears.[3] *Fleta* gives the impression that if the accused denied the charge word for word the issue would normally be settled by battle: an exception would be if the king gave his assent to a settlement.[4] References to the actual *duellum* in the records are very few and it is quite possible that the king preferred more reliable methods of establishing the guilt of his personal enemy.[5]

Treason was most clearly distinguished from other serious crimes by the punishment inflicted on the guilty party. On this the authors of the legal treatises were very much in agreement. The guilty man was to suffer physically the extreme penalty 'cum poenae aggravatione corporalis'.[6] The compiler of the *Mirror of Justices* held that judgement for lese-majesty should be executed by torment according to the ordinance and will of the king and by death. This crime he somehow distinguished from forgery [*faussonerie*] and treason [*traisson*] for which the penalty was to be drawn and hanged.[7] To the popular mind as to *Britton* a death for treason differed from one for any other capital offence in that the traitor was dragged at the horse's tail to the place of execution.[8] Sometimes the condemned man was tied to a hurdle: this was possibly less out of humanity than to provide the hangman with a living body, as Maitland was the first to point out.[9] It was in the

---

[1] Bracton, II, 337.
[2] *Mirror*, p. 53.
[3] Bracton, II, 336; *Mirror*, p. 53; *Fleta*, p. 56.
[4] *Fleta*, p. 56.
[5] I have found only one reference to an actual *duellum* in the reign of Edward I. It occurred in Jersey in 1293: *Cal. Pat. Rolls, 1292–1301*, p. 38.
[6] Bracton, II, 335. *Fleta*, p. 56, says the same.
[7] *Mirror*, p. 135.   [8] *Britton*, I, 40–1.
[9] Pollock and Maitland, II, 500. In the reign of Edward III, Chief Justice William Shareshull 'decreed imprisonment for friars and others who by placing hurdles under the condemned victims tried to mitigate the horrors of drawing':

thirteenth century that the crown first commanded traitors to be disembowelled and quartered but the authors of the treatises make no specific reference to the practice.[1]

In addition to physical punishment the penalty for treason, according to Bracton and *Fleta*, was the loss of all goods and the perpetual disinheriting of the traitor's heirs: 'Est enim tam grave crimen istud, quod vix permittitur haeredibus quod vivant'.[2] If by chance, said Bracton, the heirs should be admitted to the succession this would happen from grace rather than of right. Maitland suggested it was in the thirteenth century that the rule evolved whereby a traitor's land went not to his immediate lord but to the king. He believed this was a compromise after some sort of struggle, one which was ignored or slurred over in the legal writings of the time.[3] King John, he pointed out, in chapter 32 of Magna Carta, promised to return to the lords after a year and a day the lands of those of their tenants who had been convicted of *felonia*. Therefore for their own benefit Henry III and Edward I introduced the novel crimes of *proditio* and *seditio*. Thus the law of treason of the later middle ages was crucially affected by economic considerations. The weakness of this argument lies in the paucity of thirteenth-century treason cases, a fact on which Maitland himself remarked in another context.[4] One recent writer has stated that between 1196 and 1305 there occurred no more than a dozen examples:[5] certainly both Henry III and Edward I were reluctant to accuse men of treason and they can have derived little financial profit from that source. Where forfeiture for treason did occur the crown showed little inclination to exact the full penalty possible. The brutal simplicity of the Bractonian doctrine of forfeiture was amended and mollified. In 1306 Edward I was willing when granting away the lands which Robert Bruce had held in England to preserve the dower of Eleanor widow of Robert

B. H. Putnam, *The Place in Legal History of Sir William Shareshull* (Cambridge, 1950), p. 128. The drawing of Sir Thomas Turberville in 1295 has been described in some detail: 'Primo pelle bovis stratus, ascensis sex lictoribus equos, caudis ipsorum distractus per civitatem Londoniae, vallatus quatuor tortoribus larvatis et effigatis in serabaris et pellicis interpolatis, improperantibus ei convicia exprobrantur': *Flores Historiarum*, ed. H. R. Luard (R.S., 1890), III, 282.

[1] Below, chapter 3.   [2] *Fleta*, p. 56; Bracton, II, 335.
[3] Pollock and Maitland, II, 501.   [4] *Ibid.*, II, 506.
[5] J. G. Edwards, 'Treason of Thomas Turberville, 1295' in *Studies presented to F. M. Powicke*, p. 296.

Bruce his father.[1] In 1304 when the English king admitted John Comyn and other Scottish insurgents to his peace he said they should not be disinherited. He kept his word and his successor confirmed the concession.[2] Later on, in 1322, when Edward II had an English rebellion to deal with he continued to moderate the Bractonian dictum.[3] Only at the very end of the century, in 1397, was there a return by the crown to a policy of total forfeiture.[4]

No thirteenth-century legal writer referred to the treason of levying war against the king. In the case of *Fleta*, *Britton* and the author of the *Mirror of Justices*, this was a notable omission since Edward I, at the time when they were writing, was busy construing the offence as treason and by the time of his death had arrived at a comprehensive judicial policy on rebellion. Perhaps they did not feel the actual examples of this policy were in harmony with their writings: perhaps they were so absorbed with Bracton that they failed to notice contemporary developments, or perhaps they felt that the levying of war against the king was no more than compassing the king's death. If in fact their silence was testimony to their disapproval it meant nothing to Edward, who continually developed this extension of treason and by so doing was responsible for the judicial device of conviction by the royal record as well as for the rise of the English state trial.[5]

---

[1] *Cal. Docs. Scot.*, II, 483.
[2] *Cal. Close Rolls, 1307–13*, p. 115.
[3] See, for example, *Cal. Close Rolls, 1318–23*, pp. 576, 578, 579, 583 (Alice, wife of Thomas of Lancaster, and Christiana, wife of Edmund de Wylyngton); *Cal. Close Rolls, 1323–7*, pp. 65, 69; R. Somerville, *History of the Duchy of Lancaster* (London, 1953), I, 33–4. Usually dower and the female inheritance were protected, sometimes joint enfeoffment also.
[4] C. D. Ross, 'Forfeiture for treason in the reign of Richard II', *Eng. Hist. Rev.*, LXXI (1956), 560–75.
[5] Below, chapter 3.

3

THE ORIGINS OF THE ENGLISH STATE TRIAL

NOT UNTIL the reign of Edward I did the English kings find it necessary to treat rebellion as treason.[1] Throughout the twelfth and thirteenth centuries the levying of war against the king by his subjects, possibly the most common of later treasons, was treated with what to the modern mind seems a remarkable degree of clemency. There was no case of the execution of an earl for open rebellion between the death of Waltheof in 1076 and that of John, earl of Atholl in 1306. In its periodic disloyalty the English nobility was no worse and no better than any other similar class in western Europe, and the English kings had their moments of acute discomfort. Yet they were never provoked into the proscription of defeated partisans. It seems probable that the feudal law, which accorded a proper place to the *diffidatio*, and in a lesser degree the position of the kings of England as payers of homage to the kings of France, combined to protect those who levied war on the king in his realm. In contrast there were other crimes which from much earlier times had always been held as high treason and whose perpetrators on conviction had usually suffered death. They comprised as we have seen the compassing of the king's death, the procuring of his own or his armies' sedition, the affording of aid, whether tangibly or by mere advice, to his enemies. During the thirteenth century there was a tendency to punish these treasons more severely, and to the penalties of drawing and hanging were added on different occasions disembowelling, burning, beheading and quartering.[2] Until the reign of Edward I the men who suffered

---

[1] For a summary of the law of treason to the mid-thirteenth century, see Pollock and Maitland, II, 500–8.

[2] In 1238 an 'armiger literatus' who attempted the king's life was drawn, hanged, beheaded and quartered: 'rex eum, quasi regiae majestatis (occisorem), membratim laniatum equis apud Coventre, exemplum terribile et spectaculum comentabile praebere (iussit) omnibus audentibus talia machinari. Primo enim distractus, postea decollatus et corpus in tres partes divisum est' (Paris, *Chronica Majora*, III, 498). In 1242 William de Marisco was sentenced to be drawn, hanged, disembowelled and quartered: 'Primo igitur a Westmonasterio usque ad turrim Londoniarum, et inde usque ad illam poenalem machinam, quae vulgariter *gibbetus* dicitur, distractus, cum ibidem miseram animam exhalasset, super unum uncorum est suspensus; et cum mortuus obriguisset, demissus

such brutal execution were of little political importance, but in the process at Shrewsbury against David ap Gruffydd in 1282 the English state trial had its origins and the *quasi* treason of levying war against the king took on a new status and importance. When Edward died in 1307 at least a score of important political opponents had been executed for treason and the majority because they had levied war. They had undergone trials and punishments which in subsequent centuries were to call forth censorious criticism. The question arises whether Edward I, in whom some modern writers have detected a brutal and vicious streak, developed a law of treason in accordance with his own whim, or whether the legal process of the state trial was a natural expression of the law of the land. Before Edward came to the throne the author of the *Song of Lewes* had cast doubts on his reverence for the law: 'whatever he wants he holds to be lawful and thinks that there are no legal bounds to his power'.[1] Recently a critic has suggested that the king wilfully abused his power in pursuit of his dynastic aims and was in fact much different from the merciful, impartial and righteous monarch drawn by *Fleta*.[2] In the various trials for treason Edward was involved at a personal level, for he considered each traitor as his own private enemy. The temptation therefore to act in a despotic way against those for example who denied him what he believed was his rightful possession of Scotland was very great. Thus it is not unreasonable to hope that a study of the Edwardian treason trials may throw some light on the issue of despotism as well.

The first political trial of the reign concerned the treason of David ap Gruffydd, brother of Prince Llywelyn. David was an exceptional traitor in that he had royal blood in his veins. According to English custom he must therefore be tried before men of noble rank. In Edward's view this may have been none too satisfactory, for they might return the wrong verdict. Therefore the king proceeded carefully, calling a parliament to Shrewsbury

evisceratus est et statim in eodem loco visceribus combustis, miserum cadaver in quatuor partes est divisum et ad quatuor principales regni civitates eaedem partes, ut miserabile spectaculum illud singulos intuentes exterreret sunt transmissae. Omnes autem sexdecim socii, per civitatem Londoniarum ad caudas equorum tracti ad patibula sunt suspensi' (*ibid.*, IV, 196).

[1] C. L. Kingsford, *The Song of Lewes* (Oxford, 1890), p. 15.

[2] K. B. McFarlane, 'Had Edward I a policy toward the Earls?', *History*, L (1965), 156. See also *Select Cases in the Court of the King's Bench*, ed. G. O. Sayles (Seld. Soc., 1955), p. liii.

for Michaelmas 1283 for the express purpose of consulting about what should be done with the captive Welsh prince. Each county and twenty boroughs were asked to send two representatives and over a hundred nobles were told to attend in their own persons.[1] The role of the nobility in the subsequent judicial process is hard to explain to complete satisfaction. Three chroniclers state that David was actually judged by the nobles and another that the death sentence came as judgement 'per consideratum magnatum', yet this cannot have been the whole story.[2] More precisely, the 'continuator' of the chronicle of 'Florence of Worcester' records that 'in parliamento generali . . . in ipsa domini regis curia, praesidente in judicio auctoritate regia Johanne de Wallibus de proditione' was the Welsh prince convicted[3] and there is support for his assertion in the continuation of Gervase of Canterbury.[4] The account of the successor to William Rishanger differs slightly in that David is supposed to have been judicially condemned 'per deputatos ad hoc Justiciarios'.[5] The Waverley annalist believed that the magnates were summoned to advise on the actual physical penalties to be inflicted on the condemned man,[6] while the compiler of the Dunstable annals actually explains which punishments were related to which crimes.[7] In contrast an official record tersely announces that the king, after taking counsel with his nobles, intends to ordain what ought to be done with David: it implies that the crown will deliver the judgement itself, and not the peers of the realm.[8] No doubt Edward would have liked to proceed straightaway to a summary and certain judgement. But since the crime was held as high treason the king himself was directly involved and it was a maxim current amongst thirteenth-century lawyers that he could not be both accuser and judge in his own cause.[9] To abandon his role as supreme judge must have been unthinkable and therefore the answer which Edward devised

---

[1] *Cal. Chanc. Rolls, 1277–1326*, pp. 281, 282.

[2] *Annales Monastici*, III, 295, IV, 489, 294; *Flores Historiarum*, III, 58.

[3] *Continuation of the Chronicle of Florence of Worcester*, ed. B. Thorpe (English Historical Society, 1849), II, 229.

[4] *The Historical Works of Gervase of Canterbury*, ed. W. Stubbs (R.S., 1880), II, 292: 'Hoc judicium protulit dominus Johannes de Vaus'.

[5] *Rishanger, Chronica*, p. 104.

[6] *Annales Monastici*, II, 400: 'in curia regia tractatum est a regni potentioribus qua poena mortis plecti debuit . . .'

[7] *Ibid.*, III, 295.   [8] *Cal. Chanc. Rolls, 1277–1326*, p. 281.

[9] Bracton, II, 337.

seems to have been this. He asked the barons if David's supposed crimes amounted to treason. When they answered in the affirmative the king gave sentence through his justices. This would explain the comments of two later chroniclers, Sir Thomas Grey of Heton[1] and the author of the *Brut*,[2] who aver quite bluntly that David was sentenced at the king's command. The part played by the magnates was probably analogous to a declaration of various misdeeds as treason: sometimes it was referred to as the reputing of the king's enemies.[3] Of course since it was the crown which put the crimes before the nobles Edward was still really the accuser but the true nature of the device was cleverly disguised.

By David's rebellion Edward had been highly incensed and the relevant entries on the chancery rolls exude righteous wrath and personal hurt. David was called the last of a family of traitors: he had forgotten that the king had once received him as an exile, nourished him as an orphan, endowed him with lands and given him high position at court.[4] So annoyed was Edward by this betrayal of his confidence that he determined on an exemplary punishment. The extent to which he had been governed by precedent in the actual process against the Welsh prince is not entirely clear but in the matter of the penalties which were inflicted the contemporary chroniclers saw great novelty. The Oseney annalist states that David was sentenced to a death which was of a type hitherto unknown.[5] The writer of the Dunstable annals, as has already been noted, demonstrated how the penalties derived. Because David was a betrayer of the king, who had made him a knight, he was to be drawn at the horse's tail to the place of his hanging. This, of course, was the hall-mark of treason. Because he had killed Fulk Trigald and other English noblemen he was to be hanged alive; because he had committed the murders at Easter he was to be disembowelled and his entrails burned. Finally, because he had plotted the king's death in several different parts of the realm his body was to be quartered and limbs despatched to where they could act as a warning to others.[6]

---

[1] *The Scalacronica of Sir Thomas Gray*, translated by H. Maxwell (Glasgow, 1907), p. 4.
[2] *The Brut*, ed. F. W. D. Brie (Early English Text Society, 1906), I, 183–4.
[3] Below, pp. 27–8.   [4] *Cal. Chanc. Rolls, 1277–1326*, p. 281.
[5] *Annales Monastici*, IV, 294. In fact the same or very similar punishments had been inflicted on traitors earlier in the century. See p. 23, n. 2.
[6] *Ibid.*, III, 295.

The brutality which the crown showed to David has to be set alongside the generosity which Henry III and his eldest son displayed towards their opponents at the close of the Barons' Wars. Unlike Simon de Montfort and Gilbert de Clare before the battle of Lewes, or John Balliol in October 1295, David had not apparently defied his liege lord in formal manner and it may be imagined that this was the reason for his severe punishment.[1] But example can be taken from 1265 to show that in royalist eyes at least the *diffidatio* gave no legal protection to a rebel though it might affect the awarding of the king's grace. Thus Henry III, after the battle of Evesham had been won, addressed certain knights who refused to surrender a castle in a very revealing way. He said he ought to deal with them 'generally and severally judicially rather than mercifully', but in fact on that occasion he was merciful.[2] Another general consideration concerns the crime of levying war against the king. The rebels who defended Northampton in the spring of 1264 were said to have resisted the king in a hostile manner at a time when strong war had arisen in the realm.[3] When victory was certain the crown's servants talked more boldly of the war being moved by Simon de Montfort for the disherison of the king and the destruction of his crown.[4] This was approaching very close to the fourteenth-century treason of levying war against the king. Since there were no state trials at the civil war's conclusion the latter charge was never made in the courts and we have no means of knowing for sure if it would have been construed as treason. Most probably it would not, for although David was accused of burning the king's towns, slaying and burning many of his subjects and invading his castles, he was not accused in explicit terms of levying war against his sovereign. Private war, we should remember, was the custom of the marches until Edward I disciplined the earls of Gloucester and Hereford in 1291.[5] A third consideration in the matter of armed insurrection concerns a fairly common sanction used by the crown in the Barons' Wars. This was the reputing of a rebel as the enemy of the king. Nearly always it was done on the advice of the magnates. The procedure

---

[1] *Rishanger, Chronica*, p. 22; *Cal. Docs. Scot.*, ii, 167.
[2] *Cal. Pat. Rolls*, 1258–66, p. 488.
[3] *Ibid.*, p. 313.   [4] *Ibid.*, p. 532.
[5] See *Cal. Chanc. Rolls*, 1277–1326, pp. 334–49 for details of the great feud between the earls, the findings of a commission of enquiry and the judgement in parliament.

dated back to before the period of actual fighting, being mentioned as early as September 1261.[1] In July 1263 some knights who occupied Windsor castle were commanded to leave on pain of being reputed as the king's enemies for forcefully detaining the castle against his will.[2] In October 1264 the marcher lords who were besieging the castle of Gilbert de Clare were ordered by the king to retire from the siege and not molest the earl further on pain of being reputed as enemies of himself and the realm and thereby incurring their own disherison.[3] The knights already mentioned who were threatened in the same way after Evesham were told they might equally easily be disinherited or lose their lives: thus such reputing must have been roughly the same as being outlawed and the rebel on capture could possibly be hanged without more ado. Behind this procedure may have been the king's desire for some sort of judgement against the rebels before he took their lands into his own hands and maybe regranted them to royalists at a later date. Bracton held that no lands should be forfeited without judgement, but outlawry was always regarded as the equivalent of a judgement.[4] The contrast in the punishment meted out to the adherents of Montfort on the one hand and to Prince David on the other was very great. To make a rebel redeem his lands at seven times the annual value was as severe a punishment as any Montfortian received[5] and the crown had the utmost difficulty in separating political offences from mere looting and the settling of old scores in the 'tempus turbacionis'. For Edward therefore when he had crushed the Welsh rebellion there was in the Barons' Wars no precedent on punishment to his liking. He must needs develop a policy on rebellion of his own. The Welsh could count on no strong body of support in England and the considerations of state which had carried the day in 1265–7 no longer obtained in

[1] *Cal. Pat. Rolls, 1258–66*, p. 175.
[2] *Ibid.*, p. 271.
[3] *Ibid.*, p. 374.
[4] H. Bracton, *De Legibus Angliae*, ed. T. Twiss (R.S., 1878–83), II, 350. Reputing a man a traitor on the part of the king was analogous to the defiance of a feudal inferior by his superior, the reverse of the usual process. It was similar to outlawry at the king's command, a practice which because of Magna Carta could only operate for felony and in time of peace. Reputing was for treason and operable when the king had proclaimed open war.
[5] This was the penalty which the Dictum of Kenilworth imposed on Robert Ferrers, earl of Derby, Henry de Hastings the leader of the Kenilworth garrison, and those responsible for the mutilation of a royal messenger. See F. M. Powicke, *The Thirteenth Century* (Oxford, 1953), p. 212 n.

1283. The king could make an example of David with impunity: so he did.

At a point in time almost midway between the Shrewsbury Parliament and the famous trial of William Wallace in 1305 came the process against another Welsh rebel, Rhys ap Maredudd. As in the case of David ap Gruffydd there is little information to be gleaned about the actual trial although the enrolment of the commission of 2 June 1292 to the justices of gaol delivery who pronounced sentence does survive.[1] Rhys had been hunted by the English government since 1287 and it seems unlikely that its attitude towards him altered in the period before his capture. In July 1287 he was called a manifest rebel and enemy of the king who had made war against the king's subjects during Edward's absence abroad by means of burning, manslaughter and other excesses against the king's peace, for the keeping of which he was bound by his homage with others of the king's subjects of those parts.[2] These charges, although made in letters patent and not before a court of law, are of great interest. By declaring Rhys as a manifest rebel the crown was groping its way towards judgement by notoriety, the method of condemnation used against Roger Mortimer in 1330 and more generally to afforce charges of levying war against the king in the reign of Edward II. Common fame, that is to say ill fame, a popular notion under the common law, was being carried into the political arena, though of course Edward I would have been the last to admit that Rhys was anything more than an ordinary criminal. Making war against the king's subjects and presumably against the king himself had he been within the realm was a charge which approximated more closely still to the fourteenth-century treason of levying war against the king than did the comparable one against David. Furthermore, the factors that went to make up such war were becoming recognizable. They included wanton devastation by means of fire, the committing of manslaughter (or as we would say the killing of civilians) and some other large crime.[3] There was no unequivocal reference to a formal defiance of his overlord by the Welsh rebel, although he was reported as having maliciously withdrawn from his fealty and

---

[1] Printed from the *Close Rolls* by J. G. Edwards in 'Treason of Thomas Turberville, 1295', *Studies presented to F. M. Powicke*, p. 296.

[2] *Cal. Chanc. Rolls, 1277–1326*, p. 307.

[3] Similar crimes were imputed to John Balliol and William Wallace (*Chronicles of Edward I and Edward II*, I, 119, 141).

homage. The stress was quite as much on his breaking the king's peace; feudal obligation counted for less than it had done even ten years before.

King Edward, it is easy to see, felt a particular grievance against those who spurned his generosity. David, he believed, had returned evil for the hospitality extended to him in his youth. Rhys had been warned on more than one occasion that he should cease his disturbances and submit to the king's grace, but had ignored the suggestion. The precise terms which Edward offered are not known, but it was his practice to offer substantial inducement initially and only demand unconditional surrender when his patience was finally exhausted. Such was the procedure with William Wallace in 1304–5. In 1287 the king had probably already reached this stage and the announcement that anyone who brought him the rebel's head would receive £100 is suggestive of the final hunt for Wallace. Whether like the Scot Rhys was actually outlawed cannot be shown: there is a fair possibility that he was. In July 1287 his lands had been taken into the king's hands as forfeit and he had not recovered them when he was finally taken in 1292.[1] On capture he was conducted to York, where he was lodged in the king's gaol until he was delivered on 2 June at Edward's special command. It was no general delivery of the gaol for Peter de Campania and his fellows were appointed for Rhys's judgement alone.[2] The prisoner was convicted 'de seductione domino regi facta' and of homicides, arsons, robberies and larcenies against the king's peace and of demolishing royal castles. It was adjudged he should be drawn 'pro seductione' and hanged for the homicides and other crimes. These charges approximate closely to the misdeeds he had been held to have committed in 1287. Rhys was a baron of Wales but unlike David he never seems to have had his crimes considered by his peers: nor in the judgement was there

---

[1] *Cal. Chanc. Rolls, 1277–1326*, p. 307.

[2] 'Deliberacio gaole regis de Eboraco facta de Rees Amereduk in crastino sancte Trinitatis anno regni regis nunc vicesimo per speciale preceptum eiusdem regis coram Petro de Campania, Johanne de Lythegreynes, Johanne de Melsa et Wilhelmo de S. Quintino, justiciariis ductus fuit et convictus de seductione domino regi facta, homicidiis combustionibus, roberiis et latrociniis contra pacem eiusdem domini regis factis, et castellis eiusdem regis prostratis. Adjudicatus est quod pro seductione domino regi facta detractetur et pro dictis homicidiis combustionibus, roberiis et latrociniis et castellis suspendatur' (*Close Roll* 109 (20 Edward I) schedule to m. 5d printed in *Studies presented to F. M. Powicke*, p. 296).

such a precise connexion between each crime and a different type of punishment. He was executed on the same day as the trial on 'Knavesmire' and his body was left hanging for three days.[1] To all outward appearances, unless there was something particularly sinister in delivery at the king's special command the trial was carried out under the normal processes of the common law. The proviso is however an important one.

What crystallized Edward's theories and practices in dealing with rebellion was undoubtedly the Scottish war. How he believed the king of England should proceed against those of his subjects who levied war against him is admirably illustrated in his letter to Pope Boniface of 7 May 1301 which was primarily intended to prove his overlordship of Scotland. The Scottish revolt of 1295–6 was the matter being explained. Edward related that John Balliol and his supporters 'ex praeconcepto malitia et praelocuta ac prae-ordinata proditione, pactiones, confoederationes, conspirationes et comminationes in exhaeredationem nostram et haeredum nostro-rum ac regni nostri, contra debitum homagii sui et fidelitatis juramentum inter se inierunt' thereby 'in crimine laesae majestatis nequiter incidendo'.[2] To say they had gone against their homage and fealty was common form but the use of the term lese-majesty to describe the rebellion was a distinct novelty. It may have been a symptom of the dawning of new political concepts but it may also have been an attempt to use civilian terminology which the papal lawyers would understand. Even if it was the latter it might well have affected the thinking of the king and his legal advisers and given rise to new ideas and interpretations. With Balliol, as in the case of Rhys ap Maredudd, the king talked of the crimes being of common report, that is, notorious: similarly Balliol like Rhys had refused to go before the king to receive justice but persisted in his perfidy. In other words he had refused to submit and throw him-self on the king's mercy. Evidence was also offered that Balliol had levied war in England by burning and slaughtering as well as by committing two crimes which had not been attributed in the same terms to either David or Rhys, namely laying the country waste and committing innumerable atrocities. Similar accusations were made against William Wallace in August 1305. Edward added that the Scottish king and his supporters were considered

---

[1] *Chronicon de Lanercost*, ed. J. Stevenson (Bannatyne Club, 1839), p. 145.
[2] *Chronicles of Edward I and Edward II*, I, 118.

4

by the English magnates to have committed war under the customs of the kingdom and that he felt justified in using his might to crush the rebellion of these notorious traitors.[1] Such declaration or reputing of the Scots by the king's noble advisers showed that the device used in the Barons' Wars and against David of Wales had become established. The fact that Balliol had given Edward his formal renunciation of homage at Berwick on 5 April 1296 was not mentioned in the king's letter.[2] It may however have saved certain of the Scottish leaders from being formally tried for treason when Edward had taken Scotland into his own hands within the year. As it was there were no trials or physical punishments. Lands of a number of mesne tenants which had been taken into the king's hands were returned to their holders:[3] homage and fealty were taken from the nobility, the knights and the communities who at the same time renounced their league with the king of France.[4] The only reference to proceedings against treason occurred on the plea roll of the English army in Scotland and concerned military discipline rather than the punishment of insurrection. On 21 March 1296 Sir William de Wytyngham, who had been taken and imprisoned on suspicion of being a traitor, was accused of being a Scottish spy, of being of the affinity of John Comyn and of absenting himself from his lands to avoid serving in Edward's army against the Scots. He put himself on a jury which acquitted him.[5] In three other cases men were also accused of being Scottish spies and enemies of the king. Like Wytyngham each put himself on a jury and was acquitted.

Despite several threats on King Edward's part that various Scots had behaved traitorously, and in one instance that they should receive their proper deserts, none were in fact tried for treason before William Wallace in August 1305.[6] By that time the king had

---

[1] *Chronicles of Edward I and Edward II*, i, 118, 119.

[2] *Foedera*, ed. T. Rymer (Rec. Comm. edn), i, ii, 836–7.

[3] *Cal. Close Rolls, 1288–96*, pp. 487, 491, 495; *Documents and Records Illustrating the History of Scotland*, ed. F. Palgrave (London, 1837), pp. 175 ff. There was no general return of forfeited land until much later. The chancery rolls under 4 October 1304 refer to an ordinance by the king and council dealing with the return of the lands of Scots which had been taken into the king's hands by reason of war (*Cal. Pat. Rolls, 1301–7*, p. 261).

[4] *Cal. Docs. Scot.*, ii, 182–96.

[5] P.R.O., E. 39/93/15 mm. 1, 2d, 5. The roll is unique.

[6] See *Cal. Close Rolls, 1296–1302*, p. 168 and *Cal. Docs. Scot.*, ii, 241. Those so mentioned were Edmund Comyn and Henry de Chartres (June 1298) and Macduff (August 1297).

become very annoyed at his inability to establish a secure peace in Scotland and laid much of the blame on the shoulders of the former army leader. After a period of inactivity Wallace rejoined the resistance to Edward in the winter of 1302–3 but no longer had overall command. In the summer of 1303 the English king led an army into Scotland and in February of the subsequent year John Comyn and other leading Scottish magnates submitted. The terms they were given were generous: there was no disinheritance and forfeited estates were redeemable at varying fines.[1] Through his friends Wallace sent a request to Edward at the beginning of 1304 asking if he could 'submit to his honest peace without surrendering into his hands body or head'. The chronicler adds that he also asked for an inducement: 'that the king grant him of his gift, not as a loan, an honourable allowance of woods and cattle and by his writing the seizure and investment for him and his heirs in purchased land'. The king, we are told, was very angry and offered 300 marks to any man who killed the Scot. It is possible that Wallace had also solicited the king's peace during the year previous and that Edward had seen fit to grant him a day to make his submission, but without ultimate result.[2] The spurning of the king's generosity on two occasions and the demand for a 'douceur' may have played a part in the deliberate exclusion of Wallace from the terms of submission allowed to John Comyn and other Scots magnates in February 1304. 'Et quant a Monsieur Guilliam de Galeys', said the agreement, 'est accorde q'il se mette en la volunte et en la grace nostre Seignr le Roy si lui semble que bon soit'.[3] In other words Wallace could surrender if he wanted to but there would be no fixed terms for him: he would have to take his chance. In the St Andrews Parliament of March 1304 the peace terms were confirmed but Simon Fraser, the garrison of Stirling Castle, which was still holding out against the English, and William Wallace were specifically excluded. Against these men, we are told, Edward sought judgement according to due process and the laws of Scotland, and the parliament pronounced them to be outlawed.[4]

---

[1] *Documents and Records of Scotland*, ed. Palgrave, pp. 286–7; *Rot. Parl.*, I, 211–13.

[2] *The Chronicle of Pierre de Langtoft*, ed. T. Wright (R.S., 1866), II, 351, 353.

[3] *Rot. Parl.*, I, 213 a.

[4] *Annales Nicholai Trivet*, ed. T. Hog (English Historical Society, 1845), p. 402 n: 'Ad locum vero et diem statutem convenerunt omnes, qui vocati fuerant, exceptis Simone Frisel et Willelmo Waleys, et his qui contra regem

We have no way of telling if the victims had actually been exacted in five county courts, as would have been the case with ordinary criminals who refused to appear before the king's justices. If they had not then the procedure against them was very much akin to the reputing of the king's foes as public enemies during the Barons' Wars and again in 1295. In such circumstances the action of the St Andrews Parliament is suggestive of a fifteenth-century act of attainder. By the time of the surrender of Stirling castle on 20 July 1304 Fraser had managed to come to an agreement with Edward and Wallace alone was still an outlaw. Towards him the king's attitude was unaltered and he announced to Fraser, Comyn, Alexander Lindsay and David Graham, each of whom by then had been adjudged to exile, that if they managed to take Wallace by mid-January 1305 the captor would stand a good chance of having the sentence against him mitigated.[1]

Wallace was pursued without success for a long time but was eventually captured on 3 August 1305 near Glasgow by men who were under the orders of Sir John Menteith. He was sent under guard to Edward but the king apparently refused to see him and ordered him to be taken to London where he arrived on 22 August. Luckily, despite the dearth of legal records relating to treason in the reign of Edward I, what appears to be a copy of the official version of the judicial proceedings against Wallace was preserved by the author of the *Annales Londonienses*.[2] On the morning of 23 August, according to this source, Wallace was led on horseback to Westminster Hall and immediately called to judgement. His judges had been appointed to deliver 'prisonam nostram civitatis nostrae Londoniarum', which was in fact the house of William de Leyre, an alderman, 'juxta ordinationem vobis per nos inde injunctam' : that is to say by special royal command as in the case of Rhys ap Maredudd at York in 1292. A signification of the same date (18 August) to the chancellor gives the additional information that Wallace was to be delivered 'selonc la ley et l'usage de notre realme'. Peter Mallore, justiciar of England and one of the five judges appointed by commission, accused the captive of betraying

---

castrum de Strivelin tenuerunt; quorum petente rege judicium secundum juris processum et leges Scoticanas omnes qui convenerant concordi sententia pronunciant exlegatos.'
[1] *Documents and Records of Scotland*, ed. Palgrave, p. 276.
[2] *Chronicles of Edward I and Edward II*, I, 139–42.

his king.[1] Wallace is said to have replied that he had never been a traitor to the king of England but conceded the other crimes which were laid against him.[2] What happened next is not perfectly clear. The chronicler says that Mallore and his fellow justices 'decrcvit judicium serie qua sequitur'. He then sets down the commission of gaol delivery and says that under it the justices proceeded in this manner.[3] There follows a copy of what was probably the official record of the trial and apparently, if the chronicler was not guilty of gross omission, it was a trial without accusation in the normal manner. There was no indictment by jury, no appeal by an individual, no accusation by the king's prosecutor but merely a statement of the crimes which the crown held Wallace to have committed, terminating with the judgement 'consideratum est quod praedictus Willelmus pro manifesta seditione quam ipsi domino regi fecerat, felonice machinando, in mortem eius perpetrando, annullationem et enervationem coronae et regiae dignitatis suae, vexillum contra dominum suum ligium in bello mortali deferendo, detrahatur . . . et . . . suspendatur et postea devaletur'.[4] There is no suggestion of Wallace having an opportunity to put himself on a jury. As it stands it reads very much like the king's own record of the offences serving as immediate proof. The justices merely rehearsed the record together with the sentence which the crown had attached to it and which had no doubt been carefully devised by the king's legal advisers. The record of the king or more commonly the record of another court was often recited when an outlaw was captured and brought into court. In such circumstances there was no proper trial but merely the passing of sentence and its execution. Bracton states that when an outlaw has been taken nothing remains to be adjudged respecting him but only the execution of judgement.[5] The king's own word or record that a fact was so was the most perfect form of proof obtainable since it was incontrovertible.[6] Very possibly Wallace was treated as an outlaw for when the record had listed at considerable length

---

[1] *Documents Illustrative of the History of Scotland*, ed. J. Stevenson (Edinburgh, 1870), p. 187.
[2] *Chronicles of Edward I and Edward II*, i, 139.
[3] *Ibid.*, i, 140.   [4] *Ibid.*, i, 141.
[5] Bracton, *De Legibus Angliae*, ed. Twiss, ii, 383.
[6] T. F. T. Plucknett, 'The Origin of Impeachment', *Trans. Roy. Hist. Soc.*, 4th ser., xxiv (1942), 56–63, discusses the king's power to record and shows that by about 1339 there were some limitations to it.

the crimes he had committed in the course of his resistance it went on to state that he had been publicly outlawed in the king's court 'ut seductor, praedo et felo' according to the laws and customs of England and Scotland.[1] Furthermore he was still an outlaw and so could not be allowed to defend himself or make any response. Wallace nonetheless had already made one interjection as we have seen.

The crimes which Wallace was said to have committed had much in common with those laid against David ap Gruffydd, Rhys ap Maredudd and John Balliol, although since it was probably a copy of an official record they were given in more detail. The crown argued that Scotland had been conquered because Balliol had forfeited it by rebellion and that the king had established his peace, installed his ministers and taken the homage and fealty of the leaders of the community.[2] In perpetrating his various felonies and seditions Wallace was accused of being unmindful of his fealty and allegiance but he was not said to have broken his fealty, like David, or withdrawn from it, like Rhys. He was charged with killing the sheriff of Lanark when he was holding county court, with attacking towns and villages, issuing writs like those of the king, holding parliaments and assemblies and counselling the magnates of his party to submit to the dominion of the king of France. He was held to have invaded the English northern counties, to have burned or laid waste religious places and shrines and to have killed clergy, women and children.[3] This list of crimes bears a strong resemblance to the homicides, arsons and robberies attributed to Rhys ap Maredudd, while the next charge in the official record, that he had sought to compass the death of the king, smacks very much of the Dunstable annalist's last charge against Prince David. Plotting of this sort together with the issuing of writs and the holding of assemblies and the slaughter of clergy was specifically classed as sedition but it is noticeable that when sentence was pronounced at the end a second reference was made to two crimes of Wallace which the crown had no doubt about as being treason. These were compassing King Edward's death and bearing a banner against him in mortal war: on their account was the normal treason penalty of being drawn to the place of execution awarded.[4] The other crimes, despite the frequent insertion of the words

---

[1] *Chronicles of Edward I and Edward II*, I, 141. [2] *Ibid.*, I, 140.
[3] *Ibid.*, I, 140–1. [4] *Ibid.*, I, 141.

'seditio' and 'seditiose', were classified as acts of violence, homicides and felonies and the punishment was hanging. Men had been accused of waging war upon the king before but the Wallace record provides the first example of a lawyer's definition of this crime. It had obviously been decided that the displaying of a banner against the king in mortal war, as against the mock war of the tournament, was the vital element: no doubt because there would be many witnesses and therefore little subsequent argument. The definition was probably based on contemporary social and chivalric custom. The jurors who provided information about the feuding of the earls of Gloucester and Hereford in 1291 were concerned very much with private war in South Wales and the marches. They had also taken the display of banners as the sign of waging war.[1]

The case against Wallace was stated not vaguely or generally but in precise terminology which made a cogent legal argument. As far as the facts referred to can be checked historically they were quite accurate. Nowhere did Edward overstate his case. For example he refrained from calling the seeking of a French alliance adhering to the king's enemies and he only used the charge of treason where he knew he was on sure ground.[2] What Wallace meant by saying he had committed no treason is not self evident. It has been construed as meaning that King Edward 'had never been his lawful and natural lord and at no time had he ever sworn allegiance or done homage to him'. This, adds the writer, 'Wallace himself was unable to declare at his trial.'[3] There is no evidence for the second of these statements though Wallace may indeed have seen the charges in this light. The argument has been tendered that Wallace had never taken an oath to Edward and was not therefore one of the king's lieges: he was acting in the name of Balliol as king and had never recognized the deposition.[4] Presumably he reckoned his deeds were excused by Balliol's *diffidatio* of 1296 and he refused to accept the Scottish king's return to homage and

---

[1] *Cal. Chanc. Rolls, 1277–1326*, pp. 337, 345.

[2] To adhere to the king's enemies had been classed as treason for some time; see *Oxford City Documents*, pp. 204–5 and *Studies presented to F. M. Powicke*, p. 307. J. G. Edwards states that Sir Thomas Turberville was not the first perpetrator of this crime: 'That adhering to the king's enemies by spying was already recognised as treasonable before 1295 is clear.'

[3] G. W. S. Barrow, *Robert Bruce and the Community of the Realm of Scotland* (London, 1965), p. 194 and note.

[4] By the author of the article on William Wallace in the *Dictionary of the National Biography* (A. J. G. MacKay).

fealty in which he conceded Edward's conquest was 'of right'.[1] Certainly the name William Wallace does not appear on the list of those who offered homage and fealty in May–August 1296. King Edward on the other hand seems to have believed that those who did so offer spoke not for themselves alone but for the whole of the community. Thus, although for example for the county of Lanark about a score of barons and knights came to the king's faith and swore fealty at the end of August 1296 and Wallace was not among them,[2] yet the crown claimed less than two years later that the king was seised of the homages and the fealties of the prelates, earls, barons, knights and other nobles and of the entire communities and inhabitants of Scotland.[3] The statement can be explained as wishful thinking on Edward's part but it is more likely that he genuinely believed it. If the small number of barons and knights of Lanark or any other shire spoke only for themselves then all the lower classes of the Scottish countryside had *carte blanche* to break into rebellion whenever they felt like it with no fear of retribution. If there was no 'community of the shire' in Scotland whose representatives on occasion might act for it, nor on the other hand the more primitive idea that a lord spoke for his tenants, then Edward and his advisers were hopelessly out of touch with Scottish customs. Perhaps Wallace chose to stand by the defiance of 1296 because he considered that Balliol had been cowed into admitting that Edward's conquest was rightful and had been forced into yielding the land and people of Scotland and their homages to him. If this was the case he was ignoring the will of the 'maior et sanior pars' of the Scottish community. He may of course have felt it was not the will of the lower class. Supposing that these were the reasons behind Wallace's denial of treason, and it is only conjecture, then the arguments were finely balanced. Edward behaved with studious care before he actually used force and must have been perplexed when nationalism thwarted his plans since popular movements were not allowed for in the high diplomacy of the times.

From the political view-point the trial and sentence were ill-judged and personal animosity may have clouded the king's vision. Considered judicially the process was akin in the sentence pronounced to the one which concerned David ap Gruffydd. It

---

[1] *Rishanger, Chronica*, pp. 158, 161.   [2] See *Cal. Docs. Scot.*, II, 186.
[3] *Ibid.*, II, 252.

was, however, at once more refined and more brutal. For his treason Wallace was drawn from Westminster to the Tower of London, to Aldgate and thence to the Elms at Smithfield. 'Pro roberiis et homicidiis et feloniis' committed in England and Scotland he was hanged and disembowelled.[1] Because he had lived and died an outlaw he was beheaded. Because of his injuries to the church and its holy things the entrails which had given rise to his blasphemous thoughts were burned: this matched very closely one feature of the award against Prince David. Similarly Wallace's corpse was to be dismembered, but for sedition to the king and the people of England and Scotland, and not for compassing the death of the king. His four quarters were to be displayed in the north as a deterrence. The punishment was a brutal one and the chroniclers of the period were much impressed. Indeed they were more impressed by Wallace's execution than they had been by the drawing and hanging of the 293 Jewish and three Christian coin clippers on a single occasion in 1279.[2] Such was probably Edward's intention. The mode of punishment does not stand alone in English medieval history by any means and the lawyers accepted that it was quite within Edward's prerogative to decree. 'The judgment for lese majesty against the earthly king', writes the author of the *Mirror of Justices*, 'is executed by torment according to the ordinance and will of the king and by death.'[3]

Had King Edward ever succeeded in capturing Robert Bruce it is probable that he would have met a fate similar to that of Wallace although his crimes were quite different. What turned Bruce into a traitor in Edward's eyes was the murder of John Comyn in the Greyfriars' church at Dumfries on 10 February 1306. The deed was committed, so we are told, because Comyn would not give his assent 'a la traison qe le dit Robert pensa de faire contre le dit Roi d'Engleterre, cest asavoir de relever contre li de guerre' with the intention of making himself king of Scotland.[4] The crime was referred to as treasonable insurrection against the homage and fealty which Bruce owed to his liege lord the king of England. An entry in the chancery rolls under 5 April 1306 makes reference to the murder, the raising of war, the imprisoning of the king's ministers, the seizing of castles and towns and the usurping of the

[1] *Chronicles of Edward I and Edward II*, 1, 141–2.
[2] *Ibid.*, 1, 88.   [3] *Mirror*, p. 135.
[4] *Documents and Records of Scotland*, ed. Palgrave, p. 335.

lordship of Scotland as being to the scandal of the catholic church and the realm and the disherison of the king and his crown.[1] Five days later when Bruce's Annandale lands, now forfeit, were granted to Humphrey de Bohun, earl of Hereford and Essex, this construction was confirmed. The crime was set down as the seditious and treacherous slaying of Comyn before the high altar of the Friars Minors' church at Dumfries 'thus committing sacrilege'.[2] As in the cases of Wallace and David ap Gruffydd Edward was regarding the crimes as being not only against himself but against the church as well. Thereby the charges bore added notoriety and infamy. The legal measures which he took against the new traitor and his adherents went considerably beyond the devices used to deal with previous treasons and it is remarkable that no historian has appreciated their significance. The policy was stated in the ordinances made at Lanercost priory in the winter of 1306–7 by the king and his council 'for better assuring the peace of Scotland' and the suppression of the rebellion. All who had been involved in the death of John Comyn as well as those who counselled them were to be drawn and hanged. Any man taken by force in the war against the king was to be hanged or beheaded and all those who had stood against the king before, during or after the battle of Methven were to be imprisoned and not released without Edward's express command.[3] The ordinances were a refinement of the stern directive from King Edward to Aymer de Valence, his lieutenant in Scotland, on 28 June 1306, nine days after the rout of Bruce's army at Methven. It referred to the king's order to Valence to put to death all rebels and enemies already taken or to be captured in the future, except Bruce, the earl of Atholl and Simon Fraser, until the king had declared his pleasure on their fate.[4] Thus with regard to the Scots who had fought at Methven the ordinances were actually a step towards moderation. Very possibly this was because King Edward had been appeased in the meantime by the execution of sixteen notable rebels all but one of whom had been involved in the battle near Perth. The manner in which these men were condemned was of the utmost importance to the development of the law of treason.

[1] *Cal. Pat. Rolls, 1301–7*, p. 426.
[2] *Cal. Docs. Scot.*, II, 473; see also *Cal. Pat. Rolls, 1301–7*, p. 436.
[3] *Documents and Records of Scotland*, ed. Palgrave, pp. 361–2.
[4] *Cal. Docs. Scot.*, II, 480.

The rebels, who comprised fifteen Scots and a single English-man, were delivered from the gaol of Newcastle-on-Tyne on 4 August 1306 by Peter Mallore and his fellow justices specially assigned for the purpose. From the king the latter received certain instructions which were read openly in court. They were to the effect that John de Seton, the Englishman, was to be drawn and hanged as the king had heard that he had been present at the death of John Comyn: that Bernard Mowat was to suffer the same fate as he had been present at the death of Roger de Tany, who was on his way to the king, then involved in the Scottish war. Mowat had also burned and destroyed the possessions of the Holy Church. It was further commanded that all the other fourteen prisoners of war were to be hanged as they had borne arms against their liege lord at Methven and had been taken as prisoners of war. Also a record or copy was to be made by one of the justices of the treasons and felonies imputed by the king and thereon judgement pro-nounced as ordained. None of the prisoners was to be allowed to answer. First to appear before the justices was apparently John de Seton, who was stated to have captured and held for Robert Bruce the castle of Tibbers: he had also aided Bruce in Comyn's murder. Probably the charges were read over to the prisoner before the court proceeded to find that as the crimes were suffi-ciently notorious and manifest to the king and his court he should be drawn and hanged 'secundum (tenorem) mandati domini Regis credentie predicte'. Next Bernard Mowat was dealt with. The justices rehearsed the royal record to the effect that he had borne arms against King Edward at the battle of Methven and had feloniously and wickedly slain some of the king's liegemen who had been captured there. He had, like Seton, been involved in the killing of Roger Tany, the king's valet, and had burned and des-troyed churches. For these crimes he was to be drawn and hanged again 'secundum tenorem mandati domini Regis et credentie sue predicte'. The rest of the prisoners were charged with bearing arms with Bruce against the king at Methven. Their crimes were recorded as notorious and manifest and they were sentenced to be hanged, but not drawn, under the king's instructions.[1]

---

[1] P.R.O., J. I. 1. 1108, m. 26, 26d: 'La creaunte dunt mon sire Robert de la Warde est charge depar le Rey adire a mon sire Pieres de Maulay et a tes com-pargnons Justices assigns a delivrer la gaole le Rey a Noefchastel sus Tyne et David de Inchmartyn, Johan de Campbell, chevaliers, Johan de Somervill,

These cases are the earliest and indeed the clearest example of conviction by record to be discovered. Plucknett showed how the king and certain of his ministers had the power to convict a man by their own word, although it was usual for them to have direct knowledge of the crime, probably because they had seen it occur.[1] It is impossible to be sure how Edward got the idea of using the device to condemn the Methven rebels, but the process against William Wallace may well have played a part since it too was lacking an appeal or indictment or trial by jury. Unlike Seton, Mowat and their fellows, Wallace at his trial was referred to as an outlaw even though the outlawry was under an ordinance of an Anglo–Scottish parliament.[2] In this way the trials of 1306 were of a more summary nature than the one of 1305. Since the historical materials for the reconstruction of Wallace's trial are so few it cannot be proved that the justices who sentenced him received instructions similar to those addressed to the deliverers of Newcastle-on-Tyne gaol, but the possibility cannot be denied. Once our

Rauf de Heriz, Alisaundre le Skyrmyschour, Robert Wycher, Bernar de Morhaut, Cuthbert de Carryk, Williame de Ba, Willaime de Botharm, Roger le Taillur, Uttyng le Mareschall, Duncan Boyde, Williame Rusky, Adam Turry le Messenger, Simond Fraser et Johan de Seton est tiels cet est asaver qe Johan de Seton seit treynez et penduz pur ceo qe le Rey ad intendu, q'il fut a la mort Roger de Tany qe fut tue a la forste de Selekirke en venant de nostre Seignur le Roy qe adunk fut en sa gerre de scotz e pur ceo q'il art et destrut Seint Eglise et qe toutz les autres personns avaunt nomies soient pendus pur ceo qeux ausi bien com les avantditz Johan de Seton et Bernar portent armes contre le Rey d'engleterre lur lige seignur et furent prises de gerre. Et de cestes tresunz et feloniz lur seit le record fet par akun des Justices avantditz en la fourme susdit et sur ceo les iugementz pronunties com devant est ordine et qe nul de eaux ne seit rescewe a respouns. En tesmoigne de quele chose le Rey ad fet fert ces lettres ouvertes sealez de sun privie seal a Laysinby le prim jour D'aust lan de sun regne trentime quatre.' The sentence on Seton follows immediately: 'et recordatus eidem Johanni traditionibus et feloniis suis predictis et similiter contemptoribus tam satisfactione ecclesie quam ipso Domino Regi: Et curiae sue sunt notorii et satis manifestati consideratum est quod predictus Johannes detrahatur et praeterea suspendatur secundum tenorem mandati domini Regis credentie predicte'. A similar sentence was passed on Bernard Mowat who had been at Methven 'arma gerens contra Dominum Regem' and had killed 'nequiter et felonice' certain of the king's lieges captured on the battlefield: in addition he had committed two 'traditiones' by being at the death of Roger de Tany and through burning down some Scottish churches.

[1] Plucknett, 'Origin of Impeachment', *Trans. Roy. Hist. Soc.*, 4th Ser., xxiv, 56–63. Plucknett quotes the important pronouncement of Willoughby, J., in 1339 that 'when the king records anything of his own view, that record shall never be annulled; but when he records upon the relation of another that record can be defeated by such suit as he has here made' (i.e. by the verdict of an inquisition). [2] *Annales Nicolai Trivet*, p. 402 n.

suspicions have been aroused it is easy to imagine the trial of Rhys ap Maredudd being merely a recital of the king's record stating the Welsh nobleman had in fact committed treason, particularly as the gaol was delivered on the king's special injunction.[1] Similarly, the evidence that Edward intended to ordain what should be done with David ap Gruffydd points in the same direction.[2] One noticeable difference between the procedure at Newcastle and that used in the trials of David and Wallace was the king's failure in 1306 to announce he had consulted with his council, the magnates or parliament in advance. Since Seton, Mowat and the others had not been 'reputed' as the king's enemies the increasingly summary nature of Edwardian state trials is difficult to deny. Further support for this sombre interpretation of events is provided by a letter from Edward the prince of Wales to Aymer de Valence informing him that the castle of Lochmaben and its garrison had surrendered on 11 July 1306 quite unconditionally except that the latter were to have a fair trial.[3] The implication is that King Edward had already initiated a policy of summary execution against those Scots taken in arms who particularly annoyed him. The only evidence that can be offered to show the English king in a better light is by no means weighty. It is to be found in an entry in the chancery rolls recording that Nigel Campbell, an adherent of Bruce and a rebel and enemy of the king, had been discovered to have been in the king's peace and allegiance until 10 February 1306, the day Bruce murdered Comyn. This fact was the finding of an inquisition taken before the king's council by his order.[4] It is possible but not at all probable that those important rebels who were given a summary trial, like John de Seton, Bernard Mowat, the knights taken at Methven, even the earl of Atholl and Simon Fraser, had been the subjects of similar inquisitions which had reputed them as traitors. The inquisition on Nigel Campbell was perhaps intended to find out the date on which his lands had been forfeited to the crown, but it could also have been used as the record of the crime in a court.[5] If Robert Bruce himself had ever been captured he

---

[1] *Studies presented to F. M. Powicke*, p. 296.
[2] *Cal. Chanc. Rolls, 1277–1326*, p. 281.
[3] *Cal. Docs. Scot.*, II, 483.
[4] *Cal. Close Rolls, 1302–7*, p. 497.
[5] Edward III in 1358–61 made a great deal of use of such inquisitions to give him title to the lands of those who had levied war against him or adhered to his foes and were beyond his authority. Below, p. 89.

might have been dealt with by this process. By an inquisition taken on Edward's instructions he had been found responsible for the traitorous murder of Comyn on the grounds that the facts were notorious both in Scotland and England and could not be denied.[1] Unfortunately since neither Bruce nor Campbell was captured and sentenced their cases do not afford conclusive evidence on the judicial methods used against those who were.

Judgement for treason on the king's record was not an unnatural device of an ill-tempered and acrimonious king, although Edward was undoubtedly very bitter about the Scottish revolt, but a fairly logical development from the legal ideas of the time. In the case of the private war between the earls of Gloucester and Hereford it had been declared as the opinion of the royal council that 'the king, from whom all ministers subjected to him have record, is a superlative and much more arduous record excelling all his ministers and the processes and record of their rolls'.[2] Thus the king's own word would suffice in place of a record of outlawry and perhaps also in place of being reputed as a traitor by one's peers in council or parliament. Seton, Mowat and the Scots who had fought at Methven were however condemned on the king's record because the charges were sufficiently notorious and manifest to the king and his court. The notion of public ill-fame was used to support the king's record of a traitor's guilt.[3] To some degree this addition must have been designed to disguise the novelty of the king's record as an appeal or indictment and a verdict all in one. Certainly it did away with the need for the normal type of accusation as methods used under the common law in the same year testify. When setting out for Scotland in June, Edward had told his sheriffs 'it is not unknown to the king what is known to all, to wit how divers traitors and felons do not permit themselves to be justiced . . .' Therefore although the second statute of Westminster did not allow a man to be arrested unless indicted by twelve jurymen and the indictment testified by their seals, the king ordered all suspects and manifest felons to be taken and imprisoned.[4] Not only were the crimes of Seton, Mowat and the others notorious and manifest but they were sufficiently [satis]

---

[1] *Documents and Records of Scotland*, ed. Palgrave, p. 346.
[2] *Cal. Chanc. Rolls, 1277–1326*, pp. 343–4.
[3] Plucknett, 'Origin of Impeachment', *Trans. Roy. Hist. Soc.*, 4th Ser., xxiv, 56–63.   [4] *Cal. Close Rolls, 1302–7*, p. 396.

notorious and manifest that drawing and hanging were awarded as penalties according to the tenor of the record. In this way the degree of notoriety eliminated the need for response and for trial by jury and operated an immediate conviction. The device was simple and brutally effective and had the king been challenged on the lawfulness of notoriety working a conviction he could have answered that he was not introducing a novelty but merely extending to treason a practice used to deal with the crime of sodomy.[1] The conviction on the king's record and by notoriety of John Seton, Bernard Mowat and the fourteen Scots who had been captured at the battle of Methven had results beyond the Scottish war and the reign of Edward I. It set a fashion in dealing with traitors taken in arms which was to figure prominently in the civil wars of the two succeeding centuries.

There were other rebels who also suffered under the sterner policy against treason which King Edward implemented following John Comyn's murder. Neil Bruce, the Scottish king's brother, and Sir Alan Durward of Fichlie were drawn, hanged and beheaded at Berwick;[2] Christopher Seton, the brother of John Seton, suffered the same fate at Dumfries while Thomas Bruce, another brother of Robert, was executed in a similar manner at Carlisle.[3] Edward must have been particularly pleased at the arrest of Simon Fraser, who had been a persistent thorn in the flesh. Despite the fact that his capture and execution aroused the greatest interest in southern England there is little information available concerning the trial. The *Brut* tells us like Wallace he was taken before the king and that Edward would not see him 'but commaundede him to ben ledde away to have his dome at London'.[4] Fraser had been outlawed with Wallace in the St Andrews Parliament of 1304 but some months later was able to surrender without dire consequence. In October 1305 Edward allowed him to recover his estates at three years' purchase.[5] He joined Bruce at about the time of his coronation, was present at Methven and was captured soon after. The punishment which Fraser received was as severe as that meted out to Wallace. After being drawn through the middle of London

---

[1] *Mirror*, p. 53.
[2] *Johannis de Fordun Chronica Gentis Scotorum*, ed. W. F. Skene (Edinburgh, 1871–2), I, 342; *Flores Historiarum*, III, 135; *Scalacronica of Sir Thomas Gray of Heton, Knight* (Maitland Club, 1836), p. 131.
[3] *Walter of Guisborough*, p. 369; *Flores Historiarum*, III, 136.
[4] *The Brut*, ed. Brie, I, 201.   [5] *Foedera*, ed. Rymer (Rec. Comm.), I, 974–5.

he was hanged still on the hurdle, cut down while alive and beheaded. His entrails were cut out and burned and the body hanged once more. To the sound of a horn his head was affixed to the highest point of London Bridge.[1] Because his heart, lungs and liver were burned we may surmise he was held to have outraged the church in some way, possibly by destroying ecclesiastical fabric or holy objects. Since he was beheaded it may have been that Edward still regarded Fraser when he was captured as an outlaw: in the record of Wallace's trial decollation and outlawry were directly connected. The author of the *Flores Historiarum* on the other hand has it that he was decapitated as a murderer.[2] Another Scottish leader who was executed in 1306 was John Strabolgi, earl of Atholl, the first earl to be so punished for 230 years. Like Fraser he was sent by King Edward to London immediately on capture. At the queen's request he was excused being drawn to the place of execution. On 7 November he was hanged on a high gallows, cut down still living, his head struck off and his trunk burned.[3] The place of the treason in legal history is obscure as there is very little to be gleaned concerning the mode of trial beyond the fact that it occurred in Westminster Hall before Roger Brabazon and Peter Mallore. If we may argue *ex silentio* one fact does stand out. There is no suggestion that Atholl was tried by his peers or that they were used to repute him as a traitor, unlike David ap Gruffydd, the other noble rebel of Edward's reign. If such was the case and Atholl was convicted on the king's record then the English king had perfected a universal weapon.

The state trials of 1306, apart from those held at Newcastle-on-Tyne, throw little light on the treason policy of the English crown. Not until well into the reign of Edward's son is there evidence to show that the father's devices were more than temporary expedients manufactured *ad hoc* by an old man in a hurry. At Hilary term 1318 there occurred in the king's bench a trial of singular significance. The constable of the Tower brought into court a north country knight called Gilbert de Middleton. There was no indictment or appeal, merely as in the cases of Wallace, John Seton, Mowat and the Methven captives the reading of the king's record.[4] This

---

[1] *Chronicles of Edward I and Edward II*, I, 148.
[2] *Flores Historiarum*, III, 134.
[3] *Ibid.*, III, 135; *Chronicles of Edward I and Edward II*, I, 149–50.
[4] *Select Cases in the Court of the King's Bench*, ed. Sayles (Seld. Soc., 1955), p. 78.

stated that Gilbert was within the king's allegiance and as a member of the royal household was retained with his robes and wages. 'Felonice ut felo, seductive ut seductor' he had raised an army of Scots, who were the king's enemies, and other felons and had ridden 'ad modum guerre cum vexillo suo displicato': men in the king's allegiance he had persuaded to take oaths to him. One good reason why the king used his record rather than resort to the normal processes of the common law lay in another crime which Middleton had committed. He had robbed the cardinals Gaucelin of Eauze and Luca Fieschi, who had been sent by Pope John XXII to arrange a peace between both the rival factions in England and the English and the Scots: he had also captured and held to ransom Henry de Beaumont, his brother Lewis, who was the bishop elect of Durham, and others of the kingdom, thereby displaying Edward II's lack of effective government. Finally he had held Mitford castle by force 'in signum hostilitatis ipsius domini regis' so that it was no fault of Gilbert's that war did not break out in the realm. The listing of Middleton's crimes having been completed there followed immediately the sentence: 'dominus rex vult et precepit quod idem Gilbertus pro feloniis et sedicionibus predictis per civitatem detrahatur . . . usque ad furcas et ibidem vivus suspendatur et vivus avalletur.' After the disembowelling he was to be beheaded and his head sent to London. Other parts of the sentence confirm the similarity with the penalties imposed on Wallace. Because his heart and entrails had germinated such horrible felonies against God, the Holy Church and his liege lord the king they were to be burned under the gallows. At the very end the body was to be divided into four quarters and despatched to Newcastle, York, Bristol and Dover. From other sources it appears that although the bishop of Durham and his brother were held to ransom the two cardinals were allowed to make their way to Durham unscathed. When they had pushed on to the safer climate of York they solemnly excommunicated Middleton and his allies.[1] On 20 September, about a month after the crime was committed, writs were addressed to all sheriffs ordering proclamation to be made in all cities, boroughs, market towns and other places, announcing that the king with the advice of the prelates, the magnates of the kingdom and others of the council would

---

[1] *Johannis de Trokelowe et Henrici de Blaneforde, Chronica et Annales*, ed. H. T. Riley (R.S., 1866), p. 99.

5

ordain due punishment to be inflicted on the 'sons of iniquity' who had assaulted and robbed the cardinal legates at Acle in the liberty of the bishopric of Durham.[1] The names of the miscreants were at that time unknown. What prompted the king to seek the immediate conviction and sentencing of these men as traitors was probably his own humiliation at not being able to properly protect the visiting dignitaries. Another factor may well have been the practice of the canon law to treat attacks on cardinals as lese-majesty and worthy, so far as it was within the church's power, of disinheritance. The author of the *Vita Edwardi Secundi*, who refers to this episode, was prompted to quote the relevant constitution 'Of Penalties' of Pope Boniface VIII.[2]

The record of the crimes which Edward II sent into the king's bench at Hilary term 1318 did not stand by itself but must have been issued subsequent to his taking advice from the magnates of the realm. The connexion with the process against David ap Gruffydd and the other examples of reputing men as the king's enemies is obvious. It was also analogous to the outlawry of Wallace in the St Andrews Parliament of 1304. Since the crown did not find it easy to ascertain the malefactors' names it could not claim the crimes were notorious and manifest and afforce the charges in that way: but it did seek to emphasize that Gilbert had as his allies a number of Scots who were the king's enemies and that he and they had ridden in warlike fashion with his banner displayed. It was important to make this point since the treasons recorded by the crown in 1306 had been committed in war as had indeed those of Wallace and David of Wales. In 1327 Henry earl of Lancaster argued successfully that men could only be convicted on the king's record if their treasons had been committed in time of war, which was when the king marched with his own banner displayed.[3] The crown did not entirely accept this definition and throughout the fourteenth and fifteenth centuries continued to hold that it only needed an act of arms and a banner displayed to make a riot an act of treason.[4] In 1317 Edward II could rightly

---

[1] *Parliamentary Writs and Writs of Military Summons, Edward I and Edward II* (Rec. Comm., 1827–34), II, I, Appendix, p. 200.
[2] *Vita Edwardi Secundi*, ed. N. Denholm-Young (London, 1957), p. 83.
[3] *Rot. Parl.*, II, 5.
[4] The argument of the crown was that the raising of a banner in insurrection was treason in itself; there was no need for the king to raise his own. See chapters 4 and 7.

have claimed that he was at war with the Scots and that Gilbert de Middleton by adhering to them was taking part in that war. Because of the nature of his crime Gilbert de Middleton died a pariah. Because he had no friends the process by which he had been sentenced to death elicited no criticism at all. It was probably felt that the king had shown an unexpected gleam of majesty. The common lawyers must have accepted conviction for treason on the king's record as part of the royal prerogative for when in 1322 their advice was sought by the Despensers about the best method of trying Thomas earl of Lancaster, recently taken in rebellion at Boroughbridge, they gave their opinion that it was best that 'the kyng shulde put oppon him poyntes of traitory'. So says *The Brut*. The Despenser father and son had given thought 'how and in what maner the God Erl Thomas of Lancastre shulde bene dede withouten iugement of his peris' and this apparently was the solution recommended.[1] Lancaster was in fact arraigned and convicted by means of the king's record but there was more to it than a mere recital of his crimes on 22 March 1322. On 11 March all sheriffs had been instructed to pursue and arrest Lancaster, Humphrey de Bohun earl of Hereford, Roger Damory, Hugh Audley the younger, John de Mowbray and other malcontents as the king had pronounced them traitors after taking counsel with the earls of Kent, Richmond, Pembroke, Arundel, Atholl and other magnates in his entourage. They were to be brought to justice and condign punishment.[2] Thus when they were taken and put on trial it could be pointed out that they had already been reputed as traitors by their peers, even if this was not judgement by their peers. According to *The Brut*, whose author was well informed in the matter, Thomas of Lancaster was tried before a commission which included the elder Despenser, the earls of Pembroke, Richmond and Kent and Sir Robert Malberthorp, a royal judge. Through Sir Robert the prisoner was addressed thus: 'Thomas atte the ferst oure lord the Kyng and this court excludeth yow of al maner ansuere. Thomas, oure lorde the Kyng put oppon yow that ye have in his lande riden with baner displaiede, ageynes his pees, as a traitour.' To which, like Wallace, Lancaster interjected that he had never been a traitor, but the interruption was ignored. He was charged with robbing and murdering the king's folk, and,

---

[1] *The Brut*, ed. Brie, I, 221.
[2] *Cal. Close Rolls, 1318–23*, p. 522; *Parl. Writs*, II, I, Appendix, p. 283.

added Malberthorp, 'the Kyng also put oppon you that he des-
comfitede yow and your peple with his folc in his owne reaume;
Wherefore ye went and fley to the wode as an outlawe, and also ye
were taken as an outlaw'.[1] The king's record as shown in the *Rotuli
Parliamentorum*[2] hardly touches the latter point though it is quite
possible that the author of *The Brut* drew his information from the
tenor of the writ which might have accompanied the charges
and sentence but which does not figure in the rolls. In laying stress
on the outlawry *The Brut* was emphasizing figuratively if not
exactly, for Lancaster was never a proper outlaw in the woods, a
most important feature of the process against the earl. He was held
to be an outlaw yet the dates of his misdeeds precluded any outlawry under the common law. *The Brut* in fact must have been
referring to the reputing of Lancaster on 11 March 1322.

The trial of Roger Damory affords convincing proof that Lancaster was considered a convicted traitor before the battle of
Boroughbridge and the time of his surrender. Damory had judgement awarded against him under the king's record on Saturday 13
March 1322 in a military court held at Tutbury before Fulk
Fitzwarin the constable and John Weston the marshal. The
important part of this record is the section stating Damory went
'en la cumpaignye des traytours Attenytz Thomas jadys counte de
Lancastre et Umfrey jadys counte de Hereford tauntqe a Burton
sour Trente . . .'[3] 'Atteyntz' in the legal terminology of the
fourteenth century signified that proper legal process against the
accused had been completed and he had been found guilty: but
Lancaster was not brought before the king's judges at Pontefract
until nine days later and Hereford was killed at Boroughbridge on
16 March. The attainder must therefore have resulted from the
declaration of the magnates prior to 11 March 1322.

The version of Lancaster's trial in *The Brut* is obviously a
popularized and truncated one although accurate in the essentials.
The record to be found in the *Rotuli Parliamentorum*, which was
produced at Henry of Lancaster's request in 1327, comprises what
are really two separate sections. The first part refers to Earl

[1] *The Brut*, ed. Brie, I, 222; *Rot. Parl.*, II, 3 adds the names of the earls of
Arundel, Atholl, Angus and Warenne.
[2] *Rot. Parl.*, II, 3–5.
[3] L. W. Vernon Harcourt, *His Grace the Steward and the Trial of Peers*
(London, 1907), p. 400, where the trial is printed from P.R.O., K.B. 27/259
Rex m. 34.

Thomas's treasons, murders, burnings, depredations and other felonies from the time of the king's arrival at Burton-on-Trent: basically it concerns his manoeuvring in arms with banners displayed. It concludes with a statement that the crimes are notorious and manifest to the magnates and people of the realm and then the sentence is pronounced.[1] This should be the end but there follows a long list of Lancaster's earlier crimes, including deeds construed as usurping the royal power. Finally the sentence of drawing and hanging was mitigated to beheading.[2] The way in which the treason of levying war against the king was made the charge for which he was condemned to a traitor's death is suggestive. The crown was using charges which had been employed by Edward I to convict his enemies on his own record. It did not venture to introduce other crimes until the sentence had been pronounced. Then they were added on after, perhaps so that they might be construed as treason through their own proximity to a traitor's sentence at some future date. It may have been intended they should add to Lancaster's guilt like the statement that his crimes were notorious and manifest in the first section. It was the process against Thomas of Lancaster which first connected conviction on the royal record with trial for treason under the law of arms. The crimes laid against the earl in the first part of the record concerned the usages of war and had much in common with the trial of Roger Damory in a military court before the constable and marshal on 13 March 1322. Those nobles and knights who were the allies and supporters of Lancaster in the insurrection were condemned in like manner to the earl. Their acts of open war were recorded by the king 'by virtue of his royal power', being described as notorious and manifest to the magnates and lesser men of the kingdom. They were sentenced to be drawn for treason and hanged for homicides, robberies, burnings and other felonies.[3]

---

[1] *Rot. Parl.*, ii, 3.

[2] *Ibid.*, ii, 3 b, 4, 5.

[3] See for example *Parl. Writs*, II, i, Appendix, p. 290; P.R.O., J. I. 3/76 m. 23; the latter concerns the delivery of York gaol 24 March 1322. John de Mowbray, Roger Clifford and Jocelyn de Eyvill were the prisoners delivered 'per preceptum et recordum domini regis' before John de Doncaster and Richard de Birmingham. The process against all three was identical: 'Gocelinus de Eyvill captus et detentus in prisona Eboraci allocatus coram justiciariis predictis de eo quod idem Gocelinus dudum hostiliter et felonice cum aliis felonibus et pacis domini regis perturbatoribus castrum ipsius domini regis de Tykehull obsidebat et in homines

The trial of Andrew de Harclay, earl of Carlisle, in March 1323, illustrates a further development in conviction by the king's record. Harclay was discovered by the king's spies to have been negotiating with the Scottish enemy. Edward sent the sheriff of Cumberland, Sir Anthony de Lucy, to arrest the earl, which he did successfully. The trial was held at Carlisle before the earl of Kent, John de Hastings a baron, Sir Ralph Basset, Sir John Peache, Sir John de Wysham and Geoffrey le Scrope the chief justice, but all they really had to do was to read the king's record and supervise the execution.[1] Harclay, says *The Brut*, was 'ledde unto the barr in maner of an Erl, worthely arraied, and with a suorde gert aboute him, and hosede and spored'. He was charged with adhering to Robert Bruce, the king's enemy, and accepting him as king of Scotland.[2] According to the *coram rege* rolls the rank of earl was taken from him, his sword broken and his spurs hewn off. For his treasons he was drawn, hanged and beheaded whilst his heart and bowels, from which his traitorous thoughts proceeded, were burned.[3] The body was then quartered as a warning to others. The degradation of the prisoner was an undoubted novelty and seems to have stemmed from the special affront to the king's feelings and dignity caused by the disloyalty of one whom he had girt with the earl's sword shortly before. A second innovation lay in the omission of any reputing or outlawry of the prisoner. There was apparently no declaration by the magnates of the council of Harclay as a traitor and enemy of the king. There was nothing in fact on this

ipsius dominum regem castro existentes hostiliter et felonice insultum fecit et quosdam de hominibus ipsius domini regis infra castris existentes vulneravit et plures hostiliter et felonice interfecit. Et exinde in comitiva Thomae nuper comitis Lancastriae inimicis ac seductoribus domini regis inde comite cum multitudine armatorum versus Burton super Trentam eundo et ibidem dominum regem agrediendo ac pontem ville predicte de Burton assedendo et ipsum per tres dies custodiendo ne aliquis de familia domini regis transsiret volendo hostiliter et felonice interficiendo ac post modum in recessu apertibus predictis villam incendebat et sic in eundo versus Pontefractum totam patriam in circuitu depredatus fuit. Et sic a Pontefracto in comitiva ipsius comitis usque Ponteburgum recessit et ibidem quibusdam dilectis et fidelibus domini regis sibi de precepto suo accederet volentibus obviavit meos insultum faciendo et quia plures interficiendo manifeste et notorie pro ut quia plures comites et Barones regni testant et idem dominus Rex recordatur. Ideo consideratum est quod predictus Gocelinus pro seductione predicta detrahatur et pro homicidiis, incendiis et aliis feloniis suspendatur.'

[1] *Abbrevatio Placitorum, Richard I—Edward II* (Rec. Comm., 1811), I, 351.
[2] *The Brut*, ed. Brie, I, 227.
[3] *Abbrevatio Placitorum*, I, 351.

occasion to disguise the summary nature of conviction on the king's record. This might account for the protest of Harclay's nephew and heir Henry in a petition in the next reign that his uncle 'ne fuist unques atteint par enquest de ses piers ne des autres'.[1] Unlike the advisers of Henry of Lancaster in 1327 who thought, probably with the trials after Methven in their minds, that the method could be used but only in time of war, the younger Harclay argued that judgement on the king's record was 'encountre ley de tut temps usee'. He may quite correctly have recognized the novelty in the fact that the crime in question was adhering to the king's enemies and not the usual levying of war.

Only after Edward II had been deposed was there complaint against conviction for treason on the king's record. Any dissatisfaction with the trials of 1322–3 may well have been fanned by the methods used to condemn the royal favourites in 1326 when a number of imitations of conviction by the king's record were used by the Mortimer faction. Basically these served to implement the punishment due to men already outlawed, as for example the Despensers had been by the award of exile against them by the magnates in the parliament of 1321. In this way the conviction was by record, but of the barons and king in parliament rather than of the king himself. Like Wallace and Thomas of Lancaster the elder Despenser at his trial was not allowed to make any answer.[2] Either the barons were deliberately copying the process against Thomas of Lancaster or they understood that judgement for treason by record should follow outlawry under the common law or being reputed as a traitor by the king and his council which was the equivalent: both of these precluded any answer. From the succession of Edward III the use of the king's record in trials of treason disappeared save where the crime was one of fighting the king in open war: this of course was the use to which the device had originally been put by Edward I. In the later fourteenth century, unlike the fifteenth, such trials never occurred in any number and few descriptions survive. One clear example occurred in February 1347 and concerned two Scottish noblemen, John Graham, earl of Menteith and Duncan, earl of Fife.[3] Their crime

---

[1] P.R.O., S.C.8/50/2500 (printed in Harcourt, *His Grace the Steward*, p. 334).
[2] G. A. Holmes, 'Judgment on the Younger Despenser', *Eng. Hist. Rev.*, LXX (1955), 261–7; *Chronicles of Edward I and Edward II*, I, 317–21.
[3] *Cal. Docs. Scot.*, III, nos. 1485–7.

was that they had fought against King Edward's army at the battle of Durham and been captured 'as public rebels'. When they were taken Edward III was in France besieging Calais. Nonetheless he proceeded to sentence them forthwith under the royal record. A commission which included the justices Robert de Sadyngton, William Thorpe, William Trussel and the mayor of London was ordered to pronounce on Saturday, 24 February 1347 sentence of death as given by the king and his council at Calais. The nationality of the two accused did not serve to excuse them from a traitor's death. What mattered was that they had broken their oath to the English king, Menteith directly for he was a sworn member of Edward III's council, and Fife through disloyalty to Edward Balliol the royal pretender who in 1334 had done homage for his Scottish kingdom.

The later use of conviction on the king's record became quite naturally tied up with the law of chivalry. This was a tendency which had been apparent in the trials of Damory, Harclay and the Despensers. Hence the *genre* of treason trials under the law of arms. When in 1330 Edward III was in need of a summary process by means of which he might sentence Roger Mortimer he made use of conviction by notoriety.[1] This was simply a declaration in parliament that the crimes of the accused were notorious and manifest to all, after which the sentence was delivered. In that certain cases of conviction for treason on the king's record were afforced by the statement that the crime was notorious and manifest to either the barons or the whole kingdom this was a development from recorded treason. As with conviction on the king's record there was no chance for the prisoner to answer. The device, which was basically conviction through public ill-fame, was implicitly condemned in 1354, when Mortimer's heir got the record against his grandfather quashed.[2] Thenceforward ill-fame could

---

[1] See M. H. Keen, 'Treason Trials under the Law of Arms', *Trans. Roy. Hist. Soc.*, 5th ser., XII (1962), 85–103, which is the only treatment of the subject; Plucknett, *Trans. Roy. Hist. Soc.*, 4th ser., XXIV, 60–1. The chronicler who made the point that Mortimer was condemned unheard and did not come before his peers added that this had been the fashion since the death of Thomas of Lancaster. He held that such convictions were illegal: Adam Murimuth and Robert Avesbury, *Chronica*, ed. E. M. Thompson (R.S., 1889), p. 62.

[2] *Rot. Parl.*, II, 255–6; Plucknett, *Trans. Roy. Hist. Soc.*, 4th ser., XXIV, 60–1. Plucknett argues that the reason for the use of notoriety against Mortimer was the success in 1327 of Henry of Lancaster in getting his brother's conviction by the king's record annulled on the grounds that there was no open war at the time.

only at the very worst be made to serve as an indictment: it did not work an instant conviction.

The dominant theme in the history of treason under the first two Edwards was then the development of conviction on the king's record. There were very few cases of treason which were tried in the courts of common law or in parliament and where the method was accusation by indictment or appeal and conviction was by verdict of a jury of peers. The trial of Sir Thomas Turberville, who had adhered to Philip of France, the king's enemy, was possibly one such case, but the official record is missing and we cannot be certain.[1] Ten years later, in 1305, Nicholas de Segrave was accused in parliament of deserting the royal army in time of war and appealing to the court of Edward's former liege lord, the king of France. He confessed and submitted himself to the king, who asked the advice of his peers about the penalty which should be inflicted.[2] Edward was careful not to refer to the crime as treason but as 'laesio coronae et dignitatis suae regiae et exheredatio manifesta' which was how in the reign of Edward III the crown classified the offence of appealing to the papal curia against a decision of the king's court and the category of offence known as accroaching the royal power. There was no use of the words 'traitor', 'traitorously' or 'treacherously' because it was not politic to impose treason on a powerful English baron at that moment, nor was it wise for the crown to bring up the matter of the English king's feudal relationship with the king of France at a time when such relationships with Scotland were still at boiling point. When faced with these considerations of state Edward kept his violent temper under control, but when the stakes were not so high then he might call a traitor any man who stubbornly opposed the royal will. Thus Sir John de Lovetot, son of a justiciar, was defamed in that manner because early in the year 1300 he accused Walter Langton, bishop of Coventry and Lichfield and the king's treasurer, in the papal curia of committing adultery with Joan de Briancon, Lovetot's stepmother, of keeping her as a concubine and with Joan's assistance of having strangled his father. Lovetot had offered to prove that Langton was also guilty of simony and had held in

---

[1] *Studies presented to F. M. Powicke*, p. 307.
[2] *Memoranda de Parliamento*, ed. F. W. Maitland (R.S., 1893), pp. 255–64. Edward had defied his liege lord the king of France in 1294: see *Rishanger, Chronica*, pp. 142–3.

plurality without papal dispensation. An inquisition held under the pope's commission found that the bishop was indeed publicly defamed in England and elsewhere of these and other crimes.[1] What incensed the king was that Lovetot having procured apostolic letters concerning the bishop refused to exhibit them to the archbishop of Canterbury thereby hoping, so Edward believed, to destroy his treasurer. Hence he ordered Lovetot to be arrested as a false and untruthful man and as a traitor.[2] The king was far too astute to put the knight on trial for a misdeed which was not even remotely treason but there was in fact no need to since Lovetot failed to appear at the papal curia in 1303 and Langton was allowed to clear himself by a purgative oath before the archbishop of Canterbury.[3] Another case concerning treason where Edward indulged his temper but probably without intending to pursue the matter to the end occurred in September 1306. He commanded the English sheriffs to proclaim against the holding of tournaments before the king's war in Scotland was finished.[4] Those who so offended were to forfeit all their possessions and were to be conducted to the king under close arrest as his enemies and traitors. There is no evidence to suggest that those who disobeyed were in fact put on trial as traitors but the episode is worthy of mention as a precursor of the attempts by Edward III to afforce normal methods of accusation against those who by their riots endangered the peace when the king was waging war abroad before and after Crecy.

To conclude we cannot do better than summarize. It was Edward I who first defined the crime of levying war against the king and

[1] *Calendar of Papal Registers, Papal Letters, 1198–1304,* I, 607, 605.

[2] *Cal. Close Rolls, 1296–1302,* pp. 603, 604.

[3] *Cal. Papal Reg.,* I, 610; *Flores Historiarum,* III, 305–6. Shortly afterwards Lovetot was committed to gaol on a charge of homicide and died there: *Flores Historiarum,* III, 306. Langton was absolved finally by a bull of purgation dated 8 June 1313: *Foedera,* ed. Rymer (Rec. Comm.), II, 932–4.

In Coke's *Reports* there is mention in Caudray's case of a case very much like Lovetot's which also occurred in Edward I's reign. Apparently one of the king's subjects brought into the country a bull of excommunication against another and published it to the lord treasurer. By the common law this was adjudged treason against the king, his crown and dignity. For his crime the offender should have been drawn and hanged but at the intercession of the chancellor and treasurer he was allowed to abjure the realm: *English Reports* (London, 1907), LXXVII, 15. Whether in fact the case was Lovetot's is difficult to fathom. It is equally hazardous surmising what Coke's authority was. There may be another reference to the case in *Year Books, Liver des Assises,* 30 Edward III pl. 19: the relevant section is the comment by Thorpe.

[4] *Cal. Close Rolls, 1302–7,* p. 459.

who first classified it as high treason. The importance of the crime and the rank of those who committed it necessarily caused the evolution of new legal procedures against the offenders. There was the public reputing by the king and his magnate counsellors of the rebels as traitors: there was the use of the king's own word that the offenders were guilty. This acted as indictment, or appeal, and verdict all in one. In Edward I's time all those who suffered such summary justice were held to have levied war against the king but in the troubled years at the end of Edward II's reign there was some suggestion that conviction on the king's record was likely to be extended to deal with other types of treason as well: fortunately it came to nothing. In cases of treason of less importance, for example counterfeiting or spying on the king on his enemies' behalf, there is no evidence despite several royal threats that the policies of the first two Edwards differed from those of their predecessors.

In the wider context of political principles and government the reign of Edward I seems to have been the high point of what may be called the royal thesis of treason. For Edward high treason was directed against the king's person or his servants' alone. There was one reference during the reign to treason against the realm but it occurred in a letter to the Pope and was probably meant as propaganda or as a concession to the canon lawyers who would read it. There was also a reference to treason against the people. The body of William Wallace was ordered to be dismembered because of his sedition to the king and also to the people of England and Scotland. Here the intention was probably to gain popular approval of the execution. Only when Edward's obsession with Scotland was involved was he willing to introduce the notion that high treason could be against something other than the king's person. The use of the king's record and the charge of levying war against the king gave strength to the royal thesis of treason. The acceptance in one case at least, the one involving Nicholas de Wantham in 1285, of information as a satisfactory method of accusation may have been an attempt to develop the thesis in another direction as well. These moves do not seem to have gone unnoticed for as soon as Edward was dead there were magnates keen to expound that allegiance was to the crown rather than the king and that the king must maintain the laws which emerged from the combined wills of himself and the community of the realm. No suggestions for a statute of treason were made before the 1340s but the divisions between the king and the baronage earlier that century made it certain that no markedly royal thesis of treason would be generally accepted even if some elements were actually practised for a time in the civil wars of the 1320s.

4

THE GREAT STATUTE OF TREASONS

Perhaps no English statute of the later middle ages has yielded its secrets more reluctantly to the historian than the treason act of 1352. There have been at least as many opinions as commentators, probably more, since some criticisms have not even had the merit of consistency. To a large extent this unsatisfactory state arose because of the scarcity of evidence concerning executive action on matters of treason in the decades which preceded and followed the statute's promulgation. There seemed, so to speak, no controls to test a theory against. The executions of important men just before and after the deposition of Edward II were almost the same distance in time from the treason statute as the impeachments in the Good Parliament. In 1352 Edward III was a hero with both the baronage and the commonalty and there was very little likelihood of treasonable crimes being committed in such numbers and of such variety that the exact intention of the statute would be displayed in trial and sentence. On the whole historians have concluded that Edward's design was either legal or political, the advocates of each type of motivation being fairly equally divided. Thus Miss McKisack states that 'the primary object of the statute was probably legal rather than political; to establish a clear distinction between high and petty treason and so to settle the rules about forfeitures'.[1] Plucknett's views are very similar: 'the motives of the statute are patently to prevent the loss of escheats by treating felonies of certain sorts as treason. This is made perfectly clear moreover in the petition which led to the statute. There is no trace of political theory in the act'.[2] Miss Thornley was another supporter of this attitude, for despite her asseveration that the act was first and foremost a financial measure the tenor of her argument is that the statute was intended to provide a distinction

---

[1] M. McKisack, *The Fourteenth Century* (Oxford, 1959), p. 257.

[2] T. F. T. Plucknett, *A Concise History of the Common Law* (5th edn, London, 1956), p. 444. However, in 1938 Plucknett wrote of the statute that 'Its main concern was the type of baronial revolt which had become alarming under the reign of Edward II': see B. H. Putnam, *Proceedings before the Justices of the Peace in the Fourteenth and Fifteenth Centuries* (London, 1938), p. cli.

between offences which were treason and others which constituted mere felony, and thereby was primarily concerned with legal definition.[1]

The political view of the 1352 statute, if we may call it such, has been most forcibly stated by Miss Clarke. She was particularly interested in the state trials of the period 1321–31, being noticeably moved by their apparent illegality. Perhaps it was on this account that she suggested that 'the main purpose of the statute of 1352 was by means of statutory definition to prevent the recurrence of the reckless charges and arbitrary punishments which had ruined so many noble families in the reign of Edward II'.[2] Wilkinson subscribes to a similar opinion, holding that the statute 'did something to end the possibility of a recurrence of the blood feuds and executions which characterised the early part of the century': and by defining treason 'more moderately and clearly the statute formed an important part of a general reconciliation between king and baronage'.[3] According to Holdsworth, who was also a member of this school of thought, the king's intent was primarily to extend treason for political purposes. 'It was easier to get a conviction for treason than for any of the more precisely defined felonies' since treason was not clergyable. The crown, he pointed out, also benefited from the forfeiture incurred.[4] In contrast with these commentators Stubbs offered no explanation of the government's intent, avowing equivocally that the statute must have been based on the current maxims of the lawyers. He did not commit himself as to whether legal convenience or political necessity was the greater spur to action.[5] At first sight this diversity of interpretation is perplexing, but there is in fact a ready explanation. The statute was much admired by the lawyers of the sixteenth and seventeenth centuries and they tried to examine the circumstances of its enactment. Unfortunately historical investigation stopped there, and although the nineteenth and twentieth centuries have thrown up new commentators and new commentaries, new evidence has been

---

[1] I. D. Thornley, 'The Act of Treasons of 1352', *History*, VI (1921), 106–8.
[2] M. V. Clarke, *Fourteenth Century Studies*, ed. L. S. Sutherland and M. McKisack (Oxford, 1937), p. 132.
[3] B. Wilkinson, *Constitutional History of Medieval England 1216–1399* (London, 1952), II, 47–8.
[4] Holdsworth, *History of English Law*, III, 290.
[5] See W. Stubbs, *The Constitutional History of England* (Oxford, 1878), III, 518.

almost totally lacking. Modern historians, it may be fairly concluded, have been far too happy to rely on the works of Coke or
Hale and they have failed to put in sufficient spadework.[1]

It is a common tactic when investigating the causes of any piece
of medieval legislation to look first for information in the contemporary chroniclers. Unfortunately the decade from Crécy to
Poitiers was covered by no writer of importance. Furthermore those
who did write were interested mainly in the war with France, not
in the domestic scene. The statute of treasons was ignored
completely. We are compelled therefore to rely from the outset on
legal records. The best line of approach is to proceed from the
known to the hitherto unknown, to take the cases referred to by
other historians as leading to the act of 1352 and test their historical
validity. In practice this is not difficult since all later writers on the
subject have followed closely the work of Sir Matthew Hale, which
emphasized the importance of three legal cases arising in 1347 and
1348.[2] These, he suggested, were the real cause of the great statute
of treasons.

About one of the cases there is very little to be discovered. It is
mentioned incidentally in a *Year Book*, where Hale noticed it.
Apparently in 1347 certain of the royal justices held that an appeal
of treason lay for the murder of a man who was riding with a number
of men-at-arms to aid the king in his wars.[3] Another case which
Hale mentioned was drawn from the *Liver des Assises*. In 1348 one
John de Hill of Flaworth was indicted before Thomas de Rukeby
of the death of Adam de Walton, a royal messenger on the king's
mission. The crime was held to be one of treason and John was
found guilty and beheaded. Despite the protest of Hill's immediate
lord, who pleaded a royal grant, the royal justices decided that the
traitor's possessions had forfeited to the crown where unless they
were the subject of a new grant they would remain in perpetuity.[4]
The case on which Hale had the most evidence concerned highway
robbery on the part of Sir John Gerberge on 16 March 1347. Hale
quoted fairly accurately from the indictment in the *coram rege*

---

[1] The classical treatment of the statute of treason is in Coke, pp. 1–19, and in
Hale, I, 58–383.
[2] Hale, I, 80–1.
[3] *Year Books*, 21 Edward III Trin. pl. 16.
[4] *Year Books, Liver des Assises*, 22 Edward III, pl. 49. The case shows that
in 1348 the judges viewed high treason as being any treason which touched the
king plus the crime of adhering to his enemies.

rolls.[1] Gerberge had ridden along the king's highway in the town field of Royston clad in armour and wearing a tunic called *cote armure*, thus manifestly attired in manner of war, and with a drawn sword in his hand. He captured William de Botelisford, a Lincoln merchant, and detained him until he paid a large ransom 'usurpando sibi infra regnum regis regiam potestatem ipso domino rege in partibus exteris existente, contra sui ligeantium, et regis et coronae suae praejudicium et seditionem manifestam'. Although Hale did not mention it, Gerberge and his confederates, for there is a reference to his society or gang, were also accused of seditiously ambushing and killing at 'Shaldford Lane' in Redbourn (near Dunstable) a William Catesby and his servant. This had occurred on 22 April 1347. Thus, concluded the indictment, Gerberge is a common thief and a notorious ambusher of passages accustomed to perpetrate treasons within the realm. In court Gerberge and Alexander de Jernmouth, his esquire, refused to plead and claimed benefit of clergy, but the bench held that as it was indeed a case of treason such privilege could not be allowed. Both were therefore delivered to the Marshalsea 'ad poenitentiam', probably, that is, to suffer 'peine forte et dure' until they changed their minds and offered a plea. Two of Gerberge's valets, John Coo of Yarmouth and John de Ravengham, did put themselves on the country. They were found guilty, drawn and hanged.

The case has many interesting features. At first sight the crime appears no more than highway robbery. However, the accusation that Gerberge had worn *cote armure* 'modo guerrino manifeste' and carried a drawn sword can only be taken to mean he was charged with levying war on the king. Keen has drawn our attention to the signs which announced the waging of open war in the later middle ages. Riding with banners displayed or 'tirer canon ou engin gecter' were two of these, while a 'liege appearing against his king in arms under banners displayed was clearly levying war upon him and could be taken as a traitor'.[2] In Gerberge's case the wearing of *cote armure*, the drawn sword, the taking of ransom, concerning which the law of arms was very precise, seem to have been construed by the royal justices as tantamount to such levying of war. Since according to late medieval theory the sovereign prince alone had the right to levy open war only he could allow the holding of

[1] Hale, I, 80–1. The case occurs in P.R.O., K.B. 27/349 Rex m. 23.
[2] Keen, 'Treason Trials', *Trans. Roy. Hist. Soc.*, 5th ser., XII, 95.

men to ransom.[1] To do so without his permission in a 'war' not of his authorization was therefore lese-majesty since the taking of the ransom was the arrogation of royal power. This was probably what was referred to by 'usurpando sibi infra regnum regis regiam potestatem'. It is important to note that this usurpation, which in other cases was sometimes called assuming or accroaching the royal power, was held at the Gerberge trial to be manifest treason and therefore not clergyable. The sentences on Gerberge's two valets offer confirmation: they were to be drawn at the horse's tail to the place of execution and there hanged.[2]

This then is the sum of the evidence of a purely legal nature hitherto unearthed. Hale said there were 'like instances' but he did not give them. The cases were undoubtedly important and display just 'how uncertain and arbitrary the crime of treason was before the statute of 25 Edward III'.[3] Yet they fail to explain many of the new provisions. A more careful examination of the legal records of that time will show that for several years before 1347 the crown through its judges had been tampering with the scope of treason, particularly by accusing those who thwarted or interfered with or took the place of royal officials of accroaching, assuming or usurping the royal power. Before we can properly assess the causes of the 1352 act some consideration of this charge is essential and from a political as well as a legal point of view.

The defeat of King John in 1215 at the hands of his barons had achieved, as we have seen, the result of keeping England a feudal monarchy when elsewhere in Europe theocratic kingship was flourishing. Admittedly the English king was at the top of the feudal structure, but he was obliged to take the advice of his magnates, who were in some ways his equals. He had to govern with their cooperation even if he hankered after and made periodic sallies towards royal autocracy. The contradictory nature of the king's position was reflected in the ambiguous treatment afforded to kingship by Bracton, who felt obliged to distinguish between the power of the king in an executive capacity [gubernaculum], where he could act freely, and his authority in making and changing the law [jurisdictio], where he must act in conjunction with his

---

[1] Keen, 'Treason Trials', *Trans. Roy. Hist. Soc.*, 5th ser., XII, 96–7, quoting Honoré Bonet, *The Tree of Battles*, translated by G. W. Coopland (Liverpool, 1949), p. 175. [2] P.R.O., K.B. 27/349 Rex mm. 6, 23.
[3] Hale, I, 82.

magnates. This contractual cooperation gave rise in the thirteenth century to several political and juristic notions of which one, the concept of crown, was particularly important. The *corona* was in fact the bond between the kingdom, in the sense of those barons who must be consulted (often called the community of the realm), and the king.[1] Thus matters concerning the crown were common to the king and the community. The crown was sovereign rather than the king. It was therefore natural that the foundation of a comprehensive law of treason to protect the king should be accompanied by attempts to provide sanctions against those who endangered the crown, particularly since from 1308 or thereabouts men were distinguishing clearly between the king's person and his office. The accusation of *exheredatio coronae* became a common one in one form or another. The king might say that a man or a group of men were infringing the rights of the crown: the community of the realm might accuse the king of failing to protect the crown, or it might accuse a third party of diminishing the power or usurping the rights of the crown. The first and the last of these three offences were commonly referred to in the fourteenth century as accroaching the royal power.

To accroach royal power was a political offence and virtually unknown as a crime under the common law. Its varieties were many. One example of the type where the king accused men of usurping his rights has already been noticed and others are surveyed below. They date mainly from the period 1340 to 1350. The type in which magnates accused favourites of abusing the royal power is also very instructive and there is no shortage of examples. Most notable were perhaps the charges made in the ordinances of 1311 against Edward II's favourite Piers Gaveston and in the sentences of 1321 and 1326 on the elder and younger Despensers. Gaveston was said to have led the king into doing wrong by accroaching royal power and to have disinherited the crown by causing discord between the king and his nobles.[2] The two Despensers had also created a division between the king and the magnates but in their case by preventing the latter from giving counsel or even approaching the king unless they were present themselves. These were general charges but a number of specific accroachments, which they were held to have committed, were

---

[1] Ullmann, *Principles of Government*, pp. 177–9. Ullmann argues cogently on this matter.   [2] *Rot. Parl.*, I, 283.

also mentioned.[1] They had maliciously stopped certain magnates paying entry fines so that their lands were forfeited: they had not allowed the king to hear or do right to the magnates concerning their representation against the Despensers in the matter of the lands of the Templars. The younger Despenser had released from prison illegally John de Lacchelegh and others, condemned for their trespasses against the lady of Merk. In 1322 they had made the king destroy the barons 'against Magna Carta' and the ordinances of 1311, and had been responsible for the false judgement on Thomas of Lancaster. Furthermore they were said to have forced men to maintain them falsely in their private quarrels. If it might have been objected about some of these offences that they were committed without the king's commission or approval it certainly cannot be said about them all. A number of the misdeeds can only have been offences in the eyes of the Despensers' baronial enemies. When in 1321 the Despensers returned from exile and demonstrated in parliament the errors in the process against them they drew attention to the fact that there was nothing in the charges which touched on felony or treason, without which no one should be proscribed or exiled.[2] On this legal matter there may have been differing opinions since the point was not included in the schedule which rehearsed the errors in the original process.[3] Alternatively the Despensers may have found the weapon too useful to destroy: they accused their opponents of accroaching 'the royal power, jurisdiction and cognizance of making process and judgment of matters pertaining to . . . royal dignity' because they had gone to Westminster to award judgement on their own authority in the king's absence.[4]

The following year the crown made use of the charge when it condemned Thomas of Lancaster for having *inter alia* usurped royal power to the disinheritance of the king. Included in the crime were Lancaster's threatening to make an alliance with the Scots, his impeding men from joining the king's Scottish expedition at York and the way he had permitted his men 'to acclaim the king

---

[1] *Cal. Close Rolls, 1318–23*, pp. 492–5; Holmes, 'Judgment on the Younger Despenser', *Eng. Hist. Rev.*, LXX, 264–7; *Chronicles of Edward I and Edward II*, I, 317–18.

[2] *Ibid.*, II, 70. 'Tertio quod de cunctis sibi oppositis nihil tangit feloniam aut proditionem, sine quibus aut illorum altero nemo debet proscribi, nec etiam exulare.'

[3] *Cal. Close Rolls, 1318–23*, p. 541.   [4] *Ibid.*, p. 542.

contemptuously' at Pontefract.[1] The usurpation charges followed after the accusations of actual treason and were part of a list of additional crimes not directly connected with the earl's sentence. They were referred to rather vaguely as 'iniquitatibus, sceleribus et criminibus' and were acts of political disobedience rather than offences under the common law. In October and November 1326 at the trials of the elder and younger Despensers several charges of accroaching the royal power were mingled with those of treason and offences against the church in such a way as to give the impression they were in fact treasons.[2] In 1330 the crown recorded a list of treasons, felonies and misdeeds notoriously committed by Roger Mortimer and the lords of parliament agreed to their notoriety and adjudged him a traitor and enemy of the king.[3] The large majority of the charges involved Mortimer's accroaching the royal power and although there is every reason to suppose they were regarded in this instance as treasons rather than mere felonies the crown forbore to label each particular accroachment as treason by name and it is therefore possible to argue that the only definite treason laid against the accused was the murder of Edward II. We should remember that there is no case amongst the bloody trials of this decade which shows a man being adjudged to a traitor's death solely for accroaching the royal power. When men were drawn and hanged they had invariably been found guilty of an obvious treason like encompassing the king's death, adhering to his enemies, levying war against him or committing an offence against the royal army. Since accroaching the royal power was a relatively newly risen crime men were unwilling to rest their case on it alone. No faction wanted to use it by itself as the reason for the proscription of its enemies since the judgement might be reversed or found fraudulent at a later date.

Not until Edward III had made his claim on the French throne did the crime of accroaching or assuming the royal power arise once more. The attack by the author of the *Libellus Famosus* on Archbishop Stratford in 1341 made the charge that he had committed many acts 'in status nostri detrimentum et dignitatis regie laesionem', a crime which sounds very much akin to accroaching.[4]

[1] *Rot. Parl.*, II, 4 a.
[2] For the trial of the father see *Chronicles of Edward I and Edward II*, I, 317; for that of the son, Holmes, 'Judgment on the Younger Despenser', *Eng. Hist. Rev.*, LXX, 264–7.   [3] *Rot. Parl.*, II, 52–3.
[4] *Foedera*, ed. Rymer (original edn) V, 228.

The archbishop, however, took this to be an accusation of treason and denied he had aroused 'seditionem in populo proditorie'. He reminded the king that if the charge was treason no secular judge was competent to try him, presumably since he believed he must be tried by his peers. Since the matter was never pressed to a conclusion and no formal indictment or appeal made there is no way of telling how the king intended to construe Stratford's deeds. The letters patent of June 1346 which finally excused him were deliberately vague and spoke of his annulling the law of the realm, his hindering of the king's quarrel and the sedition, contempt, despite, scandal and setting aside of his person.[1]

On a lower level but equally significant there is mention in September 1342 of men in Cornwall assuming the royal power in usurping to themselves divers stannaries where by use of force they compelled the miners to work for them.[2] In January 1343 a commission was ordered to discover the names of a number of Cirencester jurors who had revealed the king's secrets to men who were usurping the king's rights with intent to disinherit him, that is to say men who were held to be accroaching the royal power.[3] A commission of oyer and terminer of August the same year claimed that the bailiffs of Canterbury at the instigation of the commonalty there had summoned an assembly of citizens at which unlawful confederations prejudicial to the king and his royal power had been entered into, thereby unduly usurping that royal power.[4] It is unfortunate that we do not know what penalties, if any, the crown inflicted. At the same time that Sir John Gerberge was put on trial in 1347 a member of his gang called Peter de Thorp, son of John de Thorp of Pakenham, Suffolk, was accused of having committed felony and sedition at Little Yarmouth and Gorleston on 7 April 1344. Thorp and a band of some 600 men 'cum tribus vexillis extensis ad modum guerre insultum fecerunt predictis villis' and they took sixty men captive from a church, thereby being guilty of assuming the royal power.[5] Here again there was a definite treason in the shape of levying war against the king juxtaposed with accroachment, in this case a crime resulting from the war.

The year 1347 was particularly fruitful in cases which involved

[1] Cal. Pat. Rolls, 1345–8, p. 121.   [2] Cal. Pat. Rolls, 1340–3, p. 553.
[3] Ibid., p. 66.   [4] Ibid., p. 167.
[5] P.R.O., K.B. 27/349 Rex m. 23d.

the assumption of the royal power. In July a group of miscreants at Bristol were accused of assuming to themselves the royal power, having elected one of their number as their captain, issued proclamations and boarded and plundered with armed force ships in the port of that town. The vessels were laden under the king's licence with corn for Gascony.[1] Almost at the same time, at Lynn (Norfolk), a large confederacy of evildoers acted in a similar way and when it had brought a cargo of grain ashore it offered it for sale at a price which was not the official one. The malefactors also arrested corn which had been brought to the town for purposes of sale and adjudged of their own authority certain of the bearers to the pillory. These crimes, which were referred to as misprisions, as well as accroachments of the royal power do not seem to have been construed as any sort of treason.[2] These events took place just after a tumult had occurred in the Worcestershire sessions of William Beauchamp and his fellow justices of oyer and terminer. The crown claimed that when Beauchamp was about to hold court at Tredington a large number of evildoers, assuming the royal power, entered with armed might into the house which was to be used for the purpose and prevented the justices from entering. They also placed pennons bearing their arms on the walls of the house as a sign of their rebellion 'whereby they rebelliously resisted the judges'.[3] Here once more, assuming or accroaching the royal power was allied to an accepted sign for the levying of war, which was treason. There was however no use of the word 'treason' in the description. At Boston in October 1347 those who had assisted Thomas de Okeham in his misdeeds, including the choosing of a mayor and the plundering of two ships, were indicted for sedition and felony 'regiam potestatem assumentes et ut de guerra insurgentes': the similarity between this and the previous case is obvious.[4] In contrast a case from January of the same year shows a third judicial construction upon accroachment. According to the indictment one John Litel, alias John of South Mimms, feloniously and traitorously with armed might ambushed and pillaged various people on the highway near Colney Hatch, thereby assuming the royal power.[5] Apart from the Gerberge case this is the sole example of accroaching being categorically classed as treason.

---

[1] *Cal. Pat. Rolls, 1345–8*, p. 392.
[2] *Ibid.*, p. 388. The miscreants also issued proclamations in the royal manner.
[3] *Ibid.*, p. 386.   [4] P.R.O., K.B. 27/350 m. 101.   [5] P.R.O., K.B. 9/66/65.

The punishment of Gerberge and probably of Litel too, if he was ever brought into court, achieved some notoriety, but the case which must have focused the attention of the lords and commons on the increasing use of the charge of accroachment was the one which involved the rape of Margery de la Beche, relict of Sir Nicholas de la Beche, sometime keeper of the Tower of London. The deed was committed before dawn on Good Friday 1347 at Margery's manor of Beams in Wiltshire where the king's third son Lionel of Antwerp was then staying. While his father was abroad Lionel was acting as keeper of England and the deed was therefore committed within the verge of the marshalsea of his household.[1] In the course of Margery's abduction two members of her household were murdered, several servants wounded, and her chaplain, who lay in sickbed, died of fright.[2] Other servants were kidnapped and goods and chattels of at least £500 in value were stolen. The leader of the miscreants was Sir John Dalton of Apthorp, Northants and his design was apparently to abduct Margery so as to force her to marry him.[3] The seriousness of the offence was demonstrated by the speed with which the royal officials reacted. A writ was despatched to Dalton the following day, Easter Saturday 31 March, ordering him to have Margery de la Beche before Lionel, keeper of England, and the king's council at Westminster with all possible speed, and in any case before 18 April.[4] The sheriffs were instructed to proclaim that no one was to receive Dalton and his confederates or maintain or abet them under pain of forfeiture.[5] While the pursuit went on the criminals were put in exigent to be outlawed in the court of William Thorpe and his fellows, the names having been supplied by royal writ from an indictment made before the steward and marshals of the keeper of the realm's household.[6] They were still at liberty at the beginning

---

[1] Cal. Pat. Rolls, 1345–8, p. 310; P.R.O., K.B. 27/350 Rex m. 55.
[2] Cal. Close Rolls, 1346–9, pp. 271, 305.
[3] Calendarium Inquisitionum post mortem sive Excaetarum, ed. J. Caley and J. Bayley (Rec. Comm. 1806–28), II, 296. Dalton also held land in Bispham, Dalton Hall, Whitington and Manchester (Lancashire).
[4] Cal. Close Rolls, 1346–9, p. 251.
[5] Ibid., p. 271.
[6] Cal. Fine Rolls, 1347–56, p. 31. Of Dalton and his friends' offences it was said 'which business amounts to sedition the cognisance whereof pertains to the king and no other in the realm'. The use of the royal writ to supply details of the indictment demonstrates the urgency of the matter and smacks of corner-cutting if not of actual sharp practice.

of May, when part of the gang was reported in Lancashire, wandering about and committing evil deeds by day and night 'which business amounts to sedition'. There were hopes that the miscreants would soon be captured for it was at this time that the constable of the Tower was ordered to make ready to receive Dalton and his allies and imprison them till further notice. Nothing came of it and at the end of June the situation remained the same, the criminals, as the crown was informed, being maintained by the very commissioners who had been ordered to arrest them.[1] A number of the miscreants were reported to have fled to the Scottish marches, drawing to themselves divers malefactors and perpetrating many evils. A mandate despatched to the king of Scotland asked he should not admit them but effect their arrest and have them sent to the Tower.[2] Obviously the anger of the English government had by no means abated. By July Margery de la Beche had still not been freed from her abductors and the king continued to complain that the latter were being received in divers parts of the realm by the maintenance and assent of those whose job it was to catch them.[3] The *coram rege* rolls show the trial of the principals, which was intended for the king's bench, being put back term by term.[4] The only satisfaction the crown could obtain was the forfeiture of Dalton's lands. At last the government had to recognize its powerlessness and the offenders, one by one, were allowed to purchase a pardon.

The particular significance of the Beche case lies in the charges which were laid against Sir John Dalton and his confederates. The commission to William Catesby, John de Claydon and others appointed to arrest the malefactors on 14 May 1347 said that the deed, that is to say the abduction, touched on sedition and that the other felonies and trespasses were also prejudicial to the king.[5] Elsewhere it was recorded that the affair caused a scandalous outcry to prevail everywhere amongst the people and a very grievous complaint to be made to the king.[6] Emphasis was laid on the fact

---

[1] *Cal. Pat. Rolls, 1345–8*, p. 379.
[2] *Ibid.*, pp. 319, 320.
[3] *Ibid.*, p. 384.
[4] P.R.O., K.B. 27/350 Rex mm. 48, 55, 55d, 56. Some of those who received the gang, including the prior of Upholland, were still being called into court in Michaelmas term 1351 (P.R.O., K.B. 27/369 Rex m. 26d).
[5] *Cal. Pat. Rolls, 1345–8*, p. 318.
[6] *Ibid.*, p. 310; see also *Cal. Close Rolls, 1346–9*, p. 251.

that the crime had been committed on the holy day of Good Friday 'without reverence for God, the Holy Church or the king' and furthermore to the terror of the keeper of England and the rest of the king's children who were with him and to the people of those parts. Further weight was laid to the accusations by the charge that the raiders had taken Margery and some of her servants as captives out of Wiltshire and thereby had usurped to themselves royal power in manifest destruction of the regality of the crown. The indictment in the plea rolls puts it that the malefactors by breaking into the Beche house by night when armed and arrayed made traitorous [seditioniter] insult, committed both felonies and treasons and having pillaged various goods they feloniously and traitorously took them away.[1]

The crown was badly advised by its law officers, if indeed it was they who suggested the liberal infusion within the charges of words referring to treason. The combination of insult to the keeper of the realm and danger to the royal children when the king was at war abroad must have been the cause. Precedent for such action there was none. Thomas of Lancaster had accroached the royal power by allowing his men to acclaim the king contemptuously, and several of his supporters were convicted of making insult feloniously and as enemies to the king's men in Tickhill castle. But these deeds were committed during open insurrection as could be said of a similar case in 1344.[2] Despite these liberties with the common law the crown hesitated to append the adjective 'traitorous' to the usurpation of the royal power caused by the taking of captives out of Wiltshire. To add that the crime was in manifest destruction of the regality of the crown was nearly going as far, and without actually fusing the two crimes together it left accroachment very close to treason indeed.

The royal policy was noticed and it caused some discontent. In the parliament which met at Westminster in January 1348 the commons petitioned against the excessive use they felt the king was making of charges of treason or accroaching the royal power.

---

[1] P.R.O., K.B. 27/350 Rex mm. 55, 55d.
[2] *Rot. Parl.*, II, 4 a. Those accused of insulting the garrison of Tickhill castle were Jocelyn de Eyvill, John de Mowbray and Roger Clifford: P.R.O., J.I. 3/76. In 1347 Peter de Thorp of Pakenham, Suffolk, was accused of having in 1344 with 600 men at Yarmouth and Gorleston 'cum tribus vexillis extensis ad modum guerre insultum fecerunt predictis villis' thereby committing felony and sedition: P.R.O., K.B. 27/349 Rex m. 23d.

They claimed that the royal justices were holding as treason and accroachment crimes which had never been so interpreted in the past and they asked for a declaration in parliament of what exactly the crime of accroaching included.[1] They affected to be much concerned by the loss of both escheats to the lords of the fees and of benefit of clergy to those who were arraigned. The king prevaricated, saying that each legal judgement would declare if the case was treason, accroachment or another crime. To the lower house at least, accroaching the royal power was being treated exactly as treason, although in fact for the moment the royal judges were still making a subtle distinction.

For two years there were no more provocative cases, but in the summer of 1350 the matter of accroachment came to the fore again. Two Oxfordshire justices of the peace, John Golafre and Thomas Langele, were attacked at Eynsham and chased into the abbey chamber.[2] The assailants, we are told, behaved like madmen or men possessed by an evil spirit: by their coming in large numbers in manner of war and preventing the judicial sessions they usurped to themselves power above the royal power. In August the crown described these misdeeds as 'great rebellions', a term which was used in the fourteenth century when there was collective disobedience to its authority. Rebellion in the records of the later middle ages was never a synonym for treason. Thus the case shows accroachment being once more rated as a lesser crime, but this was not because of a retreat by the government. More probably it was because the occasion did not warrant any great show of royal displeasure.

In sharp contrast was the crown's attitude in a case which came into the king's bench at Michaelmas term 1350 and involved the murder of a Hertfordshire justice of the peace. This official, John Legat, had arraigned an assize of novel disseisin against certain of his own tenants whom he claimed had disseised him in Pirton. When on his way to Hertford to prosecute his assize before the justices in their last session there, he was ambushed in a lane off the royal highway at Hitchin. The attackers, who were apparently led by Sir John de Oddyngseles, were arrayed in manner of war, usurping to themselves the royal power, and Legat was seditiously murdered: so said the indictment.[3] On capture the killers were

---

[1] *Rot. Parl.* ii, 166 b.
[2] *Cal. Pat. Rolls, 1348–50,* p. 594.   [3] P.R.O., K.B. 27/361 Rex m. 43.

put on trial and found guilty of felony and sedition. The crown laid stress on the fact that Legat had been commissioned under the great seal and that he stood *in loco regis*: this was where the treason lay. There was no suggestion that usurping the royal power by merely being arrayed for war was treasonable, though it was obviously a weighty matter which closely concerned the crown. As being arrayed for war was obviously a lesser crime than the actual levying of war, so was accroaching the royal power less than treason. In the Legat case the charge of usurping the royal power served to aggravate the accusation of treasonable murder rather as the term 'notorious' was used on occasion by juries to add strength to their indictments.

The last case of accroachment before the treason statute was probably one which concerned unlawful interference in the wool trade. At Michaelmas term 1351 an Essex jury accused one John Fitzwautier of extorting money from merchants for cocketing their wool on 18 August 1349, thereby accroaching to himself royal power. At the same time a William Baker, who had arrested four sacks of wool belonging to a Flemish merchant and refused to let him have it until he had paid a fine, was accused of the same crime. The misdeeds were referred to as felonies, trespasses and misprisions.[1] There was no suggestion they were treasonable.

Thus from the cases of accroaching the royal power which arose between 1341 and 1352 we cannot conclude the crime was tantamount to committing treason. Only in the instances which involved Gerberge and Litel was there the suggestion that the crimes were being fused, or at least confused, and even then there was a probable charge of treason by the levying of war against the king. Accroaching or usurping the royal power might take on the appearance of treason when it was committed subsequent to a definite common law treason like levying war or adhering to the king's enemies, but in fact during this period no one suffered the penalties of treason for accroaching the royal power alone. In cases where there was no actual treason adjacent it appeared as a much less important offence, being rated in two instances, as we have seen, as misprision. The way in which the clerks of chancery were wont to reel off the formula 'treason, accroachment of the royal power, felony' shows that the crime was really in a category of its own. This may have been because of its relatively recent origins. Quite

[1] P.R.O., K.B. 27/370 Rex m. 46.

possibly the king and his justices hoped that accroachment would in time become an accepted common law treason if it were associated with treason closely and often enough.[1] It cannot have been mere coincidence that these charges which were suggestive of continental practices should rise into prominence at a time when knowledge of European life and law had recently much increased.

In addition to the legal records of the several cases in which the crown accused its subjects of accroaching the royal power there is other evidence to indicate a deliberate attempt to extend the scope of treason in order to afforce the normal penalties of the common law. In his chronicle Geoffrey le Baker records that in the twenty-first year of Edward III's reign, while the king was besieging Calais, various robbers tried to profit from the situation. But the justices punished such disturbers of the peace as traitors, sparing neither layman nor cleric and arguing that they would have caused the overthrow of the kingdom to the profit of the French.[2] The chronicler pointed to the war and the king's absence from England as the reason for such a stern policy and very probably he was correct. On each occasion after 1335 that Edward left the realm on a military campaign provision was made for the speedy and efficient administration of justice in his absence. A commission of oyer and terminer issued in January 1335 stated the king wanted the trespasses in question to be punished the more speedily because some of them were committed while he was staying in Scotland to repel the Scots who had invaded the realm.[3] The similarity with the royal pronouncement in the commission of August 1350 to the justices who were to enquire into the attack on the J.P.s at Eynsham is striking. This said that 'such great rebellions and misdeeds so dishonouring to the king and especially as having been done when he is about to go forth from England for the defence of the realm and to repel his enemies therefrom greatly move him and it is his will that they shall meet with speedy punishment'.[4] In March 1346 when about to set off on the Crécy

---

[1] There is a possibility that the king's attempts to extend the scope of treason at the end of the 1340s stemmed in part from newly-acquired knowledge of French law. Some French custumals included as sedition the crimes of highway robbery and the abduction of girls. See von Bar, *Continental Criminal Law*, p. 164.

[2] *Chronicon Galfridi le Baker*, ed. F. M. Thompson (Oxford, 1889), p. 92.

[3] *Cal. Pat. Rolls, 1334–8*, p. 135.

[4] *Cal. Pat. Rolls, 1348–50*, p. 594.

campaign Edward wished to ordain for the safe custody of London and the preservation of the peace: he therefore charged the mayor, sheriffs and aldermen to punish all malefactors speedily. As a result they suppressed a riot so ruthlessly that men claimed the judgements on the troublemakers were false and erroneous.[1] Before he departed on the Scottish expedition of 1335 the king in the May parliament at York, apparently mindful that proclamation had been made many times, but with little effect, that no one should ride armed or bring an armed force to endanger the king's peace, had seen it resolved that if any men should act in this manner after his departure he should be treated as a rebel.[2] There is evidence to suggest that this ordinance was acted upon and that men were brought before the courts accused of rebellion, although what crime this was exactly is difficult to determine. The following year the crown used the same ordinance as justification for the arrest of those who had committed any trespass against the peace from the time the king had set out. When taken such men were to be committed to prison and only delivered at the express command of the king.[3]

The parliament which met at Westminster in March, 1336 produced an ordinance that the king should issue commissions for the arrest of persons suspected of trespasses against the peace.[4] The ordinance remedied one of the great weaknesses in English criminal law, the inability to arrest a suspect before he had been

---

[1] *Cal. Close Rolls, 1346–9*, p. 54. The mayor and the sheriffs attached several men who had disturbed the peace during a dispute between the fishmongers and the skinners. Some of these were adjudged to death for notorious crime at the London Guildhall. The judgements were 'by consideration of the king's court': later the king approved and confirmed what had been done. The use of notoriety is instructive. In Edward II's time the fact that a crime was notorious had occasionally been sufficient to work an instant conviction. By the reign of his son the practice had ceased although such a charge might be enough to eliminate the need for an indictment. If this was the case with the London rioters then the king was making full use of his judicial prerogatives.

[2] *Cal. Pat. Rolls, 1334–8*, pp. 200, 203, 207. Two of these commissions but not the third referred to men disturbing the peace with armed force and with banners displayed. This last qualification was the one usually used when the crown was distinguishing treasonable insurrection from mere riot.

[3] *Ibid.*, p. 284. Similar commissions of April, July, September, October, November 1336 put the statute of Northampton (2 Edward III st. 1, c. 3) alongside the York ordinance; see *Cal. Pat. Rolls, 1334–8*, pp. 287, 357, 361, 366 and also *Cal. Pat. Rolls, 1340–3*, p. 92 where the ordinance was associated with the ordinance for the arrest of suspects of 1336.

[4] *Cal. Pat. Rolls, 1334–8*, p. 290.

indicted. Although the measure did not touch on the law of treason directly it can be readily seen that the crown was radically altering the practices of the common law so as to preserve internal law and order at a time of foreign embroilment. Examples of commissions specifically under the ordinance or under a similar one made two years later are to be found every year from 1336 to 1341, when they abruptly cease, presumably because of an outcry in parliament.[1] A statute of 1341 mentions that clerks, peers and freemen had been arrested, imprisoned and put out of their goods and chattels when they had not been appealed or indicted or suit of party against them affirmed. Henceforth, says the statute, such things shall not be done.[2] Historians have usually taken the statute to refer specifically to the trial of Chief Justice Willoughby and the peremptory arrests of other ministers when the king suddenly returned from Flanders in December 1340: but the use which had been made of the power to arrest on suspicion was much wider than that. The crown claimed that these arrests were legitimate but it did not plead the ordinance of 1336: this had been withdrawn in June 1337.[3] It referred to an ordinance in the parliament at Northampton in 1338 whereby it was assented by the nobility for the maintenance of the peace while the king was abroad that robbers and malefactors of bad fame and notoriety should be arrested on suspicion.[4] This appears on the face of it to have been much less severe than the previous ordinance yet we should remember that since it was the crown which decided exactly who was of bad fame and notoriety the effect was no different. Both were intended to afforce the normal common law procedures while the king was abroad. When in November 1348 Edward proposed to set off overseas to defend, as it was put, England and his dominions, he issued a commission for the keeping of the peace in South Lynn which commanded the arrest and imprisonment of all persons notoriously suspected since it was very near to the king's heart that

---

[1] See *Cal. Pat. Rolls, 1334–8*, pp. 290, 293, 294, 296, 352, 357, 367–71, 377, 444, 513, 575, *Cal. Pat. Rolls, 1338–40*, pp. 77, 130, 145, 185, 274, 281, 352, 354, 357, 358, 359, 481, 483, 489, 555, 557, 559, *Cal. Pat. Rolls, 1340–3*, pp. 38 (where the ordinance is called an agreement), 92, 96, 107, 203–4. On 25 April 1341 (*ibid.*, p. 215) reference to the ordinance was avoided. In its place were mentioned the statutes of Winchester, Northampton and Westminster.

[2] *Stat. Realm*, I, 296. (15 Edward III st. 1 c. 3).

[3] *The English Government at Work, 1327–36*, ed. J. F. Willard, W. A. Morris and W. H. Dunham (Cambridge, Mass., 1950), III, 195.

[4] *Rot. Parl.*, II, 128 b, 130 b. It was then repealed.

his peace and the tranquillity of his people be straitly kept.[1] The commission was an isolated one but is important by its demonstration that at the time when usurpation of the royal power was a relatively common charge the king was afforcing the common law in another way, a forbidden way, and his reason lay in his fear of disorder during his absence abroad.

The dispensation of justice and the maintenance of law and order was a prime function of any medieval monarch, yet it seems as if Edward III was not interested in the internal security of England solely for its own sake. His major interest from 1337 was the war with France and his main concern was supply. To persuade parliament to grant him sufficient taxation the king must listen acutely to the popular grievances which were there revealed: a large part of these were concerned with the need for justice. Thus when Edward returned penniless from Bruges in December 1340 to revenge himself on the English administration he started off by making an example of Chief Justice Willoughby because he had sold the laws like cows. From February until at least November 1341 the courts were kept busy listening to the complaints against the oppressions supposed to have been committed by justices and royal ministers while the king had been away.[2] There were also other years which revealed a strong demand for the better dispensation of justice and the firmer preservation of law and order. The first of the three causes for the summoning of parliament in October 1339 was to arrange for the better keeping of the peace.[3] The basis of the opposition's case in 1340 was that the king's absence had caused internal order to worsen.[4] At the opening of the 1343 parliament Edward admitted that he knew the law of the land was not well kept both when he was abroad and at home and asked for the lords' and commons' advice.[5] In 1346 one cause of summons was the keeping of England and of the peace there.[6] The two parliaments of 1348 were summoned for discussion of the war abroad and the better keeping of the peace at home: this was typical of the decade.[7] A temporary break in the French war made the prime purpose of the parliaments which met in February 1351

[1] Cal. Pat. Rolls, 1348–50, p. 243.
[2] Cal. Pat. Rolls, 1340–3, pp. 110, 363.
[3] Rot. Parl., II, 103 a.
[4] G. L. Harriss, 'The Commons' Petitions of 1340', Eng. Hist. Rev., LXXVIII (1963), 651.   [5] Rot. Parl., II, 136 b.
[6] Ibid., II, 158 a.   [7] Ibid., II, 165 a.

and January 1352 internal law and order. The second of these two sessions was called

> primerement pur ceo qe nostre Seignur le Roi ad entenduz qe la Pees de son Roialme n'est pas bien garde come estre deveroit, et qe les destourbours de la Pees et meintenours des quereles et des riotes faites en pais grevont trop a son poeple, sanz ceo qe due punissement est fait de eux: Et aussint, qe l'Estatuz faitz cea en arer pur amendement des Leies de la terre et du poeple ne sont pas gardez ne usez en lour effect, ne les Juggementz renduz en les Courtes nostre Seignur le Roi . . . ne sont duement executz, solonc lour force et solonc qe la Ley vorreit.[1]

The mass of legislation in the period 1340–52 for the better maintenance of the law testifies to the effectiveness of popular protest and to the king's personal concern. To do Edward justice we should remember that he had always shown anxiety for law and order and that his war on crime in the earlier 1330s had been both ingenious and successful:[2] yet the period between Sluys and the statute of treasons shows the goal of supply brought forth more legal legislation than any number of marauding criminal bands.

The king's desire to maintain effective internal order so as to persuade the tax-paying population to part with its wealth the more readily had hidden dangers. Harriss has suggested that Edward's methods of raising money between 1338 and 1340 caused him 'to threaten what ministers, the landed classes and the men of the shires took to be their customary rights' and that 'to contemporaries in these years he appeared on the verge of despotism'.[3] In the financial field the king had made definite efforts to exploit his prerogative rights. The Walton ordinances were a step in this direction and in 1339 Edward thought to raise money by the feudal prerogatives of a tallage, a scutage and the aids for knighting the king's eldest son and *pur fille marier*. Since the internal order of England was nearly as important in the early years of the war as the collection of taxation Edward and his judges might have been expected to emphasize the royal prerogative in matters of law as well. This perhaps we can detect in the crown's tactics

---

[1] *Rot. Parl.*, II, 225 b, 237 a.
[2] For the grave problems of law and order facing the crown at the beginning of the reign see E. L. G. Stones, 'The Folvilles of Ashby-Folville, Leicestershire and their associates in crime', *Trans. Roy. Hist. Soc.*, 5th ser., VII (1957), 117–37; also my own 'The Coterel Gang: an anatomy of a band of fourteenth century criminals', *Eng. Hist. Rev.*, LXXIX (1964), 698–718.
[3] Harriss, 'Commons' Petitions', *Eng. Hist. Rev.*, LXXVIII, 632–4.

on accroachment. But Edward could never go very far in this direction since it would and did cause a popular outcry. He was in a cleft stick. He believed that law and order could be fortified by severer punishment, by changing certain crimes from felony into treason. Although the mass of the population wanted a decrease in crime it did not regard the king's solution with any favour and it was Edward who eventually gave way.

The development of the common law was also against Edward's policy. Tout has pointed to the growth of legal definition in the 1340s and the 'increasing unwillingness of the judges of the two benches to employ the large discretionary power which their predecessors had enjoyed up to the days of Edward I'. He notes that 'in 1342 a leading pleader urged that privileges allowed by statute were to be interpreted strictly and in 1346 an active judge accepted this doctrine'.[1] For Miss Putnam this period shows 'a decrease . . . in [the] powers of judges and sergeants as members of the council' and she draws our attention to another symptom of the restriction of the crown's judicial powers, the concession to a commons' petition that the points of each judicial commission were to be declared when it was issued.[2] In the spring of 1348 the king made answer to another commons' petition that 'law had and used in time past and the process thereupon used heretofore cannot be changed without a new statute'. That is to say, the crown acknowledged that law could only be changed in parliament.[3] Amongst certain common lawyers of this time it was a dictum that the king did not have certain prerogatives as of right but because they had been given him by the community.[4] The royal officials came under fire as well. In an action of replevin in 1338 a collector of taxes was found to have no warrant under seal and the court held the king's agents could not distrain without proper writ.[5] There can be little doubt that in the field of law the crown was making big concessions to public opinion and that the old freedom to manoeuvre was being closely circumscribed.

Three petitions on the roll of the first parliament of 1348 show that the complaints against the government's treason policy did not

---

[1] T. F. Tout, *Chapters in the Administrative History of Medieval England* (Manchester, 1920–33), III, 180.
[2] Putnam, *Sir William Shareshull*, pp. 41, 48.   [3] *Rot. Parl.*, II, 203 b.
[4] *Year Books, 16 Edward III, Pt. II*, ed. L. O. Pike (R.S., 1900), p. 132.
[5] As noted by G. L. Haskins in 'Executive Justice and the Rule of Law', *Speculum* XXX (1955), 536.

7

stem from 'academic interest in the clarity of law or interest in punishment'.[1] What was at issue was the nature of the forfeiture of the guilty parties' possessions. One petition has been referred to already. It stated that the king's justices were adjudging crimes as treason or accroachment of the royal power which had never been held as such before. It asked that accroaching should be defined in parliament since lords were losing their escheats. When a man was found guilty on this count the king was taking possession of his lands in perpetuity and not allowing them to go back to the mesne lords after a year and a day, as in a case of felony. The penalties were therefore those for treason yet, as we have found with the various indictments, accroaching was not identical with treason. From the earlier part of the fourteenth century several instances can be quoted to show that men were disinherited as for treason without the crime being classified as such. The penalty which the magnates awarded against the Despensers in August 1321 was disinheritance because they had disinherited the crown by accroaching the royal power.[2] In 1348 a knight and an esquire who attacked a justice in his session were sentenced to be disinherited and to be imprisoned for life: but they were not held as traitors.[3]

The issue of forfeiture or escheat occurred in two other petitions in the same parliament. A commons' petition asked if it could be declared who was entitled to the services pertaining to lands which had been forfeited to the crown for treason and granted away again without the charter specifically stating the immediate lord of the new grantee. It was also asked if such a charter could be challenged and repealed at law. The crown answered that the custom of the king's forbears was being observed and that if there was any matter which needed further definition it would be found in a new law on the subject.[4] If the king had come into the habit of retaining to himself the services once owed to the mesne lords it was in sharp contrast with the policy of the previous decade. Examples of the crown granting away traitors' lands in 1335 and 1340 show that the letters patent specifically mentioned the lands were to be held by the services due before they had come into the king's hand.[5] Very probably the king in 1347–8 had granted away

---

[1] This was first suggested by Miss Thornley ('Act of Treasons', *History*, VI, 107). [2] *Cal. Close Rolls, 1318–23*, p. 494.
[3] *Year Books*, 22 Edward III, Mich. pl. 26.
[4] *Rot. Parl.*, II, 170 a.
[5] *Cal. Pat. Rolls, 1334–8*, pp. 74, 79, 108; *Cal. Pat. Rolls, 1338–40*, p. 435.

forfeited land without making any mention of the services owed for
it at all. The other parliamentary petition of 1348 which touched
on the issue was presented by John Fitzwauter.[1] He referred to the
crown granting away forfeited land in charters which did not say
who the new lord of the grantee was. He pointed out that legal
opinion was divided on the matter and asked for a declaration by
the king. As in the other petition, it was asked if the charter could
be repealed. This time the answer came that the case would be
dealt with by the king and council. The only real difference from
the commons' petition was that Fitzwauter referred to land which
went to the crown by forfeiture of war, a penalty which resulted
from a treason which was different from other treasons in that it
did not necessarily originate in a verdict in a court. The king was
perfectly able to decide of his own will that war had in fact been
levied against him and thereby to decree forfeiture.[2] If the crown
had not made the matter clear in its charter to the grantee it was
once again quite novel since the governmental policy on forfeiture
of war had been clearly pronounced in the case of the lands of Sir
William Blount in May 1342. Lands pertaining to the king by
reason of forfeiture of war, it was stated, and granted by him to
others should be held of the chief lord by the same services as
were rendered before they came into the king's hands and the
grant by the late king (Edward II) of these lands to hold of him and
his heirs was erroneously made: therefore the king for the indem-
nity of the petitioners granted that the land in question should be
held of the chief lords of the fee by the services done before they
escheated notwithstanding his father's letters patent granting the
lands to hold of him and his heirs.[3] Nothing could have been
clearer than this as a statement of royal policy.

Another matter concerning forfeiture arose in the same year as
the three parliamentary petitions. It related to treason which did
not touch the king's person. John de Hill of Flaworth, who as we
have seen had been found guilty of killing a royal messenger, was
tenant of the Master of St Leonard's Hospital, York. The bailiffs
of that liberty claimed the traitor's chattels under a general charter.[4]

---

[1] *Rot. Parl.*, II, 180.
[2] For a reference (a land lease) to the forfeiting of land by judgement of the
king's court or by war see *Cal. Close Rolls, 1346–9*, p. 275. For a decision by the
king that war had been levied against him and forfeiture incurred see *Cal. Close
Rolls, 1318–23*, p. 522.   [3] *Cal. Pat. Rolls, 1340–3*, p. 458.
[4] *Year Books, Liver des Assises*, 22 Edward III, pl. 49.

The judges answered that in this instance the crown would have the escheat of the land as well as the chattels, because the treason touched the king directly. The charter, they pointed out, referred only to common felonies and did not include treason. They added, however, that in cases of treason which did not touch the person of the king or involve adhering to his enemies the crown in future would not take any land but only chattels as in the case of felony. Here we have the difference between great and petty treason, a distinction which was made clear in the statute of 1352 and to which Hill's case was doubtless a contributory cause.

On first inspection the great statute of treasons has no direct connexion with the fourteenth-century state trial, being over twenty years removed from the infamous cases of 1326–30. Yet very probably there was a link: one concerned not with the most famous trials of that period, but with the process against Sir John Maltravers. This knight had in 1329 helped to persuade the earl of Kent that Edward II still lived when he was already dead, thereby causing Kent's eventual execution. The crown had called the crime nothing less than a treason which was notorious to all. Since Maltravers had taken to flight there was no trial but he was attainted or convicted in parliament regardless, by what has been called the process of notoriety.[1] The victim fled to the continent where to his credit he endeavoured to win his way back into royal favour by services on the crown's behalf in Flanders. When Edward III travelled thither in 1345 he was visited at Sluys by Maltravers, who submitted himself to the royal mercy and asked for the opportunity to stand his trial in parliament and purge his innocence. The process against him, he claimed, had not been according to the law and custom of England: he pleaded especially an ordinance on this recently made in parliament. He wanted his accusers to be summoned to the next session of parliament, where the process against him could be examined.[2] On the advice, maybe even the suggestion, of the baronage Edward agreed and gave Maltravers a safe conduct so he could attend at Westminster without danger. His petition was presented in the session which met in

---

[1] *Rot. Parl.*, II, 53 b; Plucknett, 'Origin of Impeachment', *Trans. Roy. Hist. Soc.*, 4th ser., XXIV, 59–61. According to the close rolls Maltravers in 1351 was pardoned of the forfeiture incurred by reason of the death of the earl of Kent and the outlawry promulgated for that cause: *Cal. Close Rolls, 1349–54*, p. 312.

[2] *Cal. Pat. Rolls, 1343–5*, p. 535.

January 1348.[1] It claimed that the petitioner as the result of malicious information laid against him had been adjudged in absence without being indicted, attainted or appealed to reply. The king, it added, had promised in his council to do right to Maltravers and he had made a general proclamation to that intent to all men. The interest which the English magnates had in the supplicant's cause is very evident. The petition stated quite brazenly that the errors in the process of 1330 were to the danger of the baronage in time to come. Despite the unfortunate timing of the request, for Edward was under fire for his policy on treason and accroachment and was particularly in his nobility's debt as a result of the duration of the siege of Calais, the crown conceded nothing except to appoint Maltravers to a royal office outside England, namely the keepership of the Channel Islands.[2] There was, it is true, a slight thaw in the government's attitude for in August 1348 Maltravers's wife was given possession of certain of her husband's forfeited lands. If the wife died, however, they were not to go to her husband.[3] No pardon was forthcoming until 20 June 1351, when Sir John was restored to the state he had held before the judgement against him: this included the return of his lands.[4] Once again some of the magnates must have been involved for it was recorded that Maltravers had sued with great persistence through his friends both in parliament and in the king's council. Very significant was the failure either to declare the judgement of 1330 as illegal or to refer to the nature of the crime involved. Only tacitly was notoriety condemned. Whether when Maltravers's petition was acceded to the crown had already planned the redaction of the law of treason cannot be deduced with any degree of certainty. The chances are that it had but that the Maltravers case made the new law more important still.

After the statute of treasons had been promulgated royal policy changed abruptly and two of the extraordinary judgements from the early years of Edward's reign were annulled. In the parliamentary session which commenced 28 September 1354 the judgement of 1330 against Roger Mortimer was condemned as erroneous because he had never been properly accused, arraigned or given chance to make his answer.[5] Thereby judgement by notoriety was

[1] *Rot. Parl.*, II, 173 a.
[2] *Cal. Pat. Rolls, 1345–8*, p. 115.   [3] *Cal. Pat. Rolls, 1348–50*, p. 134.
[4] *Cal. Pat. Rolls, 1350–4*, p. 110.   [5] *Rot. Parl.*, II, 255–6.

specifically and overtly abnegated and brought to a finish. Concerning the many accroachments which had been laid against him nothing was said. In the same parliament Richard, earl of Arundel, petitioned the crown in an attempt to clear the name of his father Edmund who, he said, had been illegally put to death in 1327. He argued that there had been no proper legal process against his father and that no forfeiture had been adjudged.[1] He had been put to death 'voluntirment': therefore there was no legal force in the forfeiture of the Arundel estates. At Richard's request the records were searched but all that was found was a recitation of a statute of the first year of Edward's reign. This mentioned Edmund, earl of Arundel, as an ally of the Despensers when they accroached the royal power by arranging matters so that Edward II could only do as they wished. He also shared responsibility for accroaching the royal power by oppressing and disinheriting the church and the barons. The king had to agree there was nothing in this statute which said Edmund should be destroyed and therefore he was henceforth to be held as a man who had died within the law. All his lands were to go to Richard and his heirs. Mortimer and Arundel were cleared because of the lack of proper judicial process against them. Nothing was said about their crimes as such: indeed the matter was deliberately avoided possibly because the king did not wish to see the dead Mortimer's crimes found any less outrageous than they had been originally. Those who sought to rehabilitate their forbears did not apparently bring up the matter of accroaching the royal power. They either accepted that in the cases under review this crime had been the equivalent of treason or they surmised the king did not wish the question to be broached. They certainly did not believe that the statute of 1352 by its omission of

---

[1] *Rot. Parl.*, II, 256–7. Richard of Arundel had recovered his inheritance in 1331 when it was declared that the judgement on his father was to be as if it had never been given (*Rot. Parl.*, II, 33, 55). It was however stated that the restitution was of grace and not of right since the original judgement had been ratified by statute in 1327 (*Rot. Parl.*, II, 56). Despite his leading position in the opposition of 1341 he gave the crown good service in the French war. In the 1340s he became involved in litigation with the heirs of the earl of Kent. In the parliament of 1351 the restitution of 1331 was reaffirmed and it was declared the heirs of Edmund of Kent had no grounds for action against him because of his father's condemnation (*Rot. Parl.*, II, 226–7). Obviously this did not satisfy Arundel: hence the petition of 1354. Miss Clarke thought Arundel led a movement to get the law of treason settled. She believed the 1352 statute omitted accroachment because the crown feared the charge would be used against its ministers (*Fourteenth Century Studies*, p. 131).

accroachment from among the treasons gave them grounds for claiming the return of their families' forfeited lands: otherwise they would have petitioned to that effect. We can guess that their attorneys pointed to the anomalous position of accroaching the royal power in the period before 1352, then to the lack of clarification in the statute, and advised that the safest method to achieve restoration was by the way described above.

The forging, or counterfeiting of coin and any tampering with the king's image or seal had always been held as treason even if they were put into a special class by themselves.[1] They were given separate mention in the 1352 statute but this is as we should expect. Alongside these ancient treasons was set another related crime: the bringing into the realm of false money which counterfeited the money of England. Reference was made particularly to the money called 'Lushburgh', which originated in Luxemburg. This grievance was first mentioned in parliament in the session which commenced on 28 April 1343, when lords, commons and merchants petitioned that the good money was being drained away from the kingdom and being replaced by false.[2] They asked for an assay of the Flemish florin and the fixing of its value against the pound sterling: also for a new issue of gold coinage in England and Flanders of a fixed content, providing the Flemings would agree. To these demands the crown assented, as it did to the petition that no silver or sterling should be taken out of the kingdom or bad money allowed to enter on pain of life or member to the miscreant. The government was unable to fulfil the last part of this request and false coin from the towns of Luxemburg, Flushing and Foulquemont was finding its way past the official searchers by 1346.[3] In the parliament of that year complaints were made against the influx of 'Lushburgh' coin in particular and stringent action was called for. Those who introduced the coin, it was suggested, should be punished as false moneyers and those whose position and wealth precluded their indictment should be taken as notorious suspects. The king conceded the first point but refused the second.[4] In the parliament which met in January 1348 the commons again complained of the influx of coins from Luxemburg and accused

---

[1] Holdsworth, *History of English Law*, III, 289; also P.R.O., K.B. 27/242 Rex m. 21, where forging the king's money is classified as a special form of treason.
[2] *Rot. Parl.*, II, 137 b.   [3] *Cal. Pat. Rolls, 1345–8*, p. 99.
[4] *Rot. Parl.*, II, 160 b.

the judges of doing little to remedy the situation, indeed of ignoring completely the penalties ordained in the session of 1346.[1] They asked that in future the king should not pardon those who committed such deeds: deeds which were referred to as falseness and treason. In response the government issued an ordinance for the destruction of all false money and a further restriction was put on the export of English coin. The problem was too great for a medieval state to solve and the complaints against the false money of 'Lushburgh', which was probably a deliberate imitation of the English specie, continued until after the treaty of Bretigny. Cases in which counterfeiting was treated as treason were plentiful both before and after the statute.[2]

The causes of the great statute of treasons were as we have seen both numerous and complex. Some of them had been in existence well over a decade, while others were relatively newly sprung. Edward III's successes in the French war, the temporary period of truce and the Black Death combined to make the parliaments of 1351–2 particularly prolific in the matter of legislation. In Miss Putnam's view 'the great code of 1351–2 of ecclesiastical, economic and legal reforms, the last touching criminal and civil law . . .' was 'a more vital and a more far-reaching code than any in the past since Edward I or any in the future until the sixteenth century'.[3] Of the legal legislation, 'the most vital measure', the treason statute, Miss Putnam suggests, was largely the work of the judges on the council, particularly Sir William Shareshull, C.J.K.B. 'It cannot be doubted that the chief justice of the highest criminal court of the realm, perhaps in collaboration with his sole colleague Basset and also with Stonor, chief justice of common pleas, was responsible for the clear cut distinction between treason and other felonies . . .'[4] In contrast with the other petitions enacted in the parliament of January 1352, all of which came from the commons, the treason statute was not based on a petition which requested specific details. There was merely a plea for remedial legislation because different judges in their sessions were finding men as traitors 'pur diverses causes desconues a la Commune estre treison'.[5] The king was asked for his council and his nobles to declare the

---

[1] *Rot. Parl.*, II, 167 a.
[2] For example, see P.R.O., K.B. 27/349 Rex m. 20d (1347), K.B. 27/372 Rex m. 35 (1353), K.B. 27/389 Rex m. 16 (1357), K.B. 27/397 Rex m. 12 (1359), *Cal. Pat. Rolls, 1358–61*, p. 514.   [3] Putnam, *Sir William Shareshull*, p. 52.
[4] *Ibid.*, p. 54.   [5] *Rot. Parl.*, II, 239 a.

points of treason in the current session of parliament. The statute rolls talk of there being different opinions at that time as to which cases should be called treason and which not.[1]

In allowing parliamentary legislation to give a decidedly narrow interpretation to treason the king was seriously diminishing his chances of obtaining permanent forfeitures, and on the face of it, at least, undermining the royal prerogative. Previously the crown itself had decided what offences constituted treason and the yard-stick had been the political implication of each case: there had been no absolute consistency.[2] From the king's point of view treason was a casualty in a period of increasing legal definition. Those who benefited from the termination of the vague and elastic periphery of treason were the magnates. If the statute was adhered to by the king they would receive as mesne lords after a year and a day lands which would previously have gone to the crown for good.

The statute carefully distinguished between high and petty treason: the Hill case of 1347 had demonstrated the need for a clear boundary. Petty treason was to be the slaying of a master by a servant, husband by a wife or prelate by a lesser cleric. It was to be treated in all essentials as a felony.[3] High treason was henceforth to include only crimes against the king's person and his regality, yet the list was by no means a short one. There were the obvious treasons of compassing or imagining the death of the king, the queen or the royal heir, and the violation of the king's wife, eldest daughter or the wife of his eldest son. These were the only members of the royal family whose lives were sacrosanct: the mere terrorizing of the king's children as had occurred in the Beche case in 1347 would not, if it were repeated, be held more than felony. The slaying of the chancellor, the treasurer, the justices of the two benches, justices in eyre and of assize, in fact of any justices empowered to hear and determine, was made treason, but only if they were in their places performing their office. The murder of

---

[1] *Stat. Realm*, I, 319–20.

[2] Thus an Oxford clerk who claimed to be the son and heir of Edward I was executed for treason in July 1318 (*Chronicles of Edward I and Edward II*, II, 55). The king and his legal advisers may have argued that the claim to be the rightful king was tantamount to imagining the death of the present monarch.

[3] A case of treason which was not directed against the king before the statute concerned the killing of her mistress by Alice de Walburum (*Year Books, Liver des Assises* 12 Edward III pl. 30). Two cases of petty treason after the statute are to be found in *Year Books, Liver des Assises*, 33 Edward III pl. 20 and 40 Edward III pl. 25. See also Appendix II.

John Legat, had it occurred three years later, would not, if the rubric was obeyed, have been held as treason since he was at the time merely pursuing a private suit. It had always been reckoned treason to counterfeit the money of England or the king's seal.[1] This was rehearsed in the statute but the additional crime of bringing false money into the realm was also included. A direct reference to 'Lushburgh' showed whence the clause derived. Those who drafted the statute of treasons did not pretend to have listed every possible type but made provision for doubtful cases to be considered in parliament. When these arose the justices were to delay giving judgement until the case could be shown before the king in parliament and it was declared whether it ought to be judged treason or felony. In seeking the interference of parliament in matters *sub judice* this provision had something in common with the statute concerning delayed judgements of 1340 (14 Edward III st. 1, c. 5).[2] The latter provided for a parliamentary commission to have the power to call before it the records and processes of judgements which had been delayed as well as the justices concerned: it was then to take a good accord and make a good judgement, which the judges were hastily to pronounce. The closest similarity between the statutes of 1340 and 1352 concerned the difficulties which might arise. The former decreed that in any case which to the judges seemed so difficult that it could not properly be determined without the assent of parliament, the tenor of the process was to be brought into the next parliamentary session and a judgement made which the justices were to pronounce in their court. The compilers of the 1352 statute must have recognized that certain cases of treason would involve this 'difficulty' and they probably borrowed the procedure, although they seem to have intended that the justices should give the judgement and not parliament.[3] On the one hand it was a sign of the

---

[1] The statute rolls include as treason the counterfeiting of the privy seal (*Stat. Realm*, I, 319-20) which is not mentioned in the rolls of parliament (see *Rot. Parl.*, II, 239 a).   [2] *Stat. Realm*, I, 282.
[3] See S. Rezneck, 'The Early History of the Parliamentary Declaration of Treason', *Eng. Hist. Rev.*, XLII (1927), 497-513. The first crime to be so declared was the murder of John Imperial, the Genoese ambassador, in 1379. On that

were convicted were allowed to go before parliament to offer reasons why the sentences should not be carried out. Matters were further complicated by the occasion parliament sent the declaration back to the judges after the case had been examined and disputed among the lords and commons and shown to the king, saying the deed was treason and a crime of lese-majesty. It was added that no claim for benefit of clergy was to be allowed. (P.R.O., K.B. 27/476 Rex m. 31). See below, pp. 232-4.

growing prestige of parliament and its power to interfere. On the other it revealed once more the decrease in the freedom of the justices to interpret the law as they thought fit.[1] They must needs give way to the superiority of the statutes while supreme above all was the promulgator parliament.

Some of the unsatisfactory trials of the period 1322–30 the statute tacitly condemned. This was achieved by insisting that for a man to be found guilty of levying war against the king or adhering to his enemies he must be provably attainted of open fact by men of his own condition. Thus the method by which Andrew Harclay and Thomas of Lancaster and some of his adherents had been found guilty and sent to their deaths was made illegal unless, as later examples show and as Henry of Lancaster had successfully argued in 1327, it was a time of recognized open war.[2] The method condemned was the summary conviction of the accused on the king's own word that he was in fact guilty. In cases of this type there was no indictment, arraignment or putting to answer once the record of the king had been introduced. The king's record had also a particular reference to the matter of adhering to his enemies since a man who joined the Scots or the French could not easily be brought to trial. Before 1352 the king's writ, itself his record, was occasionally used to record the crime and thereby give the escheator a title to the traitor's lands.[3] There were similar examples when the crime was levying of war against the king. After 1352 the crown, no doubt in deference to the treason statute, commonly used as its title to these lands the findings of the escheator's inquest, which stood as proven attainder by men of like condition. Nonetheless the petition by William de Dacre in December 1358 suggests that the government believed the royal prerogative still gave it a good claim to these lands without any inquisition. Dacre claimed his lands had been taken into the king's hands for adhering to the Scottish enemy, without this enquiry. Edward ordered the lands to be

[1] In 1352 (25 Edward III st. 6, c. 9) the crown was compelled to stop its judges accepting indictments phrased in general terms: henceforward the details of each crime had to be included (*Stat. Realm*, I, 326).

[2] The trial of Harclay is discussed in Keen, 'Treason Trials', *Trans. Roy. Hist. Soc.*, 5th ser. XII, 88–91; for Lancaster's trial see *Rot. Parl.*, II, 3–4. See also above, pp. 50–3.

[3] See Plucknett, 'Origin of Impeachment', *Trans. Roy. Hist. Soc.*, 4th ser., XXIV, 61–3; also *Year Books, 20 Edward III, Pt. I*, ed. L. O. Pike (R.S., 1908), p. 180: '*Richemunde*: Sire vous veiez bien coment il allegge une aesioun, quele chose chiet en recorde . . .' For a typical case see *Cal. Pat. Rolls, 1348–50*, p. 246.

given back to him out of grace 'although he could retain the premises as forfeit if he wished'.[1] Despite this brave sally the government seems to have made sure that inquests were taken in subsequent cases of a similar nature. Instead of exploiting what room to manoeuvre there was in that direction the escheators sought out 'forfeited' land of another sort. The new departure was the subject of a commons' complaint in the parliament of 1361. It claimed that escheators were seizing land as forfeit to the king for treason surmised in dead persons who had never been attainted of treason during their lives.[2] The crown was trying to dig into the past and by use of a posthumous trial procedure seeking to gain considerable profit for itself. In answer to the petition the king pointed out that he and his progenitors had always been seised of these forfeitures of war and he would not therefore give up the right. Edward had in fact by means of his own royal record or through inquisition taken by his escheators, been finding scores of men of the northern shires guilty of adhering to the Scots and levying war against the English crown from as far back as the reign of Edward I.[3] None of those who suffered had apparently been provably attainted of open deed in their lifetime. The concession which Edward made in 1361 was a promise not to seek the forfeiture of lands which had belonged to those who committed their treasons of adhering to the king's enemies or levying war before the accession of Edward II. In the matter of dead traitors who had not been satisfactorily convicted in their own lifetime the statute of treasons probably restrained the use which the king had previously made of the royal record and thereby caused him to use the escaetorial inquest as his title to forfeitures.

The last few lines of the statute of treasons referred specifically to a category of crime which was not to be construed as treason. The crown declared it was not intended that those who rode armed secretly or openly so as to slay, rob, capture or kidnap should be accused as traitors. Such crimes were to be held no more

---

[1] Cal. Pat. Rolls., 1358–61, p. 130.
[2] Stat. Realm, 1, 367.
[3] The chief agent of the crown in this operation was William de Nessfield, escheator in Yorkshire, Westmorland, Northumberland and Cumberland, 1357–63: Cal. Fine Rolls, 1356–68, pp. 46, 258. The new policy seems to have begun in February 1358 and continued until circa November 1360: see Cal. Pat. Rolls, 1358–61, pp. 22, 496, 498. The subject is worthy of close study: the volume referred to is full of examples of this hitherto unnoticed aspect of the reign of Edward III.

than felony or trespass. When the criminals had been convicted their lands were to go as escheats to the lords of the fees except for the crown's year, day and waste. Forfeited lands of this type currently in the king's hands were to be released without delay. The phraseology of this special proviso indicates that when the statute was drafted in 1352 such a crime or crimes were still fresh in the popular mind. Miss Thornley, following Hale, suggested the relevance of the Gerberge case in this context and we can add the misdeeds of John Litel of South Mimms. A mandate of December 1349 referred to men going armed to the vicinity of London contrary to the statutes of Winchester and Westminster: some were of notorious suspicion, others were wandering by night.[1] Since the plague had been stayed, the king said, it was very necessary for the mayor and sheriffs to see the king's peace was inviolably kept. Criminal bands were multiplying: many men were making a living as 'gentlemen of the road' and by their interference with travelling merchants were jeopardizing the crown's economic policy and thereby the ultimate success of the French war. Between 1347 and 1350 there must have been a great deal of highway robbery but it does not seem that the government treated more than one or two of the most outstanding cases as the equivalent of treason.[2] A much more likely immediate cause of this clause of the statute of 1352 was the Beche case. At the time of the relevant parliament several of the principals in the Beams episode were still at large and were not to be pardoned until the following year.[3] Notice must be taken also of an episode at Colchester in August 1351. Lionel de Bradenham with 200 followers laid siege to the town of Colchester until the citizens paid a ransom so as to

---

[1] Cal. Pat. Rolls, 1348–50, p. 459.

[2] Gerberge and his gang, Anketil de Hoby (see below, p. 92), and Litel of South Mimms were probably all notorious criminals with long records. Alexander de Jernemouth esquire, Gerberge's right hand man, was described as a common and notorious ambusher (P.R.O., K.B. 27/349 Rex m. 6). Another member of the gang, Peter de Thorp of Pakenham, Suffolk, was referred to as being a common and notorious thief (P.R.O., K.B. 27/349 Rex m. 23d). There is the possibility that both Gerberge and Hoby had been pardoned on one occasion but had reverted to their old criminal habits: see Cal. Pat. Rolls, 1345–8, p. 532 and Cal. Pat. Rolls, 1348–50, p. 547. Hoby may well have been a member of the infamous Folville gang in the early 1330s: see Stones, 'Folvilles of Ashby-Folville', Trans. Roy. Hist. Soc., 5th ser. VII, 123.

[3] Cal. Pat. Rolls, 1350–4, pp. 431, 527. One of the abductors of Margery de la Beche must have secured a pardon almost simultaneously with the drafting of the statute: Cal. Pat. Rolls, 1350–4, p. 209.

preserve their lives and to be left alone 'as an enemy does to his enemy in a land at war, contrary to his allegiance due to the king'.[1] Bradenham eventually purchased a pardon which included not only felony but sedition.

Another case which involved capture and holding to ransom concerned a clerk called Anketil de Hoby. He was one of those who like Gerberge and Litel had been condemned for treason. The unfairness of the procedure against him was part of a complaint by the clergy in the first parliamentary session of 1352. It pointed out that he had not been allowed benefit of clergy. The answer came that the crime in question was a treason against the king and his royal majesty which had never been clergyable.[2] The crown had no intention of altering that part of the law but in future benefit would be allowed to clerks convicted of petty treason, murder or of being notorious robbers. The government set this down not in the statute of treasons but in another statute of the same year which was clearly intended to serve as a corollary.[3]

The provisions of the 1352 statute can be explained in great part by reference to contemporary legal cases. The degree to which the new law was observed by the crown is much harder to elucidate. Because the provisions were embodied in a statute this did not mean the king or his justices would automatically hold them sacrosanct. In 1343 on the advice of the magnates and those skilled in law Edward III had revoked the statute 15 Edward III st. 2 'come cel qest prejudiciel et contraire a leys et usages du roialme et as droits et prerogatives nostre seignur le roi'.[4] In 1351, according to Wilkinson, Edward evaded a demand that the intention of a statute should not be perverted.[5] In 1355 in a case involving the bishop of Ely the king went so far as to disregard the opinion of the most distinguished men of law that the temporalities of the see should not be seized into the royal hands without a proper judgement, and thereby over-rode a statute.[6] Such direct tactics were not used to abrogate the new treason legislation. But the government might have used subtler techniques. For the law to be changed the statute had to come into actual operation and cases under it had to be heard in the courts. Since a court was not bound

[1] Cal. Pat. Rolls, 1364–7, p. 54.
[2] Rot. Parl., II, 244 b.   [3] 25 Edward III st. 6, c. 4: see Stat. Realm, I, 325.
[4] Rot. Parl., II, 139 b.   [5] Wilkinson, Constitutional History, III, 332.
[6] P.R.O., C. 49/67/5.

to apply a statute if it could be shown it had never been enforced 'non-user' could mean that it lapsed.[1] It is possible though not at all probable that Edward III intended this as his policy. Not until the reign of his grandson is there evidence of the direct implementation of the 1352 act. Then the occasion was the murder of John Imperial, a Genoese ambassador, in London, which created the need for parliament to declare the crime as treason.[2] On the other hand the absence of cases under the treason statute may not be as important as it seems at first sight, since the legislation of 1352 was after all intended to reduce the scope of treason. It meant the narrowing of a category which had never been particularly wide.

The cases of treason which were prosecuted by the crown in the years immediately following the statute of 1352 concerned the counterfeiting of the king's coinage and the introduction of false money into the realm. The prosecutions could equally well have been before the statute was enacted: it is possible therefore that the old law had not been superseded.[3] Common law, so the lawyers believed, only ceased to function where it was actually contradicted by a statute: otherwise they existed side by side. The *Year Books* demonstrate actions in which litigants could choose between a new statutory remedy and satisfaction under the old common law.[4] The continuance of the common law of treason is suggested by several decisions by the king's justices. In 1353 Sir William Shareshull, after a debate with his fellow judges, ruled that to reveal the king's counsel was felony and not, as some of them believed, treason.[5] There was no reference to this crime in the

---

[1] *Year Books, 19 Edward III*, ed. Pike (R.S., 1906), p. 170.

[2] P.R.O., K.B. 27/476 Rex m. 31. See above, p. 88, n. 3; also below, pp. 113 and 180–1.

[3] For example, see P.R.O., K.B. 27/389 Rex m. 16; also K.B. 27/372 Rex m. 35 (counterfeiting the great seal). For proceedings against a false moneyer which were specifically under the treason statute, see K.B. 27/397 Rex. m. 12. But there is some evidence from the end of the fourteenth century, that the making of false coins from a false metal called 'alconamye', whatever that was, was held as only felony: Putnam, *Proceedings*, p. cli.

[4] *Year Books, 11 and 12 Edward III*, ed. A. J. Horwood (R.S., 1883), p. 438; *18 Edward III*, ed. Pike (R.S., 1904), p. 538.

[5] *Year Books, Liver des Assises*, 27 Edward III pl. 63. 'Un G. fuit endite en Bank le Roy de ceo que il fuit un des enditors que enditent certeins persons de divers felonies et scyent le counsaile le Roy discoverer que il avoit overtment entre autre monstrer que ascuns des dits gens que fuerent endits: et issint discoverer le counseyle le Roy ... il fuit arraine come de felony. Et Shard. que ascuns Justices voilent tener cest chose treason nient meins il ne fuit arraign forsque de felony et fuit acquite.'

statute of 1352, yet within a year of promulgation certain experts were ready to hold it treasonable: either they did not believe the statute superseded the common law or the crime was petty treason. The word treason was not qualified, it may be noted. How Shareshull reached his conclusion is not known. Miss Putnam suggests he was merely repeating the verdict which he had given in the Devon sessions of the peace of 1351.[1] There was no mention of piracy in the 1352 statute, yet at some time before 1366 Shareshull condemned a number of sailors who had committed the crime against other subjects of the king to be drawn and quartered for treason.[2] We must bear in mind that this too might have been held as petty treason or it might have occurred before 1352. For a crime committed in 1380, before there had been any parliamentary addition to the statute of 1352, John Haukwode was found guilty of treason because he had denied the king's laws.[3] Like the two preceding cases this one is not conclusive either. Haukwode's crime was committed on 3 September 1380, but he was not brought into court until 25 April 1384, which was after the treason act of 1381. It is possible that his deeds, which were committed during an insurrection at Salisbury, were retrospectively held as treason under that law. Other evidence for the continuation of common law treasons is similarly equivocal. A commission of July 1353 implies at first sight that not only did the old common law of treason still persist but that the crown could ignore any contradictory section of the statute if it wanted. John Pecche of London

---

[1] Putnam, *Sir William Shareshull*, p. 128.

[2] *Year Books, Liver des Assises*, 40 Edward III pl. 25. Coke believed the case was one of petty treason: Coke, p. 20. The report however merely states the crime was adjudged 'treason' (no epithet) and that the sailors were drawn and hanged.

[3] P.R.O., K.B. 27/492 Rex m. 13: 'Xii juratores ... dicunt ... quod Johannes Haukwode ... die Lune proximo ante festum Nativitatis Beate Marie anno regni Regis Ricardi post conquestum quarto in Nova Sarum, Fissherton, Aucher et alibi infra comitatum Wiltsciriam venit cum gladiis, scutis, arcubus et sagittis cum communibus predicte Nove Sarum et cum ipsis fuit consentiens, agens et negans statuta Domini Regis et iura sua ubique contra Dominum Regem insurgens et perturbatoribus pacis Domini Regis consulens et auxilians ad dictam insurrectionem faciendam; et dicunt quod idem Johannes est communis insurgens contra Dominum Regem et ministros suos proclamando in foro civitatis Nove Sarum et alibi infra comitatum Wiltsciriam ac manifeste minando quod si aliquis de ligeis Domini Regis sibi contradixit vel voluntatem suam negaverit decapitaretur.' When Haukwode appeared in court '... allocutus est qualiter de feloniis et prodicionibus predictis se velit acquitare ...' He was eventually found not guilty and set free.

was appointed to take and commit to the nearest gaol those felons and traitors who were infesting the passes in woods and other places and killing the king's lieges and merchant strangers who came to trade at the king's staples.[1] The criminals who were to be captured sound very much like ordinary highwaymen, yet the statute of 1352, as we have seen, had explicitly excluded those who rode armed to slay, rob or capture and ransom from the scope of treason. How these malefactors when taken were accused in court is unfortunately not known. Perhaps the crown was only bluffing and the actual indictments were for felony. A much more satisfactory interpretation concerns the clause in the treason statute on the levying of war. No indication was given as to how this was to be defined. The king, however, had his own rules, which do not appear to have ever been challenged. If the malefactors, who were ambushing travellers, had ridden in arms with banners displayed or shown some sign which had the same chivalric connotation, though not perhaps mere *cote armure*, then they could be taken as traitors and there would be no protest in parliament.[2] Pecche's commission therefore cannot be taken to show that the statute of treasons was ignored from its inception.

Nor does the history of accroaching the royal power support so pessimistic a view. There were no cases in the decade after 1352 in which this crime was dealt with as treason, or even put alongside treason in the indictment. On the odd occasion when it did appear it was treated as no more than felony, as for example in February 1355, when John Gotoreste, a Bristol spicer, assumed the office of mayor and had a man indicted and delivered before him.[3] It was only resuscitated in a way which connected it with treason in 1388. Then it figured not as an accusation by the crown but as a baronial charge against royal ministers and favourites. It assumed a far more potent form than earlier in the century, when although sometimes placed alongside treason it was not treasonable itself. In 1311 and 1321 the magnates had secured only the exile of hated favourites, but the Lords Appellant were determined to sentence

---

[1] *Cal. Pat. Rolls, 1350–4*, p. 514.

[2] There were however in 1401–2 two examples of men being found guilty of feloniously and traitorously lying in ambush to rob or kill along the highways and causing the depopulation of the fields, or plotting to do these things. The accused were designated as 'communes insidiatores viarum et depopulatores agrorum': P.R.O., K.B. 9/189/10 and 34. See Appendix III and below p. 134.

[3] For example, *Cal. Pat. Rolls, 1354–8*, p. 180; P.R.O., C. 47/59/2/53.

8

their enemies to death and to heap upon them as many charges of treason as possible. Since they had control of parliament and dominated the king they were able to decree that a number of accroachments were treasonable. Significantly the first of these was alienating the king from his people and allowing him to listen only to the advice of the favourites. The second was the favourites' refusal to permit the king to be counselled by his magnates. Of the total of thirty-nine articles which were laid against the favourites, the lords of parliament found fourteen to be in some way treasonable. In eight of these the crime was some form of accroaching the royal power.[1] The sentences of 1388 were reversed by Richard II nine years later and thereafter the magnates were never in a position to accuse a royal favourite of such crimes. There was, it is true, the impeachment of the duke of Suffolk in 1450, but this was perhaps more the work of the commons of parliament than the lords. Suffolk was accused of treasons and also of other crimes which were very similar to those of Gaveston, the Despensers and of Richard II's favourites. They were, however, not called accroachments but 'false deceits', 'untrue labours' and, most commonly, misprisions.[2] It was this offence which by the fifteenth century had come to embrace a number of crimes which would have been called accroachments of royal power the century before.

The change from accroachment to misprision is first detectable in the processes against Richard Lyons in the parliaments of 1376 and 1377. In the Good Parliament Lyons was accused of levying a tax on wool without parliament's assent, exporting wool and skins by routes which avoided the Calais staple, buying up the king's debts at a discount and of several other extortions, falsities, deceits and oppressions as farmer of the subsidy and the customs, taking on himself royal power. These offences were called trespasses in the rolls of the Good Parliament but were referred to as misprisions, the word used to describe misbehaviour by office holders, in a parliament of the next year.[3] This was probably a deliberate attempt by the government to play down Lyons's crimes and protect royal favourites from the criticisms of the baronage at large. Bishop Henry Despenser and the captains in command of the expedition to Flanders in 1383 woefully mishandled their affairs. They committed such offences as making

[1] *Rot. Parl.*, III, 230–5.
[2] *Ibid.*, v, 178.   [3] *Ibid.*, III, 12 b.

treaties with the enemy without royal authority, receiving pay-
ments of money from him and surrendering fortresses, food and
munitions of war, but the accusations against them in parliament
in 1383 referred to these things as being misprisions and not as
might have been the case earlier in the century, as accroachments
of royal power.[1] Only once was accroachment mentioned in the
charges: it was against Sir Thomas Tryvet, one of the captains,
whose misdeed was to have issued letters of safe conduct under the
king's seal without his authority.[2] The crimes which in 1386 were
the subject of the impeachment of Michael de la Pole, the chancellor, like those of Richard Lyons, were largely financial. He had
misspent taxation intended for military projects, defrauded the
king of his proper financial profits and granted a vast number of
pardons for treason and felony. Again the misdeeds were called
misprisions and this time there was no mention of accroachment
at all.[3]

Although the popularity of accroaching the royal power as a
royal or baronial accusation had waned, it did not disappear
entirely until the middle of the fifteenth century. In 1406 one of
the charges made in parliament against the northern rebels was that
Archbishop Scrope, Thomas Mowbray the earl marshal, and their
allies had assembled men in Yorkshire against the king's wishes
and had traitorously counselled them by speeches and proclamations to rebel, thus traitorously usurping and accroaching royal
power to themselves.[4] This was the first treasonable accroachment since 1388 and apart from the article in the act which attainted
Jack Cade in 1450 of imagining the destruction of the king and the
subversion of the realm by seditiously taking on himself royal
power, the only fifteenth-century example.[5] Soon after Cade's
revolt there came the last reference of any sort to accroachment.
The attainder act of 1459 against the Yorkists who had fought at
Bloreheath and Ludford Bridge mentioned the misdeeds committed
by the duke of York during the previous decade. One of his alleged
offences was his 'crafty labours and designs' to the 'amenusyng'
[diminution] of the royal power and authority.[6]

Why the accusation of accroaching the royal power should
appear less in the fifteenth century calls for explanation. The king

[1] *Rot. Parl.*, III, 157.   [2] *Ibid.*, III, 157 b.
[3] *Ibid.*, III, 216–20.   [4] *Ibid.*, III, 604.
[5] *Ibid.*, v, 265 a.   [6] *Ibid.*, v, 347.

made use of it on one or two occasions but there was no policy to utilize it for the extension of the law of treason as had been done by Edward III. Even the Yorkist kings made no attempts in this direction. Very probably there were more efficient weapons available. The flexibility of the treason charge of imagining or compassing the king's death permitted its application against almost any action or plan directed against the king or his government. On the other side there was no occasion in the fifteenth century when the greater part of the magnates united to attack a royal favourite, except perhaps in 1450. In that instance no use was made of accroachment as a charge. Suffolk's crimes were held to be either treasons, where in fact they did approximate to treason, or misprisions, which were misdeeds of the type called by that name by Richard II. Accroachment must also have lost its popularity because of the changing concept of kingship. The fourteenth century, even the thirteenth, had allowed a doctrine of royal capacities, that is, a difference between the king as a person and as a ruler. The argument has been offered that the origins of this thesis lay in the distinction between the spiritual and temporal status of ecclesiastics, whose effect on the lay world is to be noted in such examples as the references to the official and private capacities of the chancellor in the reign of Edward I.[1] It seems equally likely, however, that the notion of capacities arose out of the political arrangements of the thirteenth century, whereby the king ruled under the law with baronial advice, and sovereignty was vested in the union of the two, described symbolically as the crown. Baronial loyalty was therefore not to the king's person but to the crown, the office of king. In 1308, as we have seen, in the proceedings in parliament against Gaveston, it was argued that homage and allegiance were to the crown rather than to the king's person and that if the king did not guide himself by reason in the right of the crown, his subjects must lead him back to reason since he was breaking his coronation oath.[2]

The doctrine of capacities was still discernible at the end of the fourteenth century. In a *Year Book* case of 1405 there was what has been called 'a plain separation made between the rights of the king as king and his rights as duke of Lancaster'. Later in the century Chief Justice Fortescue, in his account of arguments among

---

[1] S. B. Chrimes, *English Constitutional Ideas in the Fifteenth Century* (Cambridge, 1936), p. 34.   [2] *Stat. Realm*, I, 182.

imaginary rival claimants to the throne, differentiated between the king's capacity as a private proprietor and his capacity as a public office holder.[1] The prevailing tendency in much of the fifteenth century, however, was not to distinguish different capacities but to emphasize the oneness of kingship. Royal authority was held to be indistinguishable from the royal person.[2] The king might be an infant, mentally defective or deranged, but royal authority was considered to be unimpaired and sovereignty said to reside only in the king's person. Why it was the magnates permitted this development at a time when their collective power was at its zenith is difficult to fathom: so is the method by which it was accomplished. Perhaps the law of treason played a part, particularly the finding as treason of mere slanderous words against the king by those who never intended nor had the capability to plot the king's death.[3] Perhaps the Lancastrian party at court elevated the king's position so that it should have a weapon against its baronial rivals. Perhaps it was because the magnates in opposition were for fairly long periods aligned behind their own claimant to the throne. It was no longer barons versus king as it had been in the fourteenth century but one would-be monarch and his supporters versus another would-be monarch and his. The leader of neither faction wanted royal authority impugned since he had hopes of using it himself. However, the factional wars and the resultant depositions and usurpations forced a recognition once more of the distinction between the office and person of king, one of which for the first time the common law took notice. This is demonstrated by Bagot's case which was argued in 1470.[4] Henry Bagot and William Swyrenden brought an action of novel disseisin against Thomas Ive, who had disseised them of the offices of clerks to the hanaper. Crucial in the argument was whether Bagot could bring the case at all since his letters of denizenship had been issued by Henry VI. Did the acts of a king who had usurped the throne, as the Yorkists looked at it, bind Edward IV? Was the king de iure obliged to accept the charters of his de facto predecessor? Some serjeants and apprentices argued that he was not, using the parallel of regressor and disseisor from the land laws, but the judges eventually awarded their decision to the plaintiff. Even if there was no official adoption at that time of

[1] Chrimes, *Constitutional Ideas*, p. 35.
[2] *Ibid.*, pp. 35–7.   [3] Below, pp. 116–19.
[4] *Year Books*, 9 Edward IV, Pasch. pl. 2, 20, Trin. pl. 3.

the *de iure* and *de facto* distinction made by Bagot's counsel such ideas were obviously being mooted among the legal profession. In 1485 the judges, when asked about the problem of Henry Tudor's attainder, gave the concept of the unity of the king's person and his office a renewed lease of life by affirming that any man on becoming king automatically discharged himself of his attainder.[1] Although this must have been to Henry VII's liking he was, in 1495, himself forced to admit that there could be a king *de facto* and a king *de iure*, and that therefore the office was not necessarily united with the royal person. The act of treason of that year referred in two places to the 'prince or sovereign lord for the time being', and it was he whom the subjects of his realm were bound to serve in order to defend him and their land.[2]

Accroachment of the royal power has been the object of much speculation by historians and lawyers, a great deal of it unfounded and unfortunate, as for example the attempt to see a direct connexion with the so-called common law treasons. This is the reason for the long excursus above. That accroachment did not figure in the legislation of 1352 detracts very little from the importance of the great treason statute. That act was of the greatest significance legally, politically and constitutionally. Coke cannot have been far wrong when he said its importance was second only to that of Magna Carta.

There can be little doubt that the decade preceding the statute of 1352 was crucial to the history of treason. The act did not come about because of some general affection that Edward III felt for his magnates or because secure on his throne and basking in the glory of his French victories he felt the time had come to put right some of the miscarriages of justice of his father's reign. It came as a direct result of the royal judges trying to extend the common law of treason. Their reason for so doing was the better enforcement of law and order at a time when the king was often outside the realm engaged on military expeditions. For these wars he needed supply and the taxpayer paid more willingly when law and order were maintained at a high level. To add more weight to the charges against the criminal the king's officers occasionally added that the crime was a usurpation of royal power and thereby the more serious. It was an aggravation of the accusation: it did not turn felony into treason. Men only suffered death as traitors

---

[1] *Year Books*, 1 Henry VII, Mich. pl. 5.   [2] *Stat. Realm*, II, 568.

when found guilty of committing accepted treasons although there is some evidence that the king imposed forfeiture as for treason. After the act of 1352 there were except in 1388 very few examples of the charge of accroachment but it did not disappear entirely.

The period from the outbreak of the Hundred Years War to 1352 was one of increasing legal definition which seems to have had its origins in the increase of the power of parliament as a result of the king's pressing need for taxes. The discretionary powers of the royal judges steadily declined because they hesitated to use them and the royal prerogative came under hostile scrutiny. Any definition of royal prerogative was to the king's detriment since it meant a contraction of the nebulous periphery of royal competence. It was even argued that the king did not have certain prerogatives as of right but because they had been given him by the community: presumably therefore under this theory they could be taken away again.

The statute of 1352 where it did not contravene the common law should have left that law standing. Yet if there were one or two cases where the operation of the 1352 statute is hard to trace there was certainly no group of later treasons which stood out as being offences only under the common law. The political crimes which the judges of Richard II found to be worthy of a traitor's death in 1387 were not mentioned in the 1352 act it is true but they were certainly not common law treasons either. The lawyers of the later fourteenth and the fifteenth century made no reference to common law treason. For them the law of treason was enshrined in the act of 1352, explicitly or on parliamentary declaration. Common law treason was a discovery of the royal lawyers of the sixteenth century whose exiguous historical knowledge of medieval precedent served to advance rather than diminish their fanciful claims. Finally attention must be drawn to an aspect of the law of treason about which the act of 1352 said very little. This was legal procedure. Those who levied war against the king or adhered to his enemies had in future to be provably attainted by men of like condition and cases of doubtful treason had to be declared in parliament, but in criminal process as a whole the crown still had room to move.

5

THE SCOPE OF TREASON

1352–1485

'ITEM they say when the kynge wulle shall be traytours and when he wulle none schalle be none; and that aperuthe wele hidurto': so ran one complaint of the Kentishmen in 1450.[1] Very likely 'they' were the Lancastrian courtiers and the extreme opinions which they held about the king's judicial prerogative were unlikely to have had the unreserved support of the fifteenth-century lawyers. By their complaint the Kentishmen were unwittingly drawing attention to one of the great problems concerning late medieval treason, namely the degree to which the government had to observe accepted precedent and normal legal procedure. In the matter of defining treason the law to be observed was primarily the statute of 1352 and the problem concerns how far the act was covertly altered and extended by judicial construction. The first impression is that the alterations and extensions must have been considerable since the period produced several new types of state trial, different varieties of popular insurrection and a high incidence of summary trials on the battlefield. To these must be added that number of novel crimes and situations which expose the deficiencies of any piece of legislation. On the other hand the development of parliamentary attainder during the fifteenth century might be taken as evidence against this viewpoint since attainder, it is often said, could supplement and afforce the common law and so might do away with the need for construction or alteration. We must remember that in this period the scope of treason was rarely a great constitutional issue, or at least openly so. Only in the years 1397–9 was there real concern among the magnates and it seems to have disappeared with the passing of the act which ordered that no treason was to be judged otherwise than had been ordained in 1352. There was nothing like the general horror of treason which manifested itself in the sixteenth century nor were there

[1] *Historical Manuscripts Commission, 8th Report*, Appendix, Part I, Section II, no. 267.

in the fifteenth century any confrontations with the king on one side and the magnates on the other, either of which might have led to substantial alterations in the definition of treason. The period 1381–1485 was punctuated by civil disturbance and insurrection. The parts of the 1352 statute which were most serviceable to the crown in dealing with rebels were those concerned with the levying of war against the king in his realm and the compassing or imagining of his death. By the time of Cade's rebellion and of the fully fledged attainder acts of the Yorkist era the rebels who suffered death as traitors were almost invariably condemned for one of these two crimes. Prompted no doubt by the law officers of the crown the local juries obligingly construed the offences as falling within these categories. The revolt of 1381 on the other hand demonstrated forcibly that the crown lacked a clear judicial policy on popular insurrection. There was revealed an inability or at least a failure to prime juries with suitable charges to present against the suspects. Above all there was considerable uncertainty about which crimes amounted to treason and which constituted mere felony. Thus twelve jurors from the hundred of Downhamford, Kent, found that certain rebels by their insurrection and by breaking into the house of Thomas Garwynton at Wells acted feloniously and traitorously: and that Walter Teghelere of Essex and others acted similarly when they broke into Canterbury castle and set free a number of prisoners.[1] On the other hand the jurors of Boughton who indicted John Hales, John Thacham and others of the very same crimes rated them only as felonies.[2] In general it was the attitude of the second jury which prevailed in Kent and there were relatively few charges of treason. A jury of the hundred of Westgate stolidly found the execution of the archbishop of Canterbury to be only felony.[3] Elsewhere the charge of treason was more common and took a variety of forms. The rebels might have destroyed or broken into houses feloniously and traitorously, seizing possessions to be found there as for example occurred at the homes of Sir John Cavendish at Bury St Edmunds and Richard Lyons at Lyston near Melford and Richard Imworth in London.[4]

[1] W. E. Flaherty, 'The Great Rebellion in Kent of 1381 illustrated from the Public Records', *Archaeologia Cantiana*, III (1860), 93.
[2] *Ibid.*, III, 89.   [3] *Ibid.*, III, 87.
[4] A. Réville, *Le Soulèvement des Travailleurs d'Angleterre en 1381* (Paris, 1898), pp. 177, 178, 186.

John Talmache, esquire, who was one of the trouble makers at Bury, was said to have taken a bay horse worth 20 marks 'felonice et prodiciose . . . et depredatus fuit'.[1] A George of Dunsby from Lincolnshire was held guilty of treason and felony for helping cause the revolt at Bury by his threats.[2]

In London crimes committed which were later found to be treason included breaking into and freeing prisoners in the Marshalsea prison, burning the Guildhall, plundering the Counter, entering the Tower, destroying coroners' and escheators' rolls and murdering Richard Imworth at Westminster.[3] The two aldermen John Horne and William Sibill who had given considerable assistance to the rebels were held to have behaved treasonably in inviting them to London against the king's wishes, in letting them into the city, refusing aid to guard London bridge and leaving its gate open. When the king and the mayor were returning from Smithfield on 15 June they traitorously caused Aldgate to be closed thereby stopping men from going to the king's aid.[4] Thomas Faringdon was accused of the treason of going with the insurgents to Mile End, approaching the king 'et ibidem ffrenum equi regis . . . felonice, proditorie et irreverenter in manu sua cepit'.[5] He did so in order to ask for legal satisfaction in a land case.[6] John Horne and Adam and John Fressh committed treason by treating with the leaders of the rebels. Very few indictments or appeals referred to the insurgents actually levying war against the king, possibly because the words had acquired chivalric connotations and become associated with the raising of proper armies by cliques of magnates. One record does say that the commons of Kent and Essex congregated in a great conventicle and raised themselves against their faith and allegiance 'cum vexillis armis nostris deputis et displicatis'[7] and at Bridgwater on 19 June 1381 Thomas Engilby approached the hospital of St John 'prodiciose cum vexillis nostris extensis'.[8] The displaying of banners was the accepted sign of levying war but apparently these were the only

---

[1] A. Réville, Le Soulèvement des Travailleurs d'Angleterre en 1381 (Paris, 1898), p. 178.
[2] E. Powell, The Rising in East Anglia (Cambridge, 1896), p. 127.
[3] Réville, Soulèvement des Travailleurs, pp. 186, 187, 195, 206, 212.
[4] Ibid., pp. 191–4.   [5] Ibid., p. 195.
[6] P.R.O., K.B. 27/488, Rex m. 6.
[7] P.R.O., K.B. 27/488 Rex m. 6. John Payntour and John Awedyn who carried banners were probably two of their leaders: Réville, Soulèvement des Travailleurs, pp. 209, 915.   [8] Réville, Soulèvement des Travailleurs, p. 283.

two examples. This does not mean there was an attempt to play down the rebellion. Those who laid the charges did not hesitate to stress the dreadful nature of the crimes committed for there were strong general accusations which referred to the lower classes rising in manner of war against the king and the dignity of the crown and rebelling traitorously against the king and his people and moving others to do the same.[1] There was no slavish adherence to the phraseology of the treason act of 1352. Juries, appellants and approvers were happy to call treason what seemed to them to be treason. The list of such crimes was long and some which were included were distinctly unlikely. In general treason amounted to this: the murder during the course of the rebellion of men loyal to the crown, the destruction of loyal mens' houses, of royal records and buildings and the giving of more than a minimum of assistance to the rebels. To the crown, certainly to the magnates, it must have been unthinkable that the greatest insurrection which England had ever seen and one which had caused the deaths of the archbishop of Canterbury and the treasurer could be anything less than treason. Since the government was in grave danger of being overthrown there was no time to summon a parliament in order to declare peasant insurrection treasonable and to demonstrate where riot terminated and treason began. For a short time therefore the category of treason assumed the widest proportions but because it was the lower class and not the nobility who suffered there was little chance of the verdicts being challenged in the future. The weakness of the crown's legal position in treating the revolt as treason, or at least making no effort to bring the terms of the statute of 1352 to the attention of the indicting juries, is made plain by the way in which it relied on the treason act passed by the parliament which met at Westminster in November 1381 to deal with later insurrections of a popular nature.[2] This statute was referred to at the time of John

---

[1] Powell, *Rising in East Anglia*, p. 126; Réville, *Soulèvement des Travailleurs*, p. 184 (quoting P.R.O., K.B. 27/486 Rex m. 11).

[2] *Stat. Realm*, II, 20. Not all the rebels of 1381 were accused of treason. For example, William Swepston parson of Ab Kettleby church in Leicestershire who raised men at Wartnaby was accused of breaking the statute of Northampton of 1328: Réville, *Soulèvement des Travailleurs*, p. 215.

A good example of the shapeless indictment which jurors might offer is to be found in *Calendar of Inquisitions Miscellaneous, 1377–88*, p. 102 n. There is included a rare example of the charge of usurping the royal power but without any indication that this crime was held a treason.

of Northampton's rising in London early in 1384 and the insurrections in Cheshire and Lancashire ten years later.[1] The act
was not quoted at the time of two Yorkshire disturbances in
January 1392 nor as yet were the charges which were laid against
the rebels phrased in set formulae based on the statute of 1352.
The men of the East Riding villages of Cottingham and Hessle
were indicted of having gone armed in the manner of war against
their allegiance to the king and his royal power to the town of
Benningholme like an army of traitors. Almost simultaneously other
malefactors from the lordship of Hatfield had gone armed in like
manner against their allegiance to the royalty [regaliam] of the
king: seizing royal power they had marched as would a traitorous
army to Doncaster.[2] They were not said to have levied war against
the king within his realm.

In the fifteenth century there came a change. Popular insurrection was interpreted as tending to bring about the king's destruction and therefore as falling within the clause of the 1352 statute
which referred to imagining and compassing his death. This was
in the majority of cases: in a small minority there were direct
references to the levying of war. An early example of the change is
to be found in the charges laid against those who rose in insurrection in Oxfordshire in March 1398 with John Milford a webber
of Cogges.[3] They were said to have intended to bring about the
king's death and to achieve the destruction of the kingdom and of

---

[1] See P.R.O., K.B. 27/507 Rex mm. 40–3 (printed in part by R. Bird in *The
Turbulent London of Richard II* (London, 1949), p. 137): 'ac eciam postquam
inhibitum sibi fuisset ex parte dicti consilii ibidem sub pena in statuto dicti
domini nunc regis edito apud Westmonasterium in crastino Animarum anno
regni sui quinto de congregacionibus conventiculis et insurrectionibus illicitis
ad rietum et rumores in populo faciendis contenta'.

In the statute passed against the restiveness in Cheshire and Lancashire in the
parliament of 1394 the law of 1381 was rehearsed by way of a preface: *Stat.
Realm*, II, 89. The earlier law forbade men under pain of forfeiting all they
possessed from recommencing the riots and rumours of the Peasants' Revolt.
Anyone who did so and had it duly proved against him was to be held a traitor:
ibid., II, 20. Plucknett was under the impression that the act of 1381 made it
treason to begin any riot: Putnam, *Proceedings*, p. clii.

[2] P.R.O., K.B. 9/144/12.

[3] P.R.O., K.B. 27/550 Rex m. 23. It was said that Cogges and his allies
'interligati fuerunt in mortem ipsius domini nostri Regis legis ipsius et magnatum
regni sui Anglie destrucionem felonie et proditorie contra ligeantiam suam'.
Although there was no direct reference to the treason act of 1381 the use of the
phrase 'felonice et proditorie contra dominum regem et ligeantiam suam de novo
insurrexerunt' suggests that it was still in the minds of the lawyers.

the magnates. It is difficult to be certain if the causes of this revolt were economic, social or political but those which occurred in the following thirty or so years were largely politically inspired. The planned Lollard insurrections of 1414 and 1431, reflecting the more radical and violent views which had been adopted by some members of the sect from early in the reign of Henry IV, had as their goal not only the establishment of a new faith and church but also the destruction of the royal family and the ruling class. When the Lollards were put on trial in the lay courts they were often accused of the treason of imagining the king's death.[1] After the rising at St Giles's Fields had been crushed in January 1414 those responsible were indicted of scheming to annul the royal estate, the office of prelate, the religious orders, planning to destroy churches, kill the king and his brothers and to appoint Sir John Oldcastle as regent. They had assembled 20,000 men traitorously arrayed in manner of war and had ridden in manner of insurrection against their allegiance to fight their king and commit homicide: and they had plotted and imagined falsely and traitorously other insufferable deeds.[2] In the reign of Henry IV several men were executed for high treason committed merely by the uttering of words: this was also held as imagining the king's death. The indictments said they had conspired and imagined to raise insurrection with intent to kill the king, his magnates and all his faithful subjects.[3]

In 1450 when Cade's rebellion was being put down the majority of the indictments which were presented against the insurgents emphasized the two charges of imagining and compassing the king's death and levying war against him. Other crimes might also be included: the rebels intended to annihilate good and long approved customs and laws; they had assembled in warlike array in a number of conventicles and had intended to deprive the king

[1] P.R.O., K.B. 27/611 Rex m. 7. The Lollard leaders intended 'felonie et proditorie machinando tam statum regni quam statum et officium prelatorum necnon ordines Religiosorum infra domos regni Anglie penitus adnullare ac dominum nostrum Regem fratres suos prelatos et alios magnates eiusdem regni interficere . . .'
[2] *Ibid.*, see also P.R.O., K.B. 27/617 Rex m. 4 for a similar indictment.
[3] P.R.O., K.B. 27/564 Rex m. 12 and K.B. 27/565 Rex mm. 3, 4, 4d, 5d, 11. These treasons were noted by Hale and later commented on by Miss Thornley: see 'Treason by Words in the Fifteenth Century', *Eng. Hist. Rev.*, XXXII (1917), 556-61, where the record of the trial of the friar Walter Walton is printed (560-1).

of his regality; they had imagined the destruction of the realm; they had agreed among themselves to depose the king, destroy the lords spiritual and temporal and assume the government of the kingdom; they had planned to dispossess the church and spoil the faithful lieges of the king of their goods and to kill those round the person of the king.[1] Very probably the charges were accurate but the crimes were not treason. Their listing merely displayed the width of the insurgents' designs and they were used to afforce proper charges of treason. Significantly the content of the various indictments was probably conditioned by the methods by which they were obtained. Some of the indictments were drawn up at inquests held on the special instructions of the crown where royal lawyers probably drafted the questions put to the jurors. Perhaps they made a list of crimes which the jurors merely had to approve. Other indictments were initiated and presented by juries themselves. By the mid-fifteenth century most of the cases which involved treason were of the first type and this probably accounts for the similar phraseology of each indictment and the emphasis on imagining the king's death and levying war against him as well as a conciseness and relevance in all supporting data. No longer were there produced, when the real crimes were of the gravest type, lists of minor offences full of inherent contradictions. The words 'traitorous' and 'traitorously' were not bandied around lightly but were used with some precision.[2] The smooth competence must have stemmed as much from the awareness that almost any rebellious act committed in popular insurrection could be construed as either imagining the king's death or levying war against him, as from dealing with the steady increase in treason which the century had brought.

Few cases of treason came before the courts between 1352 and the end of the reign of Edward III. Those which did were not of a type to test and clarify the new statute except in the matter of adhering to the king's French and Scottish enemies. In that particular case the relevant clause was interpreted quite widely and was even found to include as treason the exporting abroad of corn to

---

[1] P.R.O., K.B. 9/47/3, 4, 5: K.B. 9/48/6, 15. These indictments are printed by R. Virgoe in 'Some Ancient Indictments in the King's Bench referring to Kent, 1450–1452', *Kent Records*, XVIII (1964), 214–65.

[2] For example, the indictments against Eleanor duchess of Gloucester in 1441: P.R.O., K.B. 9/72/1, 2, 3, 4, 5, 6, 9, 11, 14.

the king's foes.[1] In the matter of legal procedure on the other hand care was taken to see that those accused were provably attainted by men of their own condition. The reign of Richard II in contrast was of the utmost importance in the development of the law of treason, producing experimental constructions, declarations of doubtful cases in parliament and new statutes. In 1399 a return was ordered to the unsupplemented rules of the 1352 statute but by then the law of treason had been decisively moulded by events.

The first important matter to arise was the surrender of castles in France to the French enemy on terms which cast a doubt on the loyalty of the English captains involved. It was a common practice when fairly forced to surrender their charge, for them to accept sums of money towards their expenses during the siege and for the payment of their troops. Parties in England, not only the crown, were inclined to take an unfavourable view of these arrangements and cry treason. In 1374 so famous a captain as Sir Robert Knolles felt compelled to seek an extensive pardon which included all seditions, adherence to the king's enemies, receiving the enemies' assent, counsel and favours, castles, fortresses and prisoners surrendered without licence or sold, and all other offences against the crown, the common law and the statutes.[2] At the time of the Good Parliament the issue of castle surrender acquired added notoriety when Sir John Annesley brought an appeal of treason against Thomas Caterton, a lieutenant of Lord Latimer, for his conduct at St Sauveur in the Cotentin.[3] In 1380 trial by battle in the court of chivalry was awarded and was witnessed, according to

---

[1] There was the case of Hugh Mongowe of Northumberland 'communis latro et notarius' who adhered to the Scots between 1364–6: K.B. 27/439 Rex m. 18. Also Sir John Minsterworth who on 18 April 1377 was convicted of treason before a special commission at the London Guildhall and was drawn and hanged the same day. According to Fabyan his crimes were keeping his troops' pay for his own use and later fleeing to the French court and fighting on the French side: *The Brut*, ed. Brie, II, 332; R. Fabyan, *Newe Chronycles of England and of France*, ed. H. Ellis (London, 1811), p. 487. In March 1377 a commission of oyer and terminer was appointed on information that William Fyfhyde had traitorously carried corn without the realm to foreign parts for the aid and sustenance of the king's enemies during the war with France: *Cal. Pat. Rolls, 1374–7*, p. 492.
[2] *Cal. Pat. Rolls, 1374–7*, p. 70. By convenant with the king Knolles had undertaken to lead an expedition to France and had received certain lands from him. These were resumed into the king's hands on council's advice when Knolles's conduct became known but were restored on his pardon.
[3] *Historia Anglicana*, ed. H. T. Riley (R.S., 1863–4), I, 431.

Thomas Walsingham, by more people than had attended Richard II's coronation.[1] It does not seem the prosecution was prompted by the crown but other cases show that both the royal advisers and parliament were much disturbed by the crimes without quite knowing whether they were treasonable or not. William Weston, who in 1377 surrendered Otherwick castle without the king's orders, was tried in parliament and sentenced to be drawn and hanged: the penalty was as for treason although the lords avoided classifying the crime as such.[2] In the pardon which Weston obtained in December 1377 there was no mention of treason, merely a reference to his being adjudged to sentence of death.[3] Similar crimes committed by other captains and lieutenants suggest the same vacillation and doubt. Because he lost Becherel Lord Latimer was guilty of misconduct.[4] For neglecting the castle of Marck in the Calais march and going to England when he was governor so that as a result it was delivered to the French by his lieutenant, Sir Robert Salle obtained a pardon for negligences, misprisions and trespasses. The crime of the lieutenant on the other hand was described as treachery and rebellion.[5] When Henry Despenser, bishop of Norwich, was called upon to explain his conduct on the Flanders crusade before the parliament which met in October 1383, the chancellor pronounced that if money was permitted to be taken from the enemy then any traitor who deserted or sold castles would be able to excuse his treason.[6] One of Despenser's captains, Sir William Elmham, who had received 1400 francs of gold from the French for surrendering certain Flemish towns, was found guilty of misprision and merely suffered imprisonment until he had paid a fine.[7] For all the threats and

---

[1] *Historia Anglicana*, ed. H. T. Riley (R.S., 1863–4), I, 431; *Cal. Pat. Rolls, 1377–81*, p. 485.

[2] *Rot. Parl.*, III, 10–11. Something of a precedent for the cases of the 1370s may be found in the penalties incurred by Thomas de Ursewyk and William Mareschal and others over twenty years previously. They had apparently delivered the town of Belleville and other fortalices of the inheritance of the lady of Cliczon in Poitou, then in the king's hands, to the French. Thereby they incurred the forfeiture of their bodies and goods: *Cal. Pat. Rolls, 1348–50*, p. 532.

[3] *Cal. Pat. Rolls, 1377–81*, p. 124.

[4] *Cal. Pat. Rolls, 1381–5*, p. 282.

[5] *Cal. Pat. Rolls, 1377–81*, p. 201.   [6] *Rot. Parl.*, III, 158.

[7] *Cal. Pat. Rolls, 1381–5*, p. 414. See also *Rot. Parl.*, III, 156–8: Sir Thomas Tryvet, Sir William Farndon, Sir Henry Ferriers and Robert Fitz-Rauf esquire were accused with Elmham of receiving monies for surrendering fortresses. They said they did not know they had done wrong: Elmham claimed the money

despite the sentencing of at least one soldier to the normal penalties for treason parliament did not insist on these crimes being permanently classified as treason nor did the crown wish to do so. Obviously the misdeeds of Weston and Gomeniz, of Tryvet and Elmham did not amount to adhering to the king's enemies. There was a big difference between common though unacceptable customs of war and the wilful support of the king's enemies of which for example Sir John Minsterworth had been guilty in the previous decade. The crimes of the English captains were really breaches of military contracts made with the king and as such triable before council or in the court of chivalry. It is unlikely they were justiciable under the common law or the statute of 1352. In the later years of Richard's reign the penalty for yielding a fortress in suspicious circumstances was the total forfeiture of possessions.[1] Very probably the captains' lives were safe but this was not certain. Even in the fifteenth century captains had cause to tread warily: in 1457 the earl of Warwick sought assurances from the crown that if he acquired a castle near Calais from the French and afterwards lost it again he would not be impeached of treason.[2]

To the law of treason the importance of the sentence on William Weston and the allowing of the appeal against Caterton lay in the demonstration that there were crimes which were treason in all but name which lay outside the common law, being in fact offences against the king's majesty and prerogative. Very similar were the crimes which were declared to carry the penalties of treason by the judges in 1387. The royal prerogative powers had become a matter of vital concern to the crown when it was forced to appoint the commission of government at the end of November 1386.[3] In the same parliament King Richard protested in person that nothing done during the session should prejudice his prerogative or the liberties of the crown.[4] The royal judges advanced the opinion that those who had forced the king to consent to the making of the statute or who prevented him from exercising his prerogative or

was taken either as ransom for prisoners or to purchase victuals for their men. All were found guilty. Four were imprisoned at the king's ransom and had to pay to the crown the sums they had received: Farndon was held to have incurred the penalty of forfeiture.

[1] See for example *Cal. Pat. Rolls, 1381–5*, p. 526 (the earl of Northumberland); *Cal. Pat. Rolls, 1385–9*, pp. 495, 522 and *Cal. Pat. Rolls, 1388–92*, p. 372 (John de Atherston).   [2] *Cal. Pat. Rolls, 1452–61*, p. 413.
[3] *Rot. Parl.*, III, 221.   [4] *Ibid.*, III, 224.

9

had ignored the king's proposed parliamentary agenda and sub-stituted their own, should be punished as traitors. When asked what the punishment should be for those who impeded the king from dissolving parliament or who impeached the king's ministers without his consent or who proposed that the act by which Edward II was adjudged in parliament should be held as a statute, they gave the same reply.[1] The misdeeds in question, as Chrimes has pointed out, fell into the category of 'accroaching the royal power'.[2] This description had been used by the royal lawyers both in Edward II's reign and immediately prior to the 1352 statute of treasons. Only in the second period does it appear these crimes came before the courts of common law. As has been shown above a close inspection reveals that in fact the words 'accroaching' or 'assuming' the royal power were used in the majority of instances merely to describe an accepted treason or felony and to afforce the gravity of the offence. In two cases only was there danger of treason and 'accroaching the royal power' being drawn together and confused. After the statute the practice ceased.[3] There never had been a case before the courts of common law wherein a man was sentenced for 'accroaching the royal power' by committing a crime which was not a felony or a treason: it could not stand by itself. Quite obviously accroachment of the royal power, that is to say the infringing of the king's regality and prerogative, was an offence in its own special category. Thus in February 1401 the earl of Northumberland, then constable of England, was com-missioned to hear and determine divers unaccustomed cases con-cerning the estate, fame and condition of the king's person and the dignity of the crown. The crimes, so it was stated, were such that by their nature they could not be discussed or determined by pretext of the office of constable or by the common law but only by the king's hearing or commission. The cases referred to could only have concerned accroaching the royal power. Perhaps they might also have been dealt with in parliament but no king if he were sensible would permit such delicate issues to be argued over in public.[4]

In the 'Merciless' Parliament just over a year after King Richard

---

[1] *Stat. Realm*, II, 102–4.
[2] S. B. Chrimes, 'Richard II's Questions to the Judges, 1387', *Law Quarterly Review*, LXXII (1956), 383.
[3] See chapter 4, pp. 62 ff. above.   [4] *Cal. Pat. Rolls, 1399–1401*, p. 458.

consulted the judges, the Lords Appellant brought charges of accroaching the royal power against five of the king's close advisers. The king's justices and sergeants and other legal experts declared that in so high a crime as was alleged in the appeal, which touched the person of the king and the estate of the realm, judgement should only be by the law and the course of parliament. The lords in parliament declared that the matters contained in fourteen of the articles which were laid against the accused were treasonable.[1] This they could do under the proviso in the 1352 act relating to doubtful cases: it had previously been used in the case of John Imperial in 1379.[2] Nonetheless the Lords Appellant were careful to reserve these new treasons solely to the judgement of parliament by ordaining that no justice should have the power to render judgement in cases of treason other than he had had at the beginning of the parliament.[3]

In the parliament which met in January 1394 the king and the lords declared that Sir Thomas Talbot and others by making a conspiracy to slay the dukes of Lancaster and Gloucester and other great men of the realm and doing all they could to accomplish their design were committing high treason against the king's person and the realm. This was in response to a 'bill' which requested the declaration of the penalties that the nature of the offence required.[4] Talbot's insurrection could fairly be called the levying of war tending to the destruction of the realm, a phrase which was finding its way more and more into treason records at this time, but it was not really war directed against the king. Richard was in rather an embarrassing position as Talbot believed he was saving the crown from treasonable deeds in France.[5] The precedents of offences declared treason by the parliaments of February 1388 and 1394, neither declaration being exactly in accord with the intention of those who had drafted the statute of 1352, probably decided Richard's reaction to the petition of Thomas Haxey in 1397. This clerk asked the commons of parliament to consider the great expense arising in the king's household from the multitude

---

[1] *Rot. Parl.*, III, 236, 237. For the 'law of parliament', see p. 168, n. 3.
[2] P.R.O., K.B. 27/476 Rex m. 31, 31d; *Rot. Parl.*, III, 75 b. Imperial had a two-year safe conduct.
[3] *Rot. Parl.*, III, 250 a.
[4] P.R.O., K.B. 27/532 Rex m. 16; *Cal. Pat. Rolls, 1391-6*, p. 294.
[5] I have argued to this effect in 'The Northern Rebellions in the later years of Richard II' *Bulletin of the John Rylands Library*, XLVII (1965), 254-74.

of bishops and ladies in attendance and ordain a remedy. The king was furious and persuaded the lords to declare that anyone who should excite the commons or others to make remedy or reform any matter touching the king's person, his government or his regality, should be held as a traitor.[1] This was the zenith of declaration of treason by parliament, for Richard and his advisers had devised more serviceable weapons and later kings found a combination of judicial construction and attainder act to be usually sufficient for their needs.

In the second parliament of 1397, preparatory to an appeal of treason being brought against the Lords Appellant of 1388, a new law of treason was enacted.[2] Like the declaration of 1388 and the one of 1397 against Haxey but unlike the statute of 1352 this act was particular not general. It was not really concerned with any future treason, only with the particular misdeeds which had been committed by the Lords Appellant and which the king was keen to label as treasonable. Thus those who compassed or purposed the the king's death or to depose him or to renounce their liege homage and those who raised men and rode against the king in open war within the realm were to be judged guilty of high treason. These were the very deeds which the Lords Appellant were supposed to have perpetrated in the period before and after their insurrection at Harringay in 1387. Two of the treasons, compassing the king's death and levying war, were included in the statute of 1352 which in 1388 at least was still regarded as the primary law on treason.[3] Why then did Richard II rehearse these crimes? Perhaps it was as a parody of the crimes declared treason by his opponents in 1388 but with an act instead of a declaration by the lords of parliament whom he would not wholly trust.[4] It is more probable the answer

---

[1] *Rot. Parl.*, III, 407–8.
[2] *Stat. Realm*, II, 98–9.
[3] It is not true that Richard 'added four new points of treason to the statute of 1352' as has been suggested: see Ross, 'Forfeiture for Treason', *Eng. Hist. Rev.*, LXXI, 574. Only compassing the king's deposition or compassing to render up liege homage were novel. It has been argued the omission of the words 'overt deed' was the reason for the new act. This view is based on a misreading of the 1352 statute: see pp. 122–3.
[4] There is mention in the patent rolls that the parliament of 1397–8 declared the usurping of royal power in 10 Richard II, the insurrection at Harringay and the issuing of the commission for the governance of the realm as treason: *Cal. Pat. Rolls, 1396–9*, p. 272. Anyone who in future sought to institute another such commission and was convicted of it in parliament was to be adjudged guilty of high treason: *Rot. Parl.*, III, 350.

is to be found in the careful pronouncement of the degree of forfeiture to be inflicted on those who should be found guilty. In 1388 the Lords Appellant and their advisers had specified the forfeiture of the victims' fees simple and the lands which were held by others to their use: their fees tail were however untouched.[1] In 1397 Richard went further, deciding that the traitors should lose fee simple, the lands held to their use and fee tail as well: furthermore the judgements were rigorously executed. Like the Lords Appellant in 1388 Richard, ostensibly at the request of the commons, had it enacted that anyone who sought to annul any of the proceedings of the 1397–8 parliament and was convicted of it in parliament should be executed as a traitor.[2] The final addition made to the law of treason in Richard's reign concerned Thomas Mowbray, duke of Norfolk and the man who appealed him of treason, Henry, duke of Hereford. When the proposed trial by battle at Coventry was stopped by the king, Mowbray was exiled for life and Hereford for a term of ten years. If they had not quit the realm by a set date they were to incur the penalties for treason. The same punishment was threatened if they attempted to communicate with each other or with Thomas Arundel, the former archbishop of Canterbury, while in exile, or in Mowbray's case if he did not reside in 'Almayne, Berne and Hungry'.[3] If either of the accused or their representatives sought pardon or licence to return he would suffer the penalties of treason also, a provision which had a parallel in the treason laws of classical Rome. In April 1399 Henry Bowet, one of the king's chaplains, who had counselled Hereford when he petitioned after the Coventry judgement for the power to succeed by attorney to any inheritances coming to him, was condemned as a traitor by the king on the assent of the parliamentary commission, which had by that time taken the place of parliament. Despite the measures which were taken by Richard II to protect and perpetuate his own interpretation of the law of treason it was doomed to be short-lived. In the first parliament of the next reign the proceedings of the session 1397–8 were annulled while those of the 'Merciless' Parliament were

---

[1] Ross ('Forfeiture for Treason', *Eng. Hist. Rev.*, LXXI, 560–75) has investigated the ramifications of the Lords Appellants' forfeiture policy. He argues that they followed established practices where possible: when none existed they concocted equitable principles.
[2] *Stat. Realm*, II, 98–9.
[3] *Rot. Parl.*, III, 384 a.

reaffirmed.[1] Thenceforward no appeals of treason were to be brought into parliament and no one was to be judged for treason except as provided by the statute of 1352. This was said to be because in the previous parliament[2] 'plusours peines de traison feurent ordeinez par estatut parensi qe y navoit aucun homme qe poie savoit coment il se deust avoir, de faire parler ou dire pur doubte de tielx peines'.[3]

The initial eagerness of Henry IV to return to the statute of 1352 did not stop his judges introducing one most novel and important construction.[4] This was treason by words. Miss Thornley pointed out that in 1402 there occurred at least five such cases of treason, four of which were connected with the affair of the false Richard. She suggested that on four occasions the offence was the speaking of words: in the fifth in addition to speaking, a letter was produced, probably written by one of the accused.[5] One of the prisoners, a friar, admitted that in May 1402 on being given the news that King Richard was alive in Wales he informed a fellow Franciscan and together they despatched a third to go to Wales to assure the ex-king of their support. In the king's bench the judges were of the opinion that the words were intended to excite the people against their king to the destruction of the realm and the friar was sentenced to be drawn and hanged and quartered. At Easter term 1402 John Sperhauk of Cardiff admitted that at Baldock he had heard a tailor's wife say the earl of March was the

[1] *Rot. Parl.*, iii, 425–6.

[2] *Ibid.*, iii, 442. Appeals of treason and felony were to be tried and terminated by the good laws made in the time of the king's progenitors, except those which arose outside the realm.

[3] *Stat. Realm*, ii, 114.

[4] Furthermore there is evidence of a temporary return to a device of the 1340s. Two cases in 1401–2, which admittedly seem to be unique in the fifteenth century, show Henry IV and his judges going openly against the 1352 statute. Several men were found guilty of treason for highway robbery and causing the depopulation of the fields or for plotting to do these things. They were all persistent and notorious offenders: P.R.O., K.B. 9/189/10 and 34.

It is probable that those accused and convicted included men in holy orders since in the parliament of September 1402 the bishops petitioned that clerics had been tried for treasons and felonies which did not touch the king's person before secular courts and had not been allowed benefit of clergy. The accused, it was stated, had been called 'communes latrones', 'depopulatores agrorum' and 'incidiatores viarum'. The king promised such terms would not be used in future indictments or accusations but that if by chance they were, then benefit of clergy would be allowed: *Rot. Parl.*, iii, 494.

[5] Thornley, 'Treason by words', *Eng. Hist. Rev.*, xxxii, 556–7. There had been cases of treason by words in the thirteenth century but none since.

rightful king, not Henry IV, who was not the son of John of Gaunt anyway. She held that Owen Glendower was no traitor but a loyal subject and that the king had failed to keep to the agreement he had made with the commons when he returned to England in 1399. Sperhauk confessed he had repeated these words to others in Cambridgeshire. The justices conferred with the king's council and decided the words had been spoken wilfully from the defendant's own mouth and were intended to excite the king's lieges against their lord 'que alta et maxima proditio sunt'.[1] Again the sentence was drawing, hanging and quartering. How the king played a part in the construing of the words as treason is revealed in a chronicle which is rather at odds with the legal records. We are told that a Franciscan lay-brother of the Aylesbury convent came to the king and accused one of his fellows of saying that he rejoiced to know that King Richard was still alive. Henry had the man, no doubt Sperhauk, brought before him and inquired if the charge was correct: the friar admitted it. 'You have declared that Richard is still alive and you have excited the people against me' said the king and asked whom the friar would support if he saw Richard and himself fighting each other on a field of battle. The friar said Richard. Henry retorted that the friar therefore wanted his death and those of all the lords of the kingdom.[2] The response came back that he merely wanted to make Henry the duke of Lancaster. Whether the interview took place before the council or in private audience we are not told and it is equally difficult to discover its exact position within the legal process. It may have occurred before the friar was sent for trial in the king's bench, or possibly at the time the justices conferred with the council. If the chronicler is accurate then the verdict that the crime was exciting the people against their king came originally from Henry himself. Before his reign the charge had never been construed as treason if indeed it had figured in indictment or appeal at all. The novel crime must

[1] P.R.O., K.B. 27/564 Rex m. 12: 'Per quod viso recordo predicti Coronatoris in hac parte habitaque super eisdem cum consilio domini Regis plenarie deliberacione videtur Curie et toti consilio domini Regis quod ex quo idem Johannes ligeus homo domini Regis sit et ipse verba predicta in publico ex suo proprio capite sciencia et voluntate narravit tanta mala inhonesta de eodem Rege loquendo affirmando et quasi pro vero advocando ad intentionem et voluntatem excitandi ligeos ipsius Regis de eorum bono zelo et voluntate contra dominum suum ligeum naturaliter debitum que alta et maxima proditio sunt.'

[2] *Eulogium Historiarum*, ed. F. S. Haydon (R.S. 1863), III, 390.

have found its way into the plea rolls through the king's personal interest and intervention. There, after the details of the legal process in the five cases had been given once, they were set down again a second time and the treasons labelled as conspiring and imagining to raise a new insurrection with the intention of killing the king, his magnates and all his faithful subjects.[1] It had been felt necessary to classify the crimes under already existing arrangements. In this there could have been little difficulty since the king's cross-questioning had shown clearly that the crime was ultimately a matter of intending the king's death.

In 1444 there occurred another case of the same sort. At an inquisition taken at Reading the jurors said that Thomas Kerver, a gentleman of Reading, who for a long while had been seeking to diminish the king's dignity and who had subtly and traitorously sought to deprive him of his prosperity and rule by means of provoking discord and war in the kingdom between the king and his lieges, had on 13 April 1444 wished and desired the death of the king and the destruction of the kingdom. In the abbey church at Reading Kerver had quoted with approval to John Baynard, servant of the abbot, the sermon given by John Curtis, a Dominican, on Palm Sunday before the royal court at Abingdon. The text had apparently been 'Woe to thee O land when thy king is a child'. Kerver had maliciously said that it would have been worth more than £100,000 to the kingdom had the king been dead the last twenty years. On the following day when going out of the hall of the abbey Kerver said to Thomas Codryngton, another of the abbot's servants, that it would have been of more value to the realm than £100,000 if the king had never been born. The jury also stated that on numerous occasions Kerver had said that the French dauphin had personally invaded and conquered the English lands in France and that if King Henry had possessed similar qualities he would have held those lands in peace. The jury held that in making such statements Kerver intended the king's subjects should withdraw their love from him and rebels be encouraged in their felonies and treasons. The chancery rolls in a reference to the pardon of Thomas Codryngton show that the crown interpreted the crimes as the compassing and imagining of treason presumably in the shape of compassing and imagining the

[1] P.R.O., K.B. 27/564 Rex m. 11.

king's death.[1] Kerver was sentenced to be drawn, hanged and quartered.

At the beginning of the reign of Edward IV Oliver Germaine of Tisbury, Wiltshire, was accused with others of conspiring to imagine the death and destruction of the king on 14 May 1461 at Wilton where 'in prophesiis ut falsi heretici' they announced that Henry VI was still the king and should have his crown. They did so, it was said, with the intention of withdrawing the cordial love of the people from King Edward. For these offences Germaine and his associates were each sentenced to a traitor's death. In the eighteenth year of the same reign John Alkerter, a former servant of the earl of Warwick, was outlawed, having been indicted for traitorously creating discord between the king and his people. He was accused of having said that Edward IV was responsible for the murder of both Warwick and the duke of Clarence. Again the crime was held to amount to causing the people to withdraw their cordial love from the monarch thereby compassing his death. In the same year Thomas Hever was indicted and outlawed for saying treasonably that the king would never have the cordial love of the men of Kent and also that if the bishop of Bath should die in captivity the archbishop of Canterbury should arrest the king.[2]

In each of these five cases it appears that the mere uttering of words was held as treason and that seditious speech was not

[1] P.R.O., K.B. 9/245/46 and 47. I am indebted to Dr R. L. Storey for drawing my attention to this record and to P.R.O. C. 81/1370/13 which shows the crown did not want the pardon which was given to Kerver to be known generally. See also *The Brut*, ed. Brie, II, 485. Kerver was drawn, hanged, let down and returned to prison: *Cal. Pat. Rolls, 1441-6*, p. 278. For mention of Codryngton's pardon see *Cal. Pat. Rolls, 1441-6*, p. 295.

[2] P.R.O., K.B. 9/122/15; K.B. 9/135/47; *The Third Part of the Reports of Sir George Croke*, ed. H. Grimston (London, 1683), pp. 121-2.

There are several other less well documented cases involving spoken words which may have touched on treason: see *Cal. Pat. Rolls, 1446-52*, p. 135; *Issues of the Exchequer*, ed. F. Devon (London, 1837), p. 398; *Six Town Chronicles*, ed. R. Flenley (Oxford, 1911), pp. 128, 129; Stow, p. 415; *State Trials*, ed. T. B. Howell (London, 1816), I, 894 b.

A more famous case concerned Thomas Burdet a Warwickshire esquire who was supposed to have been guilty of wishing the death of Edward IV for killing his favourite buck in Arrow park: R. Holinshed, *Chronicles of England, Scotland and Ireland* (London, 1808), III, 345; Stow, p. 430. However the indictments in the *Baga de Secretis* show Burdet was in fact sentenced to be drawn and hanged for prognosticating by the magic arts the deaths of Edward and his eldest son and for disseminating treasonable tracts in Holborn: *Reports of the Deputy Keeper of the Public Records: Third Report* (London, 1842), Appendix II, pp. 213-14.

merely ancillary to other treasons such as levying war against the king, adhering to his enemies or imagining or compassing his death but was itself the imagining or compassing of the king's death. In Sperhauk's case the king's council and the judges of the king's bench decided the accused had spoken in public wilfully and knowingly the evil and dishonest words about the king from his own head. His intention, they suggested, was to excite the king's lieges against their rightful ruler and that was treason.

If it was treason to speak certain words then it might be expected that the government would put the same construction on the drafting and circulating of seditious writings. In all probability this was what happened although as with spoken treason it is difficult to discover cases where the accusation was based solely on treasons of this sort and was not supported by other types. In 1414 John Wyghtlok, once a groom and yeoman of Richard II, and his allies, who still believed Richard II was alive, conspired King Henry's destruction. It was stated that between 14 March and 23 May while in sanctuary at Westminster they gave vent to some very disrespectful words about the king and his father. They also fixed schedules on the doors of buildings in public places at Bermondsey and elsewhere and on a church door at Westminster in disrespect of the king and the parliament which was then in session, whereby they refused and revoked the allegiance they owed to the crown. The schedules stated that Richard II was alive in Scotland and Wyghtlok had seen him. The latter had written that if this statement was false he should be taken out of his confinement and led to the vilest of deaths. According to the legal records all of Wyghtlok's deeds were performed 'traitorously'. [1] Unfortunately for the history of treason by written words, the conspirators had sought aid from the king of Scotland and had advised him to make war against their own country. Thereby they were doubtless guilty of adhering to the king's enemies which was a category of treason in the 1352 statute.[2] At the time of Jack Sharp's rebellion at Abingdon in 1431 John Keterige revealed to the mayor of Salisbury that John Longe of Abingdon had delivered to him several seditious writings. These were described as treasonable

---

[1] P.R.O., K.B. 27/609 Rex m. 14.
[2] *Ibid.* They had received Sir Andrew Lake, a Scot, and had conducted him to Westminster, so it was said, to explore the council of the king for the evil of the realm. Wyghtlok and his allies had refused a general pardon.

and since a reward only payable on the conviction of the miscreant was actually paid it does seem that a man was found a traitor for the writing and publishing of words; there is no indication how the treason was construed.[1] In 1453 Sir William Ashton and Sir William Oldhall with over a score of their followers were indicted of having on 6 March at Bury St Edmunds traitorously fabricated bills, ballads and writings in rhyme and displayed them on doors and in windows. The writings averred that King Henry on the advice of Suffolk, Lord Say and the bishops of Salisbury and Chichester had sold the kingdoms of France and England so that the French king should rule them. They were also accused of writing to the men of Kent advising the levying of war against the king and the giving of assistance to the cause of the duke of York. As in Wyghtlok's case the matter was not solely one of written words for Ashton and Oldhall were said to have also traitorously rallied men at Bergholt to the king's destruction. In the next reign William Belmyn, a Norwich mercer, was indicted of having with Robert de Ryddesdale published and proclaimed in May 1469 certain treasonable articles so as to stir up war between the king and his lieges and deprive him of his regality. Belmyn pleaded not guilty but the verdict of the jury is not known. The most notorious case of treason by words in writing, that of William Collingbourne in 1484, was an instance where indictment and sentence were for other treasons as well. The legal record is not to be found in the class of ancient indictments or in the *coram rege* rolls but Holinshed gives a version which he claimed to have found in a 'register booke of indictements'. According to this in July 1484 Collingbourne with various associates had sought to send messengers to Henry Tudor and to other attainted traitors then in Brittany, advising invasion before mid-October and promising to raise insurrection and to levy war on their arrival. Furthermore on 18 July in the parish of St Gregory's in Farringdon ward Collingbourne 'devised certaine bils and writings in rime, to the end that the same being published might stir the people to a commotion against the king'. The same day they were fastened on the doors of St Paul's. 'Thus farre the indictment', says Holinshed, 'but whether he was giltie in part or in all, I have not to saie'. It would

---

[1] *Procs. and Ords.*, IV, 99–100. A royal proclamation of April 1450 said the king would deem anyone found reading or publishing the seditious schedule or bill to be the author: *Cal. Close Rolls, 1447–54*, p. 194.

also be of great interest to know for sure if the rhyme was held as imagining the death of the king.[1]

Miss Thornley, following Coke, believed that the 1352 act excluded treason by words since it demanded an overt act.[2] Because of this she was forced to postulate the survival of common law treasons: 'By the common law words could constitute high treason and were punished as such'.[3] Rezneck opposed this thesis. He argued that there was no need to introduce the common law. Words themselves were regarded as the overt act of treasons imagined or compassed. He did not believe there had been a single case where words had been held as treason in themselves without there being a conspiracy in addition. The examples of Sperhauk and Kerver in particular suggest that this line of reasoning is fallacious. In holding that the statute of 1352 allowed for treason by words Rezneck was very probably correct but not for the reasons he specified. A careful reading of the text reveals that the drafters intended the phrase 'overt act' to refer not to imagining or compassing the king's death but to adhering to his enemies in the realm or giving them aid or comfort within the kingdom or outside it.[4] An examination of

[1] P.R.O., K.B. 9/118/30; K.B. 9/86/22 and 38; Holinshed, *Chronicles*, III, 422–3. There is however, as Gairdner first noted, a reference to Collingbourne's sentence in the controlment rolls (P.R.O., K.B. 29/115). For Croke's version of the indictment, see the appendix.

Rezneck points out that in 1416 John Benet was executed as a traitor for circulating schedules full of sedition and in 1456 John Holton a lawyer was convicted of treason for presuming to raise his voice to the skies and to write bills against the royal person: S. Rezneck, 'Constructive treason by words in the fifteenth century', *American Historical Review*, XXXIII (1927–8), 549.

[2] Thornley, 'Act of Treasons', *History*, VI, 108; Coke, pp. 13–14.

[3] Thornley, 'Treason by words', *Eng. Hist. Rev.*, XXXII, 557; Rezneck, 'Constructive treason', *American Historical Review*, XXXIII, 544–52.

[4] These were the crimes the statute made treason: 'quant homme fait compasser ou ymaginer la mort nostre seignur le roi, ma dame sa compaigne, ou de lour fitz primer et heir; ou si homme violast la compaigne le roi ou leisnece fille le roi nient marie, ou la compaigne leisne fitz et heir du roi; et si homme leve de guerre contre nostre dit seignur le roi en son roialme ou soit aherdant as enemys nostre seignur le roi en le roialme donant a eux eid ou confort en son roialme ou par aillours et de ceo provablement soit atteint de overt faite par gentz de lour condicion; et si homme contreface les grant ou prive sealx le roi ou sa monoie, ou si homme apport faus monoie en ceste roialme contrefaite a la monoie Dengleterre . . . en deceit nostre dit seignur le roi et son poeple; et si homme tuast chanceller, tresorer ou justice nostre seignur le roi del un Baunk ou del autre, justice en eir et des assises et toutes autres justices assignez a oier et terminer esteiantz en lours places en fesantz lours offices': *Stat. Realm*, I, 319–20. If we look both before and after the phrase 'provablement . . . atteint de overt faite' it is obvious the words refer quite specifically to giving aid to the king's enemies

the background of the statute shows that in the middle years of the fourteenth century the crown was wont to claim as forfeit the lands of those northerners who had adhered to the Scots and levied war on their behalf, solely on the word of the king that they were traitors. An inquest taken by the escheator to discover the facts had often been avoided, presumably under the legal maxim that adherence to the king's enemies was a matter of royal record.[1] A case in a fifteenth-century *Year Book* is additional proof that imagining and compassing the king's death needed no overt act. In 19 Henry VI Neuton J. offered as his opinion, and it was not contradicted, 'si home ymagyn le mort de Roy et ne fait pluys il serra traye et pend et disclos'. Nothing could be clearer than that.[2]

The fifteenth-century use of act of attainder like the history of treason by words shows in general a determination to adhere to the statute of 1352. This is hardly surprising where the relevant act of attainder supplemented the trial or outlawry of a traitor in a court of common law but it is less expected when there had been no previous judgement of any sort and the attainder was, so to speak, extraneous to the common law. As in indictment or appeal in the common law courts the crimes listed in an act of attainder were usually several and the treasons were normally shown by use of the words 'traitorous' or 'traitorously'. In the act of 1483 the duke of Buckingham and his supporters were said to have traitorously imagined and compassed the king's death and levied war against him.[3] Richard III, according to the act of 1485, had traitorously levied war against his sovereign lord, that is to say Henry Tudor.[4] In 1478 the duke of Clarence's varied and exotic crimes were described generally as purposing the destruction of the king by inducing his subjects to withdraw their hearts from him: this amounted to alienating the monarch from his people, the offence of the traitorous friars in 1402.[5] In the 1461 act of attainder which was aimed against Henry VI, the ex-king was held guilty of among

and possibly to the levying of war in the kingdom and adhering to his enemies. They do not refer to any other listed crime.

[1] I have discussed this matter in chapter 4 above, p. 90.

[2] *Year Books*, 19 Henry VI Mich. pl. 103: 'Donc il fuit demand si on sera mort pur chose q'il ne jamais fist. Neuton dit ouy, qe on sera mort, trait et pend et disclos pur chose q'il ne fist jamais, en fait, ny consentat ny aidat. Come si on ou sa femme imagine le mort le Roy et ne ad fait plus, pur ce imaginacion il sera mort come devant'.

[3] *Rot. Parl.*, VI, 244–9.   [4] *Ibid.*, VI, 276 a.

[5] *Ibid.*, VI, 193–5.

other crimes levying war against his sovereign Edward IV, imagining his death and adhering to the Scots, who were the king's enemies.[1] In 1459 in the great attainder act passed in the Coventry Parliament after the battles of Bloreheath and Ludford the duke of York and his followers were charged with levying war against King Henry at Ludford bridge: three other Yorkists were attainted of imagining and compassing the king's destruction. Many other of the duke of York's misdeeds were mentioned in the act but none was described as traitorous in itself.[2] Despite the efforts of the parliamentary commons William, duke of Suffolk was never the subject of an attainder act but the crimes of which he was impeached all came under the 1352 statute. His accusers claimed he was guilty of 'ymagyning and purposyng falsely and traitorously to distroy youre moost Roiall persone and this youre said Reame' by comforting the duke of Orleans and other Frenchmen. He was also said to have traitorously adhered to the king of France by counselling him to make war against Henry VI and by telling him secrets of the English council.[3] In a primitive form of attainder act in 1400 the earls of Kent, Huntingdon and Salisbury, Lord Despenser and Sir Ralph Lumley, were declared and adjudged by the Lords as traitors because they had levied war against the king.[4] The posthumous attainder of Jack Cade in 1453 as a result of a petition by the commons differed from other attainder acts in the novelty of two of the treasons propounded. These were that Cade had by imaginative language seditiously made commotion, rebellion and insurrection, and had falsely and traitorously imagined and forged against the king's estate and prerogative false and untrue articles and petitions.[5] If the first of these crimes was akin to treason by words the second was unique and probably resulted from the very novelty of Cade's deeds and the fact that the attainder was suggested by the commons. This was the one of the few

---

[1] *Rot. Parl.*, v, 476 b.

[2] *Ibid.*, v, 346–50.

[3] *Ibid.*, v, 177 b, 178. He had traitorously delivered Maine thereby adhering to the king's enemies and traitorously counselled the duke of Orleans to provoke Charles VII to go to war with King Henry thereby adhering to, counselling and comforting the French king. Traitorously he had told Charles of the provisioning and defence of various towns so 'beyng adherent to your seid grete Enemye'. He had also traitorously given information to Charles about the king's instructions to his ambassadors and had traitorously taken rewards from the French to restrain the passage of English armies to France.

[4] *Ibid.*, III, 459 b.   [5] *Ibid.*, v, 265 a.

occasions when something like accroaching the royal power was mentioned in a fifteenth-century treason charge and of all the many crimes referred to in the various bills of attainder it alone was obviously outside the 1352 act.

Quite different from the usual type of attainder act, which was basically political, were a small number of others which awarded the penalties for treason against those who were thought guilty of lesser crimes but who in most cases could not be brought to justice. It was agreed in parliament that if these men after proper warning failed to appear in court at a set time they should be attainted of treason although the actual offences were not remotely treasonable: William Pulle of Wirral, Cheshire, for the rape of Isabel relict of Sir John Boteler (1436), Philip Eggerton of Spondesley (Salop) for waging war on John Stucche and for several murders, felonies and trespasses (1439) and Lewis Leyson of Glamorgan for the rape of Margaret relict of Sir Thomas Malefaut (1439).[1] An attempt by the commons in the parliament of 1433 to have John Carpenter of Bridham adjudged a traitor for the murder of his wife was refused but it showed the way for the later attainders of this type.[2] These were all desperate measures to obtain a remedy which it was thought the common law could not or would not provide and the

---

[1] *Rot. Parl.*, IV, 497 a, V, 17, 18 a, 14 b, 15. For example, William Pulle was said to have 'the said Beseecher felonousely and moste horribely ravysshed and her naked except hir Kirtyll and hir smokke ledde with him into the wylde and desolate places of Wales; of the which rape he to fore the Kinges Justices atte Lancastre is endited'. The sheriff was to issue a proclamation every market day for two weeks commanding his attendance before the justices of the county palatine. If he still did not appear he was, in the next session, to stand attaint of high treason.

[2] *Ibid.*, IV, 447 b. Carpenter had disembowelled his wife to see if she was pregnant. The petition read: 'Please hit to youre rightwisnesse to considere the horrible murdure foresaid and by auctoritee of this youre hie Courte of Parliament to ordaine that the said John Carpenter may be juged as a Traitour and yat youre Jugges have power to yeve Jugement upon hym to be drawne and hanged as a Traytour in eschewyng of such horrible mourdours in tyme coming: Saving allwey to the Lorde of the Fee eschetes of his landes after yere, day and wast'. In this case the penalties were to be as for petty treason.

The crown refused to implement the petition on the grounds that it was against the liberties of the church. Apparently the deed had been committed when the couple were on what was supposed to be a pilgrimage. In the parliament of 1445 the commons petitioned that John Bolton, who had been accused of murdering a woman he had unsuccessfully tried to rape, should suffer the penalties of high treason if found guilty in the courts. Bolton, who had been pardoned once, was committed to gaol for life at the king's command: *Rot. Parl.*, V, 111.

intention in each case was to force miscreants who had ignored exaction and outlawry to appear before the royal justices. Suspended attainder for treason played an important part in the development of the political attainder act but it only had a short existence itself for there were no examples after 1440.

One form of treason which seems to have had its origins in the fifteenth century was the use of necromancy for traitorous purposes. It involved using the magic arts to communicate with the dead in order to make predictions. Two of the most celebrated cases concerned women of high station. Queen Joan, second wife and widow of Henry IV was arrested on 1 October 1419 as a result of an accusation by her confessor, John Randolf, a Franciscan, that she had compassed the death and destruction of the king 'en le pluis haute et horrible manere qe l'en purroit deviser' and that it was publicly known.[1] By a contemporary chronicler the ex-queen was said to have sought 'by sorcerye and nygromancye fforto have dystroyed the kyng'.[2] Randolf was examined by the king himself and then imprisoned but neither he nor his royal mistress appear to have stood trial.[3] The sorcery and necromancy sponsored or at least supported by Eleanor Cobham, duchess of Gloucester, in 1441 led on the other hand to a thorough legal investigation which displayed the exact nature of the crime. London jurors, no doubt at the crown's prompting, indicted the duchess of plotting to make herself queen. She had failed in her endeavour, it was stated, because Henry VI continued to prosper. Therefore she sought the assistance of Roger Bolingbroke, a clerk of her household, who was 'a great astronomer' and famous for his knowledge of the black arts. Bolingbroke was said to have contacted demons and other malign spirits in earth and air on several occasions between 29 June 1440 and 23 March 1441 and with Thomas Southwell, parson of St Stephen's Walbrook and a canon of the king's chapel, to have tried by astrology to discover when the king would die, 'which was

---

[1] A. R. Myers, 'The Captivity of a Royal Witch', *Bulletin of the John Rylands Library*, XXIV (1940), 264; *Rot. Parl.*, IV, 118 b. In the fourteenth century there does not seem to have been such a crime as traitorous necromancy. In 1324 Master John de Nottingham, who had agreed to a suggestion that by his arts he should kill the king, the earl of Winchester, Sir Hugh Despenser, the prior of Coventry and others, and had made seven wax images for the purpose, was appealed merely of felony: see *Select Cases in the Court of the King's Bench*, ed. Sayles (Seld. Soc., 1955), pp. 154–7.

[2] *The Brut*, ed. Brie, II, 444.

[3] *Issues of the Exchequer*, ed. Devon, p. 365; *The Brut*, ed. Brie, II, 423.

forbidden'. The charge was also made that on 27 October 1440 in St Sepulchre's parish in Farringdon ward Bolingbroke and his allies, acting on Eleanor's instructions, feloniously and traitorously disclosed that the king would soon meet his death, intending by this prognostication 'ab ipso Rege cordialem amorem retraherent et idem Rex per notitiam illorum detectionis et manifestionis caperet talem tristitiam in corde suo' and so quickly die.[1] No proper legal record of the trial of Bolingbroke and Southwell, which was before an impressive commission of oyer and terminer, has survived, nor has that of the duchess of Gloucester before the council. We cannot therefore know for sure how these treasons were construed in court. Very likely it was as imagining or compassing the death of the king. Bolingbroke at least suffered the normal penalties for high treason.[2] In trying to destroy the cordial love between the king and his people the conspirators were committing an offence similar to that of the friars in 1402, namely the alienating of a monarch from his subjects. Foretelling the date of the king's death was to occur as treason again.

In 1477 Doctor Stacey, 'nobilis astronomis', Thomas Burdet esquire, a member of the household of the duke of Clarence and Thomas Blake, an Oxford associate of Stacey's, were accused of calculating the nativities of the king and the prince of Wales in order to find out when they were going to die. This crime had apparently been committed on 20 April 1474. On 6 February and 20 May 1475 Stacey and Blake once more calculated the royal deaths despite, as the indictment put it, the determination of the Holy Church and the opinions of divers doctors forbidding any liege man thus meddling without the permission of the princes themselves. Another charge stated that on 26 May 1475 in the hope of destroying the cordial love the people had for the king and thereby shortening his life by sadness, Stacey, Blake and Burdet declared to others that the prince of Wales was to die very shortly.[3] The similarity between these crimes and those of the duchess of

---

[1] P.R.O., K.B. 9/72/14.

[2] Stow, p. 381.

[3] *D.K.R.: Third Report*, Appendix II, pp. 213–14. Furthermore, at Westminster on 26 May 1475 Stacey, Blake and Burdet, it was stated, treasonably declared and made known to Alexander Russheton and others that according to their calculations the king and the prince of Wales would soon die, intending to withdraw thereby the cordial love of the people from the king so he would grow sad and perish.

Gloucester, Bolingbroke and their confederates is very noticeable and the indictments of 1477 appear to have been modelled on those of 1441. Burdet, Stacey and Blake were tried one at a time before a commission of oyer and terminer containing a score of magnates and judges and found guilty of treason. Apparently Burdet was the chief culprit and Stacey and Blake had assisted him in imagining and compassing the death of Edward IV by black magic. The charges that conspirators were trying to destroy the cordial love existing between the king and his people are particularly noteworthy. They show that the fourteenth-century political offence of creating a division between the king and his subjects, even if it did not take the form of accroaching the royal power, was still in mens' minds. The importance of these indictments on the practical side was their demonstration that almost any exciting or stirring of the king's subjects against the government could be interpreted as treasonable.

Not only by the statute of 1352 or construction thereof was treason defined in the fifteenth century. There were other statutes which, because they legislated for particular circumstances that were likely to occur only infrequently, were of less importance. In the parliament which met at Leicester in April 1414 it was decreed that those of the king's subjects who in future ignored the safe-conducts issued by the crown and the truces made with enemies and who slew, robbed and spoiled men who were travelling under such protection, should be judged for high treason. To implement the statute conservators of truces were to be appointed with power to enquire by land and sea and to punish under the law of the king's admirals. Amongst English laws concerned with treason the act was quite distinct in its obvious derivation from contemporary European conventions. These were themselves expressions of an international law which was historically descended from the *ius gentium* of the Roman Empire and was to be found in the middle ages set down in the corpus of canon and civil law. International law divided into a number of special categories like the law merchant, the law of the sea and the law of arms, which contained not only law of Roman origin but also a body of customary usage. Safe conducts and truces, their maintenance and infraction were a most important part of the law of arms and the law of the sea and a complex system of regulations and provisos concerning them had grown up. The gravity of the offence of breaking truces and safe conducts depended on the rank of the grantor for it was his promise which had been broken and his honour which had been injured. If the truce or safe conduct had been given by a royal lieutenant the penalty was likely to be death but if it was the act of the king then the punishment was likely to be as for treason since the king's majesty had been infringed. This was the custom on the continent and Henry V in 1414 was obviously influenced by it. There were precedents in English history, it is true, for calling truce and safe conduct breaking treason, but they were only two in number and parliamentary declaration had been necessary on one of the occasions. John Imperial, an accredited Genoese ambassador, had been murdered in London in 1379 and the crime decided as treason by parliament because the king's letters of safe conduct had been infringed. In 1392 a Bristol merchant was accused of treason because he plundered contrary to a truce a barge from La Rochelle. The misdeed was committed off the coast of Brittany and is unlikely to have been justiciable under the common law. The statute of 1414 was probably intended to remedy an obvious weakness of that law and the king's method was to borrow, as had been done on earlier occasions to meet other legal problems, from a source which was basically Roman. The mention of conservators of truces, who were judges for the hearing of individual complaints about infractions, and the reference to marque in the supplementary act of 1416 (4 Henry V st. 2, c. 6) showed definite borrowing from the law military.[1]

The statute of 1414 generated much criticism among seafaring men who wished to retaliate against their foreign competitors and in the parliament of 1429–30 the commons requested the law should be annulled so that Scottish pirates could be dealt with in a suitable manner.[2] This was refused as was a similar petition in the parliament of 1433 but in 1436 when the matter was raised yet again the crown made slight concessions.[3] In 1442 it was decreed in parliament that the 'ordinance' of 1414 on truces was to last for a further twenty years but the government, aware of the law's unpopularity, consented to the pardon of those who had already

---

[1] *Stat. Realm*, II, 178; M. H. Keen, *The Laws of War in the Late Middle Ages* (London, 1965), pp. 11–13, 206 and *passim; Rot. Parl.* III, 75; *Cal. Pat. Rolls, 1391–6*, p. 280.
[2] *Rot. Parl.*, IV, 351 a.
[3] *Ibid.*, IV, 452, 500 b.

suffered pains and penalties under it.[1] Finally in the parliament of 1450-1 a form of outlawry process was added to the 1414 act whereby accused parties who failed to appear to answer before the chancellor on a set day were to stand convicted of treason.

Another statute (4 Henry V c. 6) which dealt with the less important aspects of high treason legislated on the clipping, washing and filing of coins.[2] Here, despite the ordinance of 1399, the law makers were consciously supplementing the statute of 1352: 'qe nulle mencioun ent [that is, of clipping, washing and filing] est fait en la declaracioun des articles de traisoun faitz en la parlement tenu l'an vingt et quint del noble Roi Edward . . . mesme nostre seignur le roi, voillant ouster tiele doute et le mettre en certein, ad declaree . . . qe tieux tonsure, loture, et filer soient adjuggez pur traisoun'.

Similar in intent was the addition to the law of treason made in parliament of 1423-4. The commons asked that if a man who had been indicted, appealed or taken on suspicion of high treason escaped from prison it should be adjudged treason: their reason for so doing was that the statute of 1352 did not declare how the crime should be rated.[3] They were arguing that crimes unmentioned in 1352 could nonetheless be treason and that the original statute was not necessarily exhaustive. The 1424 act seems to have been inspired by the recent escape from the Tower of London of a number of important conspirators including Thomas Payn, Oldcastle's secretary, Thomas Excestre of Ireland, who had tried to spy on the king's council and Sir John Mortimer, who had aspired to the throne as heir of the earl of March. Detailed investigation shows that it was Excestre and Mortimer who created the need for legislation.[4] Since they had not been judged in a court and were merely in custody on suspicion there could be no removal of the case from a lesser court to parliament for purposes of declaration as had been provided for in 1352. Instead the crime had to be

---

[1] *Rot. Parl.*, v, 63 b. *Stat. Realm*, ii, 358-9: this act was intended to last five years.   [2] *Stat. Realm*, ii, 195.

[3] *Rot. Parl.*, iv, 260 b.

[4] See *Year Books of Henry VI, I Henry VI*, ed. C. H. Williams (Seld. Soc., 1933), pp. xxiv-xxvii; *Cal. Pat. Rolls, 1422-9*, pp. 134, 186; Stow, p. 364. Mortimer was a particular object of the king's hatred and his imprisonment had been most severe: see *Rot. Parl.*, iv, 160 b and *Procs. and Ords.*, ii, 311. According to one chronicle, Mortimer had broken out of the Tower of London in 9 Henry V to be recaptured in Wales and put back: *Chronicle of the Grey Friars of London*, ed. J. G. Nichols (Camden Soc., 1851), p. 15.

classified as treason by means of an act.[1] It is possible that the 1424 statute did not break entirely new ground since Stow mentions that at the time of the 1414 parliament at Leicester a porter of the Tower of London was drawn, hanged and beheaded 'for consenting to one that brake out of the Tower named Whitlocke'.[2] John Wyghtlok, a suspected but perhaps not a convicted traitor, did indeed escape from captivity there but at Trinity term 1413: he got out through the 'false covin of two gaolers and the negligence of the under-constable'. According to the plea rolls the latter was found guilty of misprision and fined 1000 marks.[3] There is no mention of a porter or of the penalties inflicted on the two gaolers but Stow may be correct. If he was then it is further evidence of Henry V and his advisers creating treasons outside the 1352 statute. The act of 1424 was remarkable in that first of all it referred to men imprisoned for high treason and then it decreed that by escaping they were guilty of treason *tout court*, the adjective 'high' being omitted. Furthermore, as Stow first noted, the penalties of forfeiture were to be those for petty treason, the traitors' possessions going to their immediate lords and not necessarily the king.[4] There is no evidence of other cases under the 1424 act in the period before 1485: this may have been because the crown made sure there were no ex-tended periods of captivity between arrest and trial and therefore there was less opportunity to escape.[5]

In the parliament of 1429-30 the commons petitioned success-fully for the law of treason to be extended to include arson. Their request was prompted by a local crime wave. In the town of Cambridge and the counties of Cambridge and Essex people had been forced to pay money under the threat of having their houses and goods burned and destroyed.[6] In the parliament which met at Westminster in January 1442 the commons obtained an ordinance to the effect that Welshmen who seized Englishmen's goods in

[1] Rezneck, 'Early History of Parliamentary Declaration of Treason', *Eng. Hist. Rev.*, XLII, 506-7, discusses this example of declaration but without offering any solution or commenting on the nature of the crime.
[2] Stow, p. 345. However, in July 1392 aiding a prisoner who had been con-victed of treason to escape from York gaol was called felony: P.R.O., J.I. 1./1145 m. 4.   [3] P.R.O., K.B. 27/609 Rex m. 14.
[4] *Rot. Parl.*, IV, 260 b; Stow, p. 364.
[5] This was probably prompted by a petition of the commons: *Rot. Parl.* IV, 292 b.
[6] *Rot. Parl.*, IV, 349 b; *Stat. Realm*, II, 242-3. Such crimes had also been practised in 1411: *Cal. Pat. Rolls, 1408-13*, p. 316.

Herefordshire, Gloucestershire and Salop and took them to the Welsh marches and to Wales were to be adjudged guilty of high treason. The law was not to last indefinitely but for a period of seven years: in fact it expired in November 1449.[1] Another addition to the law of treason was made in October 1460 when Richard, duke of York came to an agreement with Henry VI over the succession to the crown. Within the memorandum which was presented to parliament was a clause which stated that if any person imagined or compassed the death of the duke and be provably attainted of open deed done, by men of his own rank, he should be deemed guilty of high treason.[2] Thus for the duke's death at the battle of Wakefield weeks later men were attainted of treasonable murder once Edward IV had come to the throne.[3] In formulating this novel treason the lawyers fell into the error of associating the crime of compassing the death of the heir to the throne with the need for an overt act: there was no association of overt act with imagining and compassing the death of the king in the act of 1352. The ground for later misrepresentation of the law of treason was thus prepared.

On nearly every occasion when the accepted penalties for treason were imposed the crime came under the 1352 statute either directly or by construction: if it did not then very likely it was covered by one of the minor acts of the fifteenth century. There were nonetheless a few instances where the normal penalties for treason were threatened or inflicted when the crime did not seem to fall into one of those categories. In 1399 John Hall, a servant of the duke of Norfolk, confessed to keeping cave when the duke of Gloucester was murdered at Calais in 1397. The king and the lords temporal in parliament found Hall guilty and decided that he deserved the worst death possible as the duke was so high a person. He was therefore sentenced to be drawn, hanged, disembowelled and quartered.[4] In the parliament which met in Coventry in October 1404 the commons granted the king two tenths and fifteenths which were to be spent only on the defence of the realm. None of the crown's creditors were to be paid from the sum: if they made any demand or actually procured payment for themselves then 'ils et chescun d'eux encourgent la peyne de treson'.[5]

---

[1] *Rot. Parl.*, V, 54 a, 151 a, 155 a.
[3] For example, *Cal. Pat. Rolls, 1461–7*, p. 521.
[5] *Ibid.*, III, 546.

[2] *Ibid.*, V, 375.
[4] *Rot. Parl.*, III, 452.

In 1422 the chief justice of the king's bench commanded the sheriffs of London to keep very careful guard over Thomas Payn, then a prisoner in Newgate, on pain of being deemed guilty of treason if he should later escape, be recaptured and be convicted of that offence: if he was not then they would suffer the penalties of law which would be both arbitrary and severe.[1] In the cases which involved Isabel Boteler (1436), John Stucche (1439) and Margaret Malefaut (1439), the crown, as we have already seen, acceded to parliamentary petitions requesting that if the accused did not appear in court within a certain period he should stand attaint of high treason.[2] Similarly under the statute de riottis of 1453 failure to appear in council or chancery after proper warning could result in the same total forfeiture as was often decreed against traitors by attainder act.[3] Apparently there was nothing to stop parliament awarding the penalties for treason whatever the actual nature of the crime and this licence was frequently exploited. In the parliament of 1455-6 the commons requested the crimes of clerks should be punished in this way. They pointed out that murders, manslaughter, rapes and robberies were increasing daily and that the perpetrators were mostly clerks emboldened by their immunity from the common law. The commons suggested that those who had once been convicted of these offences and handed over to the ordinary, and then were indicted or appealed of another similar crime, should have it treated as high treason.[4] Another petition which concerned crime and the church was put forward by the commons of the parliament of 1467-8. They asked that all robberies committed after 29 September 1467 in any church 'of eny Coupe, Pixe, or other thyng whereyn the seid blessed Sacrament hath or shall be put or closed, be demed high Treason; and that all Robbours atteint of any such Robberies have Jugement to be brent'. The king refused the request.[5]

Cases of treason which no construction on the statute of 1352 and no later act can explain, and which were not merely examples of the penalties for treason being awarded out of context by parliament, were very few in number. The plurality of charges against most of those accused, some touching treason, some not, makes it difficult to show that a man was condemned as a traitor for one

---

[1] Procs. and Ords., III, 4.
[2] Above, p. 125.
[3] Rot. Parl., v, 266 b.
[4] Ibid., v, 333.
[5] Ibid., v, 632 b.

particular crime and not another: only when the crime stands by itself can we be sure of the way it was interpreted. Thus Thomas Fort, son of Thomas Fort of Llanstephan (Carmarthenshire), who was pardoned early in February 1389, had been indicted for treason and felony in that of his own authority he had given a and safe conduct to John de Ispannia, a subject of the king of Castile, and Leon, the king's enemy, taken him into service and shown him secrets in various South Welsh castles. If the treason referred to was the giving of safe conduct the crime was outside the 1352 act but the revealing of the secrets of the Welsh castles on the other hand could conceivably have been interpreted as aiding the king's enemies.[1] There were in contrast cases which seemed to ignore the 1352 statute where the crime was clearly labelled. Two bands of notorious malefactors, who had lain in ambush near Tottenham and Iseldon in October 1401 and March 1402 respectively, were indicted and found guilty of having intended to rob and slay traitorously the common people, labourers in the fields and other of the king's lieges, and also of actually committing one traitorous robbery in each case: this despite the deliberate omission of highway robbery from the 1352 act.[2] A crime treated in its own day as treason but which seemed to the Tudor lawyers to lie outside the statute occurred in 2 Henry IV: it was referred to by Sir Thomas Bromley C.J.K.B. at the trial of Sir Nicholas Throckmorton in 1554. He said that a man who took the great seal of England from one document and put it to another was adjudged a traitor.[3] Perhaps the case was not within the express words of the act about counterfeiting the great seal but no great construction was needed to make it so. The crime attracted sufficient notice when committed to gain a place in the *Year Books*.[4] In the parliament of 1406 the lords declared as treason the giving of letters under seal of arms by the earl of Northumberland to Sir Henry Boynton and others, for the purpose of treating with the Scots and French. Negotiating with the king's enemies was hardly the equivalent of adhering to them as the crown doubtless realized and there

---

[1] *Cal. Pat. Rolls, 1388–92*, p. 9. Patently the crime was a degree different from that committed by Robert de Pillington of Scarborough: see *Cal. Pat. Rolls, 1381–5*, pp. 190–1.
[2] P.R.O. K.B. 2/189/13 and 34. See Appendix III. They had also attacked men of law, which may have been their undoing.
[3] *State Trials*, ed. Howell, 1, 892.
[4] *Year Books*, 2 Henry IV, Trin. pl. 25. See Appendix III.

were no later examples of this interpretation.[1] An entry in the patent rolls dated 10 December 1406 refers to one Simon Hasilden of Newbury (Berkshire) as being lately indicted and convicted of clipping the king's coined money of gold and silver and afterwards by judgement being drawn and hanged, that is to say suffering the penalties for treason.[2] Later on this or similar judgements may have been questioned since a statute (4 Henry V c. 6) was passed to supplement the act of 1352 and remove any doubt about clipping, washing and filing.[3] There was therefore some excuse for the charges made against Hasilden. In 1414 another supplementary statute was enacted by parliament, the subject being the breaking of truces which the king had made with other nations.[4] Yet more than twenty years before, in June 1392, John Merkeley of Bristol had been indicted because at Penmarch in Brittany he traitorously plundered contrary to the truce the barge captained by John Janewe from La Rochelle.[5] Perhaps the argument of the crown in this case was that the crime was committed abroad and was therefore not justiciable under the English common law, being rather a treason against the king's prerogative and the supranational laws of war. Even in 1392 there was a precedent for charging those who broke safe conducts with treason. In 1379 when the suspected murderers of John Imperial of Genoa were brought into court the matter was moved before parliament and the crime declared treason. Emphasis was laid on the fact that the dead man had been given safe conduct and royal protection as an ambassador.[6]

Even in the mid-fifteenth century when the quality of government was declining there were relatively few occasions when the charge of treason was legally unwarranted. One of these was

---

[1] *Rot. Parl.*, III, 605 a. In 1323 Andrew de Harclay, earl of Carlisle had been accused of making an illegal truce with the Scottish enemy. It has been suggested that the charge of treason was based on this misdeed: Keen, 'Treason Trials', *Trans. Roy. Hist. Soc.*, 5th ser., XII, 97. It seems more likely the treason was adhering to the king's enemies however.

[2] *Cal. Pat. Rolls, 1405-8*, p. 278.

[3] *Stat. Realm*, II, 195: 'Item pur ceo qe devaunt ces heures grande doute et awereuste ad este le quell la tonsure, loture, et fylynge de la moneie de la terre duissent estre adjuggez tresoun, ou nient, a cause qe nulle mencioun ent est fait en la declaracioun des articles de traisoun en la parlement tenu l'an vingt et quint del noble Roi Edward . . . voillant ouster tiele doute et le mettre en certain, ad declaree en cest present parlement qe tieux tonsure, loture et filer soient adjuggez pur traisoun'.   [4] *Stat. Realm*, II, 178.

[5] *Cal. Pat. Rolls, 1391-6*, p. 280.

[6] P.R.O., K.B. 27/476 Rex m. 31d.

mentioned by a London chronicler who gives the information that in 18 Henry VI 'whas a man drawyn, and hangid, and hedid, and quartered, and sett up at diverse placis; for he toke up bestis and all maner of vetayll in the contre in the kynges name, and whas but a thef, and so robbid the contre with treson'.[1] This is all that is known of the crime. It is conceivable the man had forged the commission and its royal seal, or one or the other. If this speculation is correct then the crime was not novel at all. There was apparently another doubtful case in 1454. Richard, duke of York granted Thomas Courtenay, earl of Devon, a charter of pardon at Michaelmas term 1453, presumably for the charge of insurrection of which the earl had been indicted in the Somerset county court. According to Vernon Harcourt this caused a charge of treason to be laid against the duke himself:[2] perhaps it was the one of which he cleared himself by a declaration of loyalty in parliament.[3] Since York was nothing more than a member of the council at the time he may have been held to have usurped the king's prerogative. Another example is referred to by the chronicler Stow. He states that in February 1480 five notable thieves were put to death in London for robbing St Martin's-le-Grand and other churches. 'For the which three of them were drawne to the Tower and there hanged and brent, the other two were pressed to death'.[4] In 1467, as we have seen, the crown had refused a petition by the commons to make such robbery treasonable so that unless the miscreants had committed an additional crime like counterfeiting money the penalties for treason were incurred for nothing more than felony.[5]

From this review of the evidence we may fairly conclude that most English kings of the period were happy to abide by the definition of treason embodied in the act of 1352. They did so not so much out of a desire to keep closely to the law, although that may occasionally have played a part, as for example in the earliest years of Henry IV's reign, but because they found no need to extend the law. Most treasons worthy of the name and a few

---

[1] *Chronicles of London*, ed. C. L. Kingsford (London, 1905), p. 147.
[2] L. W. Vernon Harcourt, 'The Baga de Secretis', *Eng. Hist. Rev.*, XXIII (1908), 518 n. Courtenay was indicted for treason for rising with Lord Cobham at Ilminster on 18 February 1452; the indictment was sent into parliament in January 1454; P.R.O., K.B. 9/105/46. I must thank Dr R. L. Storey for this reference.   [3] *Rot. Parl.*, v, 249 b.
[4] Stow, p. 431.   [5] *Rot. Parl.*, v, 632 b.

that were not could be placed by means of judicial construction within the two classes of compassing the king's death and levying war against him. The extension of treason by parliamentary statute on a small number of occasions in the first half of the fifteenth century was concession to the parliamentary commons over grievances which were particular and limited: there was no introduction of new principles. In contrast with ideas proposed by subjects the only king who may have had ideas of extending the law of treason was Richard II. He sought to preserve, define and even increase the royal prerogative. He and his advisers appear to have been working their way towards a law of treason which went beyond the common law *dicta*. They aimed at the prerogative law of treason, one which was to be enforced not so much in the common law courts as in parliament and by special commissions.

The definition of treason contained in the 1352 statute was in the political sense essentially a conservative one. The main concern was to protect the king's person, those who dispensed justice in his stead and his immediate family. There was little emphasis on treason against the state. This interpretation was echoed in the stress placed on imagining and compassing the king's death during the next two centuries and the tendency to interpret all betrayals and attacks on the king or the realm as falling into that category. Parliamentary attainder affected the scope of the law of treason remarkably little. No doubt this was because before 1459 attainder acts were used only to supplement common law verdicts already given, to deal with dead traitors' lands or in a suspended version to bring ordinary malefactors before the courts. After 1459 acts of attainder were promulgated against enemies of the king who had not been before any court at all and who had not even been outlawed, but by then a custom of conforming to the common law of treason had been established.

Since the king's lawyers were able if they wished to construe a great many crimes as compassing the death of the monarch it is obvious that it was not the scope of the law of treason which restricted any despotic tendencies in this field. It was in fact more by the legal procedure necessary to try a traitor that any tendency to override the law was limited. It was the courts, particularly the juries, which restricted autocratic practice and in this they were assisted by the remarkable reverence which the English of the later middle ages had for proper legal process.

6

TREASON BEFORE THE COURTS

1352-1485

UNDER the common law at least the process of trial in cases of treason hardly differed in essence from that employed when the charge was felony or trespass. Treason had been clearly marked off from felony by the statute of 1352 but apart from allowing for the declaration of certain crimes in parliament no special procedures had been laid down. From the prisoner's viewpoint the only noticeable difference in being tried for treason was that he could not plead benefit of clergy and, if found guilty, he was dragged to the gallows behind a horse. Those accused of treason could not be tried under the peace commission but since justices of the peace regularly received commissions of oyer and terminer which remedied this deficiency there was little difference in this respect either. Because of the nature of the offence the king's officers seem to have worked with more than their usual application to ensure that charges were precise and that jurors were suitable and informed. This, no doubt, was one of the reasons why those who were tried for treason were usually found guilty whereas those accused of felony were in the majority of cases acquitted.

In the fourteenth century trials for treason and felony, if they were not the result of an appeal by an individual, were begun by one or by several juries of the locality presenting the misdeeds of the accused. How far the choice of charge was left to the jurors and how far matters were decided in advance by the law officers of the crown is hard to determine. It probably varied with the importance of the offence and the offender but in general there seems to have been less interference in the fourteenth than in the fifteenth century. The verdict was given by a second or petty jury which was not supposed to contain any member of the first jury. By the mid-fifteenth century procedure had changed. Presentments initiated by a jury were much less common. More frequent was the formula 'inquiratur pro domino Rege' which may be taken to signify that the indictment was drawn up by the crown lawyers either from the answers to questions put to the jurors at an inquest or as a result of the examination of suspects. The list of offences was then shown to a grand jury which answered either that it was a true bill or it was not. If true then the accused was taken before a second or petty jury for verdict. Indictments were also drawn from two less common sources. One was accusation by an individual which had previously taken the form of an appeal. In the later fifteenth century this tended to be superseded by the bill of indictment which like the findings of an inquest was vetted by a grand jury.[1] Sometimes the justices of oyer and terminer, before whom treason was usually tried, offered charges themselves as a result of information volunteered to them or unearthed by their own investigations.

In some of the cases of treason where the crown allowed a jury to initiate proceedings by means of presenting an indictment there was pressure brought to bear. A good example occurred at St Albans soon after the failure of the great revolt of 1381. The king proposed to visit the town himself in order to punish those who had been in rebellion but Sir Walter atte Lee who lived in that area and feared for the havoc any royal army would create obtained permission for a personal attempt to make peace between the abbey and the rebels. At 'Derfold' wood he told the peasantry he would endeavour to protect them from a descent by the king's forces and at the same time swore in a jury for the purpose of indicting the insurgents.[2] This jury however reported that there was nobody it wished to accuse as all the local men had been loyal to the king. Another meeting also failed to give Lee any satisfaction and it seemed as though the insurrection might be renewed. He therefore ordered the seizure of William Grindcob and two other rebel leaders. Eventually the king and Chief Justice Tresilian arrived and sessions were held in the St Alban's moot-hall. First Grindcob, John Ball and two more prominent rebels were sentenced to death for treason and then Tresilian summoned a jury of twelve to indict other insurgents.[3] The jurors said there was no one whom they could indict as all in the town were loyal. The chief justice answered that if they did not supply him with the

[1] B. Lyon, *A Constitutional and Legal History of Medieval England* (New York, 1960), p. 637. Fifteenth-century criminal procedure still awaits proper investigation.

[2] *Historia Anglicana*, II, 22–3.   [3] *Ibid.*, II, 24–32.

names they themselves would be punished with the very punishment which those they ought to have presented should have had. He showed them a roll which he said contained the crimes of all their neighbours listed by loyal men of the countryside and suggested they should indict quickly to save their own lives. They did so and the indictments were then shown to a second jury of twelve which was asked to give its opinion about those who had been accused. The second jury, seeing the list was a true one, said it agreed with the indictment and would have made accusation in the same manner had it been given the task. Therefore the chief justice kept the second jury as the petty jury 'ad dicendum veredictum de praefatis personis'. When the question of guilt was actually put to it it did not dare to give a verdict different from the one already offered. Finally Tresilian showed the indictments of the first jury to a third jury which had made its own presentments: the reason was 'ut nullus damnaretur nisi per ora triginta sex virorum'.[1] By asking one jury to pronounce on the veracity of presentments made by another the original charges, if the response was positive, were afforced. Thereby the freedom of the petty jury to return a final verdict of not guilty must surely have been curtailed. The success of measures like this in 1381 probably pointed the way to the crown introducing charges itself at inquests and then getting a grand jury to pronounce whether they were true or false. Again the petty jury found itself with less chance to return the acquittal which local opinion generally favoured.

There were two other notable occasions when attempts were made to persuade juries to indict for treason against their natural inclinations and about which contemporary criticism survives. In 1452 when in his camp on Blackheath the duke of York complained to Henry VI by letter that when he was in Ireland on the king's service 'certaine commissions were made and directed unto divers persons which for the execution of the same, sate in certaine places and the iurers impanelled and charged, to the which iuries certaine persons laboured instantly to have me indited of treason'.[2] In 1468 in the *cause célèbre* of Edward IV's reign there occurred another example. Sir Thomas Cook, a London mercer, was accused by John Hawkins, a servant of Lord Wenlock, who had been put to torture in the Tower of London. He was said to have given assistance to the king's enemy ex-Queen Margaret through

[1] *Historia Anglicana*, II, 35–6.   [2] Stow, p. 394.

Hawkins and a confederate named Hugo Mulle. Quite commonly under the common law a confession turned into the approving or appealing of the criminals' associates but in Hawkins's case this was not so.[1] Perhaps it was because the matter had been dealt with by the council. Thus it was found necessary to indict Cook by presentment of a jury. Says Stow 'a jury by means of Sir John Fogge indited him of treason after which an oyer determiner was kept in the guild-hall'.[2] The plea rolls confirm that Cook was so indicted although naturally they omit any reference to labouring.[3] Contemporary and Tudor opinion did not approve of pressure being brought to bear on juries to indict but nonetheless at this time it was entirely lawful for parties and therefore for the crown to endeavour to convince the petty jurors before they met and there was no law to say that the presenting juries should not be prompted either.[4] In the fifteenth century the crown was still able to do whatever was not definitely forbidden by statute or common law and there were no set rules on indictment at all.

If charges of treason were not laid by means of an indictment then they were initiated by appeal, that is to say the accusation of a single person. Generally speaking appeal of felony was in retreat before indictment during the later middle ages yet appeal of treason showed strong powers of survival. Many appeals of treason came from the mouths of approvers, that is to say from men who admitted their own treason and accused others of participating in the crime. Such men were usually hoping to prolong their own life by the information they gave the crown.[5] Thus in 1381 John Wrawe, the rebel leader at Bury St Edmunds, appeared before the sheriffs of London and the city coroner and acknowledged himself to be a felon and traitor by describing his misdeeds. He then approved Thomas Halisworth, Geoffrey Denham and Robert Westbroun, who had been members of his band, as well as Thomas Langham of Bury, Robert Tavell of Lavenham and John Talmache

[1] P.R.O., K.B. 27/830 Rex m. 41; *Letters and Papers illustrative of the Wars of the English in France*, ed. J. Stevenson (R.S., 1864), II, II, 789–90.
[2] Stow, p. 420.
[3] P.R.O., K.B. 27/830 Rex m. 41. The jury found Cook guilty of giving shelter to Hawkins and Mulle but not guilty of adhering to Queen Margaret and sending her words of comfort.
[4] K. W. M. Pickthorn, *Early Tudor Government: Henry VII* (Cambridge, 1934), p. 80.
[5] *Cal. Pat. Rolls, 1413–16*, p. 151.

esquire.[1] Another approver, John Bakere, before execution declared the names of those who helped him decapitate Robert Hales, the treasurer, on Tower Hill.[2] Some of those who became approvers were acknowledged to be acting 'pro utilitate regni Anglie et distrucione inimicorum domini regis'.[3] To trace the eventual fate of many approvers of treason is difficult but if their own treasons were not considered exceptionally heinous and the information supplied was valuable then they might perhaps be pardoned. There was no idea however that the giving of information entitled the approver to be forgiven forthwith. An example of a traitor who probably saved his own life by the valuable information he was able to proffer was John Peyntour of Fenny Stratford, Buckinghamshire. He was indicted by jury in June 1419 for sweating and clipping English money, an offence under the treason act of 1416. He confessed to these crimes and then for the good of the king became the king's approver. At Northampton before Thomas Covele, the coroner in the king's bench, he appealed a number of yeomen who in 1415 had commissioned him to paint banners, pennons and *cote armours* for use in an attempt on King Henry's life which they explained to him. Other men he appealed for delivering counterfeit money.[4] On the advice of the council, which must have been moved by the importance of the confession, the king took Peyntour under his protection for three years, meaning three years in the Tower. On the other hand an approver of treason might be drawn and hanged first and his accusations investigated later. John Veyse of Holbeach, when in Huntingdon gaol in Henry IV's reign, appealed before the sheriff and one of the coroners no fewer than fifty-nine prominent ecclesiastics including the abbots of Ramsey, Crowland and Louth and the priors of Walsingham, Norwich and Spalding. The abbot of Ramsey and Veyse appeared before the justices of gaol delivery: the abbot was acquitted and Veyse sentenced to be drawn through Huntingdon and then hanged. The others were not forgotten for they were the subject of several later commissions of oyer and terminer designed to investigate Veyse's accusations.[5] A man who

---

[1] Réville, *Soulèvement des Travailleurs*, pp. 175–8 (quoting P.R.O., K.B. 27/484 Rex mm. 26, 26d.).   [2] Réville, *Soulèvement des Travailleurs*, p. 205.
[3] For example *ibid.*, p. 182.   [4] *Cal. Pat. Rolls, 1429–36*, p. 592.
[5] *Cal. Pat. Rolls, 1405–8*, pp. 227, 236; Trokelowe, *Chronica*, pp. 415–16. The chronicler says that Veyse, who was a notorious thief, was found guilty because he failed to recognize those he accused.

on indictment or appeal approved others not as assisting him in his treason but as being in fact the real perpetrators was subject to those rules which governed ordinary appeals, with one exception. If the details he gave were insufficient to warrant the accused man's arraignment then there was no trial by battle as between men whose word was equally acceptable. The approver was immediately sentenced and executed.

If on an appeal of treason there was insufficient evidence to prove the case, if it was one man's unsupported word against another's and if they were both of good repute and not outlawed or indicted for felony, then trial by battle might result. The reign of Richard II saw the growth in number of appeals of treason which were laid with the full intent of going to trial by battle. The appeal of treason of Thomas Caterton by Sir John Annesley and the resultant *duellum* in 1380,[1] the battle between John Walshe and his Navarrese appellant in 1384,[2] the one intended between the dukes of Norfolk and Hereford at Coventry in 1398 and the appeals in the parliaments of 1388 and 1397 must have played a part in the increasing popularity of this mode of trial. Men who laid charges with this intent explained why they wanted to resort to arms. Richard Clyveden of Bridgwater hoped that trial by battle and not verdict of jurors would be awarded on his appeal of Sir William Cogan because the latter was richer than he was and presumably would offer gifts or bribes to judge or jury.[3] In 1395 John Cavendish, who had been appealed of treason by Richard Piryman before the council, asked that the case should go before the constable's court because if it went to common law he would be condemned by the procuring of the jury of inquest.[4] There can be little doubt that Richard II encouraged such appeals and was keen to see them dealt with in the court of chivalry. In March 1397 as a result of complaints it had received that the constable and marshal of England were not doing their duty in appeals of treason the council ordered them to execute the duties of their offices properly in the future.[5] The commons of parliament had not been happy

---

[1] *Cal. Pat. Rolls, 1377–81*, p. 485.

[2] *Chronicon Angliae*, ed. E. M. Thompson (R.S., 1874), p. 361.

[3] *Rot. Parl.*, III, 105–6. This appeal was either made initially in parliament or later repeated there. It is stated that Clyveden 'mist avaunt en Parlement une Bille' which accused Cogan of aiding the Bridgwater rioters at the time of the great revolt.

[4] *Procs. and Ords.*, I, 77.   [5] *Ibid.*, I, 65.

with the increasing activity of the constable's court. In 1379 they petitioned unsuccessfully against its dealing with appeals of treason and felony done in England:[1] in 1384 however the court was barred from entertaining any plea which touched on the common law at all and in 1390 the commons obtained statutory definition of its judicial competence.[2] Included were all matters pertaining to arms and war with which the common law did not deal. In addition any man who felt a case in which he was involved should go before a court of common law was to be provided with the means to bring it before council in the first place. Presumably it would then be allotted to the court which expert opinion thought most suitable. By the last two or three years of Richard's reign these rules were being ignored either through the king's personal predilection or because of the natural popularity of appealing to arms among the upper classes. Apparently the crown gave rewards to those who appealed and conquered. Sir John Annesley received an annuity after he had beaten Thomas Caterton[3] and Hugh del Hall in February 1397 was granted 100 shillings a year for life, theoretically on account of the costs he sustained in conquering with John de More two traitors appealed by them of treason.[4] In September 1398 a significant entry was made on the patent rolls about men who were prosecuting, as it was put, unusual causes and matters which touched the king's person and the royal dignity. The duke of Albermarle as constable was commissioned to hear such cases, to discuss them in accordance with the demands of justice and the laws and customs of the court of chivalry and to determine them. If the cases were by their nature unable to be determined by the constable in virtue of his office or under the common law but only by the king's audience on his special commission then he was to substitute others to hear them in his stead despite any statute to the contrary. One of the forty-four articles of indictment brought against Richard II at the time

---

[1] *Rot. Parl.*, III, 65 b.
[2] *Ibid.*, III, 202 b; *Stat. Realm*, II, 61–2.
[3] P.R.O., E. 403/481 (6 March 1381),/502 (22 April 1384),/521 (16 November 1388).
    The entry under 16 November 1388 actually mentions the battle with Caterton. The annuity was theoretically to Annesley and his wife Isabella in part compensation for her lost Norman inheritance: Annesley continued to receive it after her death : E. 403/538.
[4] *Cal. Pat. Rolls, 1396–9*, p. 72.

of his deposition was to the effect that the crown had arrested men who were said to have spoken in derogation of the royal person and had put them on trial in the court of chivalry. There they were not allowed to answer except to plead not guilty and subsequently defend their word with their bodies. This was thought iniquitous 'quod accusatores et appellatores eorum essent juvenes fortes et sani et illi accusati senes et impotentes mutulati vel infirmi'.[1] The crimes of those who were appealed seem in general to have been construed as treason.

An act was passed in the first parliament of Henry IV's reign which excluded appeals of treason from parliament and limited the competence of the court of chivalry to those examples which had their origin outside the realm. Furthermore no one in any court was to be condemned unheard.[2] But appeals of treason even if for a period they did not figure in the court of chivalry did not cease. One example seems to have been concerned with the affair of the 'false Richard'. John Bernard of Offley (Hertfordshire) in 1402 admitted he had helped to disseminate the story that King Richard was still alive and had promised to raise men on his behalf. He then appealed his original informant William Balsshalf and the pair were brought into the court of chivalry and given a day.[3] A duel followed. Later examples help to establish that appeals of treason were still, in the fifteenth century, able to be settled by trial by battle. The only difference between the Bernard case and the fourteenth-century examples was that in 1402 the appeal was laid in a common law court and only the actual battle was under the authority of the constable. The royal justices, in Henry IV's reign at least, seem to have had little hesitation in awarding trial by battle and the king must have agreed with them. In the same year as the trial of Bernard one chronicler reports a case in which a woman accused an aged Franciscan friar of the Cambridge convent of speaking certain treasonable words against the king. The justice before whom the case was tried apparently ordered the friar to fight the woman in judicial battle with one hand bound behind his back. However the friends of the friar eventually persuaded the woman to withdraw her accusation and the archbishop of Canterbury pacified the king.[4] Another case is described in The Brut. In the eighth year of the reign a man who was called

[1] Cal. Pat. Rolls, 1396-9, p. 505; Rot. Parl., III, 420 b.   [2] Rot. Parl., III, 442.
[3] Cal. Pat. Rolls, 1401-5, pp. 99, 116.   [4] Eulogium Historiarum, III, 389.

'the Welsh clerk' appealed a knight of treason and they were joined in a fight to the death at Smithfield.[1]

It was the reign of Henry VI which witnessed the zenith of this latter-day trial by battle on appeal of treason. As in the reign of the king's grandfather there was still opposition: in the parliament of 1429–30 a petition was presented with the intention of prohibiting appeals of treason done within the realm from being brought before the court of chivalry. The crown gave an evasive answer.[2] The following year there was a trial by battle at Smithfield following the appeal of treason by John Upton against John Downe, both of whom came from Faversham (Kent). Upton, says Stow, 'put upon John Downe that he and his compiers should imagine the king's death [on the] day of his coronation'. The chronicler connected the battle with the appointment of Richard, duke of York as constable of England.[3] In 1438 John Belsham attempted to appeal Sir William Wolf by petitioning the king directly. He failed, probably because he himself had been appealed and indicted of a murder and it was recognized he made his own appeal out of malice. Before the crown decided to settle the matter by inquest Sir Henry Brounflete had been appointed to discharge the office of constable and to discuss the treasons mentioned by Belsham, according to the law and custom of the court of chivalry.[4] There was every likelihood that Wolf's supposed treason had been committed inside the realm. During the year 1446 the lists at Smithfield were prepared for judicial battle on at least two occasions. In one trial John Davy, who had appealed of treason his master the London armourer William Catour, was the victor; quite possibly his task was made easier by the victim starting the duel the worse for drink.[5] In the other case Thomas FitzThomas, prior of Kilmaine, the appellant, and the earl of Ormonde, the accused, never came to actual blows because the king 'commanded they should not fight and tooke the quarrell into his hands . . . at the instance of certaine preachers and doctors of London'.[6] Seven years later on 11 May 1453 there occurred another notable appeal of treason. In the constable's court in Whitehall John Lyalton appealed Robert Norreys and the 25 May was given as the day

1 The Brut, ed. Brie, II, 368.   2 Rot. Parl., IV, 349 b.
3 Stow, p. 371; Cal. Pat. Rolls, 1429–36, p. 38.
4 Cal. Pat. Rolls, 1436–41, pp. 265, 316.
5 Procs. and Ords., VI, 55, 59; Stow, p. 385.
6 Stow, p. 385; Procs. and Ords., VI, 57, 59.

they should do battle at Smithfield.[1] The contestants petitioned the council for a monetary grant to buy arms and armour for the battle; one even asked for a pavilion.[2] It seems very likely that in fact they welcomed this mode of trial and had agreed betwcen themselves to appeal to arms.

During the Yorkist period there were very few appeals of treason in the courts of common law. The most notorious case occurred in parliament. In the session of 1478 King Edward personally accused his brother Clarence of several treasons. The duke denied all the charges and offered, if only he might obtain a hearing, to defend his cause in battle: it was to no avail since everything was rounded off by a bill of attainder.[3] In the common law courts appeals in general were giving way to bills of indictment brought forward by individuals.[4] These were first vetted by a grand jury and if they were found to be true then the matter went before a petty jury for the pronouncement of verdict. In cases of suspected treason the king and his legal advisers apparently preferred inquest by jury to the accusation of a single individual. Thus Peter Alfray, John Plummer and Sir Gervaise Clifton, who were accused by Cornelius the servant of Sir Robert Whittingham of adhering to Queen Margaret by receiving letters from her, and Sir Thomas Cook, the London mercer, who was accused of similar crimes by John Hawkins, a scrvant of Lord Wenlock, were not the subjects of appeals by men who might have been expccted to turn approver but were indicted of their treason by jury.[5] Perhaps because the crown used force to extract the confessions from Cornelius and Hawkins it dared not put them in court as approvers: yet if the required information was so difficult to obtain it seems unlikely it would have been known to the jurors. They must surely have needed prompting.

The principal judicial instrument which the English government used in the late fourteenth and the fifteenth centuries to deal with treason was the commission of oyer and terminer. It might be addressed in minor cases to the local justices of the peace but

[1] *Procs. and Ords.*, VI, 132, 136.
[2] *Ibid.*, VI, 137, 139.
[3] *Chronicle of the Abbey of Croyland*, ed. H. T. Riley (London, 1854), pp. 479–80.
[4] Lyon, *Constitutional and Legal History*, p. 637
[5] *Letters and Papers illustrative of the Wars in France*, ed. Stevenson, II, II, 789–90; P.R.O., K.B. 27/830 Rex mm. 23, 41.

when the matter was important, and treason was usually important by its very nature, then it was customary to select magnates and men high in the royal service. Sometimes as many as thirty commissioners were appointed. If the crime was not one of general insurrection but perhaps an isolated example of plotting the king's overthrow then the commission which heard the case might closely resemble the royal council or at least a section of it. This was what happened at the trial of Sir Thomas Cook in 1468 and at those of Thomas Burdet and Doctor Stacey in 1477.[1] When noblemen were involved and the issue touched on peerage then trial was usually before the lords in parliament. The commission of oyer and terminer was a surprisingly flexible instrument and in the fourteenth and fifteenth centuries, at least, the best weapon the king possessed. It was able to divide itself into small units of two, three or four commissioners and thereby to hold investigations and hear pleas in several different places at once. It was usual for one member of each group to be a justice of either bench although he was not necessarily the chairman of the session.[2] The powers of the commissioners were great: on those they found guilty they could inflict any penalty they wished. Despite or more probably because of its wide competence the oyer and terminer commission was highly regarded by the populace at large. In 1410 a petition in parliament asked for a permanent one to be set up beyond the Trent.[3] This was a complete reversal of the popular attitude at the beginning of the fourteenth century when petitions were against special commissions.[4] In the vast majority of cases oyer and terminer commissions operated under the common law. One which did not was issued to the earl of Northumberland in February 1401. He was to hear and determine divers unaccustomed

---

[1] *Letters and Papers illustrative of the Wars in France*, ed. Stevenson, II, II, 789–90; *D.K.R.: Third Report*, Appendix II, pp. 213–14. See also P.R.O., K.B. 9/13/63d for a very strong commission appointed in January 1468 to deal with treasons, felonies, murders, riots, routs and nearly every other crime including the giving of livery.
[2] *The Great Chronicle of London*, ed. A. H. Thomas and I. D. Thornley (London, 1938), p. 206, shows that the mayor of London was the chairman of the bench which tried Cook.
[3] *Rot. Parl.*, III, 624 a.
[4] See the statute 2 Edward III c. 2: 'et qe les oiers et terminers ne soient grauntees forsqe . . . devant les Justices de lun Baunk et de lautre ou les Justices errantz; et ce pur ledit et orrible trespas et de lespeciale grace le Roi, solonc forme de statut de ce ordene en temps meisme le ael; et nemie autrement': *Stat. Realm*, I, 257–8.

cases concerning the estate, fame and condition of the king's person and the dignity of the crown although they were such that by their nature they could not be discussed or determined by pretext of the office of the constable or by the common law of the realm but only by the king's hearing or commission.[1] In the last twelve or so years of the reign of Henry VI there were a number of occasions when commissions of oyer and terminer were set up with the power to take inquests themselves, not simply to deal with indictments already drawn up.[2] Either the government suspected that the local magnates and officials would labour and induce the jurors of presentment to indict their enemies or it believed there was little chance of the proper miscreants being accused at all. The supporters of Jack Cade had for the most part to be ferreted out by means of inquests, not by the more spontaneous method of presentment. The case of Eleanor Cobham, duchess of Gloucester, in 1440–1 demonstrates very well the value of the inquest. Having received information of Roger Bolingbroke's necromancy and the patronage and support afforded him by the duchess the impressive commission which had been set to enquire was able to ask the jurors what seem to have been a carefully planned series of questions. The answers left no doubt about the treasonable nature of the offence and Eleanor's guilt.[3] When it came to sentencing those who had been found guilty of treason a commission of oyer and terminer invariably had the power to impose the death penalty. This usually took the form of drawing and hanging. The commissioners were not however allowed to receive fines or ransoms without express permission. One of the few exceptions was made in August 1382 when John of Gaunt and six other justices of oyer and terminer in Yorkshire were empowered to take fines before as well as after conviction and to respite execution of judgement at their discretion.[4]

There were other special commissions which dealt with treason

---

[1] *Cal. Pat. Rolls, 1399–1401*, p. 458. The commission was similar to the one directed to the duke of Albermarle in September 1398: *Cal. Pat. Rolls, 1396–9*, p. 505.

[2] *Cal. Pat. Rolls, 1446–52*, pp. 285–320; *Cal. Pat. Rolls, 1452–61*, pp. 124, 306, 348, 440, 444, 488.

[3] For example P.R.O., K.B. 9/72/14. Stow says (p. 381) the earls of Huntingdon, Stafford, Suffolk, Northumberland, and other notables were commissioned to enquire into treasons and sorceries and that Bolingbroke and Southwell as principals and Eleanor as accessory were indicted before them.

[4] *Cal. Pat. Rolls, 1381–5*, p. 157.

150 THE LAW OF TREASON IN ENGLAND

as well as those of oyer and terminer. At a time of crisis their members might be given quite exceptional powers. A commission to William Walworth, mayor of London, and others in June 1381 commanded the recipients to settle and pacify the rebels 'juxta eorum demerita ac mandatum nostrorum, secundum legem regni nostri Anglie vel aliis viis et modis per decollaciones et membrorum mutilaciones prout melius et celerius juxta discreciones vestros vobis videbitur faciendum castigandum'.[1] At the beginning of October in the same tumultuous year Thomas of Woodstock, earl of Buckingham, and other magnates were ordered to inform themselves concerning those insurgents who had gone from Kent to Essex intending to incite rebellion, and to arrest them. They were given the power to destroy all rebels and traitors in Essex and to certify their proceedings thereon to chancery.[2] In March 1398 Edward, duke of Albemarle and Thomas, duke of Surrey were commissioned to follow and arrest all traitors to be found within the realm of England and after they had informed themselves of their treasons and convicted them by their acknowledgement or otherwise, to chastise them at their discretion according to their deserts.[3] Another commission with unfamiliar powers was appointed after the Lollard rising at St Giles's Fields in 1414. The patent rolls state that because the king had taken part against those men who had traitorously planned his death, the commissioners were to enquire the names of those not yet captured, to arrest those whom they might find guilty and imprison them until the king gave orders for their punishment.[4] A commission issued in July 1471 to the earl of Essex, Lord Mountjoy and Sir William Bourchier was unique in the fifteenth century. The recipients were directed to enquire into several insurrections in Essex, to arrest the offenders and to punish them themselves or to deliver them for punishment to the constable of England.[5] It was the last suggestion

---

[1] Réville, *Soulèvement des Travailleurs*, p. 234.
[2] *Cal. Pat. Rolls, 1381–5*, p. 79.
[3] *Cal. Pat. Rolls, 1396–9*, p. 365.
[4] *Cal. Pat. Rolls, 1413–16*, p. 177.
  A commission to Chief Justice Gascoigne and others in November 1405 was intended to supersede judicial process which had already begun. They were to inspect certain indictments of felony and treason already laid before the sheriff of Lincoln at Caistor and Spital, to address those who had been detained in prison on the charges and to deliver them according to the law and custom of the realm: *Cal. Pat. Rolls, 1405–8*, p. 148.
[5] *Cal. Pat. Rolls, 1467–77*, p. 287.

which was so exceptional as it demonstrated a new type of co-operation between the common and civil laws. Seventy years be-fore, in July 1398, it was the common law officers who executed the death sentence of the civilians. The sheriff of Leicester was ordered to receive from the mayor and bailiffs of Nottingham William Aleyn of Ashby-by-Lutterworth who had recently been 'impeached' of treason before the constable and marshal of England in the court of chivalry and had confessed.[1] The prisoner was to be drawn through the middle of Leicester to the gallows and there hanged and beheaded: his head was to be placed openly on one of the gates of the town.

In dealing with treason the role of the king's council was im-portant without being vital. Often it acted as a clearing house, directing matters which were thought to be treasonable to other judicial organs for determination. On occasion it would appoint a number of its own members to act as the requisite commission of oyer and terminer. Commissions of this type were necessary because the council was unable to inflict punishments of the severity of those awarded under the common law. It could im-prison and it could fine but it could not decree judgement of life or limb. The king therefore had little desire to stage treason trials before it, and only on a single occasion within this period may one have occurred. This was on the appeal of John of Northampton, the former mayor of London, by his secretary Thomas Usk at Reading in 1384. Initially forty eminent London citizens had been ordered by the king to enquire into recent riots and dissensions in the city. When they had done so and had made their report a number of them were ordered to appear with the mayor before King Richard and the council at Reading.[2] There Usk as an approver made accusations which approximated to treason: 'Ego Thomas Husk proditor civitatis Londoniae et totius regni scienter scripsi ea et celavi quae Johannes Northampton cum omnibus fautoribus in destructionem et enervationem civitatis praedictae proposuit ordinare'. Northampton denied the charges and offered to prove their falsity in trial by battle. This was ignored and the king found the ex-mayor to be guilty. So says the unknown Westminster chronicler.[3] Northampton claimed that the king should not have proceeded to judgement in the absence of the

[1] *Cal. Pat. Rolls, 1396–9*, p. 433.   [2] *Cal. Pat. Rolls, 1381–5*, p. 470.
[3] *Polychronicon Ranulphi Higden*, ed. J. R. Lumby (R.S., 1886), IX, 45–6.

duke of Lancaster. Richard answered he was completely competent in the matter and ordered Northampton to be hanged,
drawn and quartered. But the queen interceded and the punishment was altered to imprisonment for life. Thomas Walsingham
slightly differently says that the judge [*justiciarius*] told Northampton that he must refute the crimes imposed on him by combat or
he would be drawn, hanged and quartered under the laws of the
kingdom. He adds that to this the ex-mayor made no answer and
that perpetual imprisonment was decreed.[1] Whatever punishment
Richard wished to impose initially he had in the end to settle for
one that was within the power of the council. Despite the suggestive details of the chroniclers the chancery rolls referred to
Northampton's crimes as being not treason but misprision, the
term used when the offence was serious misbehaviour in office.[2]
As such the crimes tried before the council contrasted with the
treasons of which Northampton was accused before the steward
of the household in the Tower on 12 September 1384 under a
commission of gaol delivery.[3] Two confederates of Northampton,
Richard Norbury and John More, were also appealed by Usk.
They were brought before the king and council not at Reading but
at Westminster where the accusation was read and the indictment
declared by William Cheyne, recorder.[4] Both pleaded guilty. They
were imprisoned in the mayor of London's custody and later
committed to the Tower where like Northampton they were
arraigned before the steward of the household and other justices.

It was the task of the council in cases of suspected treason not to
arraign or try the suspect but to examine him or perhaps to declare
whether the crime was treason or not. It might also direct the
matter to another court for proper trial. Great value was placed on
its examination of treason suspects since intelligent interrogation
might bring to light all sorts of hidden danger to the crown. In
May 1401 the sheriff of Suffolk and several of the local gentry
were commissioned to summon Adam Payn, parson of Brampton

---

[1] *Historia Anglicana*, II, 116. In an undated petition to parliament which may
have originated after this episode but before Northampton was imprisoned in
Corfe castle, he claimed he had been tried by the mayor of London, who had no
right to do so: see Bird, *Turbulent London of Richard II*, p. 142.
[2] See Appendix I. The term made more frequent appearance when accroaching the royal power ceased to figure in indictments.
[3] *Cal. Close Rolls, 1381-5*, pp. 484, 465; *Cal. Pat. Rolls, 1381-5*, p. 470.
[4] *Cal. Pat. Rolls, 1381-5*, p. 470; *Cal. Close Rolls, 1381-5*, p. 478.

church, and examine him about the words spoken by Friar Hedersete concerning Richard II and the estate and person of Henry IV. If Adam was unwilling to be questioned by them he was to be brought before the king and the council.[1] In May 1453 Robert Ponynges was ordered to be arrested and brought before the council on suspicion of treason because the king had heard that he had been attempting to stir up rebellion in various parts of the kingdom.[2] Similarly in August 1462 an order was given to arrest and bring before the king and council certain men who were stirring up insurrection and circulating rumours in support of the king's enemies near Staines, Egham and Thorp.[3] There were also commissions of the same type issued in the summer of 1471 after Edward IV had regained control of the kingdom.[4] The notorious case of Eleanor Cobham offers an example of how the council operated in matters touching treason and shows the sequence of legal process which might follow. Soon after the magical practices of Roger Bolingbroke had been brought to light he was examined by the council and persuaded to confess his crimes and accuse the duchess of Gloucester. Two or three days later Eleanor was summoned before a number of important churchmen including the archbishops of Canterbury and York and the bishop of Winchester to answer to twenty-eight charges of necromancy, witchcraft, sorcery, heresy and treason with Bolingbroke acting as a witness against her. This account is given by Stow and the author of *The Brut*: there is unfortunately no official record with which to compare it. Very likely the clergy were only investigating heresy and perhaps witchcraft. They would not have been investigating treason since it was not clergyable. After the two examinations the mayor of London, the earls of Huntingdon, Stafford, Northumberland and other magnates were given power on 28 July 1441 to take inquests into the treasons, sorceries and other crimes against the king's person.[5] By means of the findings

[1] *Cal. Pat. Rolls, 1399-1401*, p. 518. The Lancastrian kings were very touchy about popular criticism of their conduct. For example in October 1419 Henry Ducheman, a haberdasher of Southwark, was sent before council for merely speaking disparagingly of Henry V's conduct at the siege of Rouen: P.R.O., E. 175/File 3/21/1 and 2.
[2] *Cal. Pat. Rolls, 1452-61*, p. 173.
[3] *Cal. Pat. Rolls, 1461-7*, p. 206.
[4] *Cal. Pat. Rolls, 1467-77*, pp. 285-8.
[5] *The Brut*, ed. Brie, II, 478-82; Stow, pp. 381-2; *The English Chronicle from 1377 to 1461*, ed. J. S. Davies (Camden Soc., 1856), p. 58.

Roger Bolingbroke and Thomas Southwell were indicted at the London Guildhall as principals and the duchess as an accessory.[1] Eventually Bolingbroke was drawn and hanged, Southwell died a fortuitous but natural death in the Tower and Eleanor abjured her heretical deeds before the clergy. She was not put on trial for treason possibly because there were no satisfactory precedents for the trial of peeresses for felony and treason.[2] The role of the council was to elicit information, particularly when important people were suspected and the matter touched the king's person. Then the best way of bringing the suspects to justice was decided.

There were at least two occasions when appeals of treason were made before the council. At the time of the Good Parliament Sir John Annesley appealed Thomas Caterton of treacherously selling the fortress of St Sauveur to the French during the previous year. Annesley had acquired the castle through his wife, who was a coheiress of Sir John Chandos, the original owner.[3] The incident played a vital part in the impeachment of Lord Latimer and other royal favourites but because of considerations of governmental policy trial by battle was not awarded until 1380: it took place before the constable of England.[4] In the other case John Cavendish of London was appealed before the council on 27 March 1395 by Richard Piryman. What type of treason was supposed to have been committed is unknown but apparently Piryman appeared before a number of lords three times for purposes of explaining his case. The only other piece of information available shows that Cavendish petitioned for the cause to be tried before the constable and not in a court of common law.[5]

The council had also to deal with matters of treason by way of declaration. This was in spite of the proviso in the statute of 1352 that crimes which seemed treason but were not obviously so

---

[1] The inquest's findings are in P.R.O., K.B. 9/72.

[2] This was remedied in the parliament of January–March 1442: see *Rot. Parl.*, v, 56 b. In future, women of high estate indicted of treason or felony were to be 'mys a respoundre et adjuggez devaunt tielx juges et peres de le roialme si come autres peres de le roialme serroient sils fuissent enditez ou empeschez de tielx tresouns ou felonies faitz ou en apres affairez et en autiel manere et fourme et en null autre'.

[3] *Historia Anglicana*, I, 431; *Cal. Fine Rolls, 1369–77*, p. 349. I have investigated the incident and its constitutional repercussions in 'Appeal and Impeachment in the Good Parliament', *Bulletin of the Institute of Historical Research*, XXXIX (1966), 35–46.

[4] *Cal. Pat. Rolls, 1377–81*, p. 485.   [5] *Procs. and Ords.*, I, 77.

should go before parliament to be declared felony or treason and then referred back to the justices. An inquest into treasons, lollardies and felonies taken in Herefordshire on 11 January 1419 revealed crimes which the jurors were not sure how to classify although they were patently close to treason: 'et de hoc petunt discressionem consilii domini regis et iusticiorum suorum'. The misdeeds amounted to being in touch with Sir John Oldcastle, at that time an outlawed traitor, without reporting the matter to the law officers of the crown. The five men who had been accused were brought into the king's bench at Easter term 1419 but released on bail until the subsequent Michaelmas. In the meantime the justices of the king's bench conferred with the council, 'et quia videtur curie et consilio predictis quod nulla prodicio in inquisicionibus predictis versus ipsos seu eorum aliquem reperitur seu continetur ad ipsos seu eorum aliquem per legem terre Anglie inde arrenandos consideratum est quod ipsi eant inde sine die'.[1] It would seem probable another case occurred in July 1442. Master Richard Wogan was imagined by the earl of Ormonde, lieutenant of Ireland, to be guilty of treason and was indicted in Ireland of the same. Apparently the jurors dared not acquit him for fear of the earl but Wogan went to England and appeared before the king for declaration of the matter: eventually he was pardoned.[2] It is most unlikely that the council was not consulted on the issue of declaration. As well as deciding whether a crime was treason or merely a lesser offence the council might settle the manner of the punishment. A commission addressed to the earl of Oxford and certain gentlemen and officials in Essex at the time of Oldcastle's rebellion ordered them to find out the names of all those Lollards who had traitorously planned the king's death, to arrest those not in custody who had been found guilty and to imprison them until the king gave orders for their punishment by the advice of council.[3] There was also an example of the council hearing a statement of innocence of treason delivered by an important nobleman. On 1 February 1453 Ralph Lord Cromwell thought it necessary to make a declaration of innocence concerning the crimes which had been imputed to him by Master Robert Colynson. This priest,

---

[1] The relevant section of the *coram rege* rolls has been published by H. G. Richardson in 'John Oldcastle in Hiding, August–October 1417', *Eng. Hist. Rev.*, LV (1940), 432–8.   [2] *Cal. Pat. Rolls, 1441–6*, p. 91.
[3] *Cal. Pat. Rolls, 1413–16*, p. 177.

who was a notorious and accomplished criminal, claimed that he had confessed the traitor John Wilkyns at Dartford when he was being carried to execution on a hurdle. He said Wilkyns had accused Cromwell of treason. Before the council the magnate utterly denied the charge, arguing that Colynson had not been with Wilkyns at the time he stated. He was allowed to produce witnesses to prove his contention.[1] There was no suggestion of arraignment: Cromwell refuted the charges of treason quite voluntarily and his denial was later embodied in an act.[2]

Fewer still than the number of treason cases which went before the council were those dealt with in chancery. The council's normal fare was cases of riot, crimes that were novel and for which there existed no accepted procedure and suits which had their origin outside the realm. From these categories a few cases of treason might be expected to emerge. In chancery on the other hand the staple diet was civil cases, particularly where surety for future good conduct was involved, and equitable cases concerning property. Only in the cases which were transferred from the king's bench out of term time and in causes involving piracy were treasons likely to occur. In fact there survives only a single clear reference to a treason case in chancery during this period. In February 1383 the sheriff of Cornwall and others were instructed to arrest John Treverthean the elder and his associates and bring them before the king in chancery to answer for certain treasons.[3] This may have been a case of suspected piracy and quite possibly it was one dealt with out of term time.

Another court which handled treason only very occasionally was that of the steward and the marshal of the household. One such session was held at Oxford castle in the presence of Henry IV on 12 January 1400. An inquest jury indicted Sir Thomas Blount, Sir Alan Buxhill, Sir Benedict Sely and several squires and henchmen of the rebel earls of levying war on the king, intending to kill him. When the accused were arraigned Blount for some reason did not put himself on the country: nonetheless he was

---

[1] *Cal. Pat. Rolls, 1452–61*, pp. 93–102.

[2] In 1451 an attempt was made by the duke of York in seeking a general reform of the administration of justice to extend the council's jurisdiction over treason. He asked for the issuing of privy seal writs in cases of suspected treason but got no satisfaction: Stow, p. 395. The government restricted the use of the writs to cases of riot: *Stat. Realm*, II, 361–2.

[3] *Cal. Pat. Rolls, 1381–5*, p. 257.

sentenced to be drawn, hanged, decapitated and quartered. The rest, save for Buxhill who was acquitted, were all found guilty by jury and suffered the same fate although their followers were merely imprisoned.[1] The household court was only used of necessity: very likely Henry was still not sure that his throne was safe. The king's own presence was a safeguard against any later charge of illegality since he could 'record' by his own word the guilt of the captive rebels if he so wished. Although he did not do so he did play a personal part in the trial by telling the court that John Ferrour had saved his life when the Tower of London was besieged in 1381. Thereby the rebel was granted his life but forfeited all his possessions. Vernon Harcourt pointed out that in 1405 following the unsuccessful northern insurrection Archbishop Scrope 'was tried before a full palace court assisted by peers of the realm'.[2] The steward of the household may have been the chairman of the court but nowhere is it stated to have been the court of the household. More likely Scrope was condemned by a commission of those peers and justices who were to hand.[3] The steward of the household but not his court was involved in the second trial of John Northampton in 1384. The ex-mayor of London was transferred to the Tower at the beginning of September 1384 where he joined his former associates, the two mercers Richard Norbury and John More. The king commissioned his judges 'ad procedendum juridice contra praedictos super tam notoriis criminibus et excessibus publice appellatos ac etiam notorie diffamatos'.[4] This may have meant the justices were to proceed to judgement by way of notoriety, that is merely to pronounce sentence, the notorious nature of the crime having worked instant conviction and removed the need for a petty jury. But it is more probable the notoriety of the offences merely served in place of an indictment.[5] That there

---

[1] P.R.O., E. 37/28. This household court was also used to try Lollard suspects and others at Leicester in 1414: P.R.O., K.B. 27/612 Rex mm. 12–17.

[2] Harcourt, *His Grace the Steward*, pp. 373–4.

[3] *Cal. Pat. Rolls, 1405–8*, p. 65. The court of the lord high steward, which I have omitted, was investigated by Vernon Harcourt. It is possible that the origins of the court are to be found not in 1399 or 1415 but in the trial, supposedly for treason, of Thomas Lord Camoys in 1406 before the earl of Kent as high steward of the realm: see E. Hall, *Chronicle*, ed. H. Ellis (London, 1809), p. 26. Camoys's crime was presumably his suspicious behaviour at the time of the French attack on the royal flotilla in the Thames.

[4] *Polychronicon Higden*, IX, 47.

[5] On this point, see Plucknett, 'Origin of Impeachment', *Trans. Roy. Hist. Soc.*, 4th ser., XXIV, 60–1.

was something exceptional about the trial is certain. Chief Justice Tresilian feared to give judgement, believing or affecting to believe the right belonged to the mayor of London.[1] Thus on 12 September Northampton, Norbury and More appeared before a commission of gaol delivery whose chairman was John de Montagu, steward of the household, and whose other members were Tresilian and Sir Robert Bealknap C.J.C.P. When examined the accused confessed the charges to be true and put themselves on the king's mercy. They were sentenced by Montagu to be drawn and hanged but the chancellor arrived with a royal pardon and the sentence was altered to imprisonment.[2] The part played by the steward of the household was novel. The previous occasion he had been employed to deal with treason he had represented the king and conducted the prosecution against the two captains Weston and Gomeniz when they were accused of traitorously surrendering their castles to the French in the second parliament of 1377.

The role of the court of chivalry in the jurisdiction of treason was a complex one. Undoubtedly its competence in matters of arms ensured its use in times of open insurrection and furthermore the constable of England or his deputy, who were the chief officers of the court, very often presided in *ad hoc* military courts. The suggestion has been made that those proceedings were under a supranational law of arms founded in the canon and civil laws.[3] It is certain that by the second half of the fourteenth century they were not according to the English common law for they were of a most summary nature. The trial was merely a matter of reading out the king's record to the effect that the accused had committed certain treasons and then judges pronounced sentence. In the later fourteenth and the fifteenth centuries the constable and his military courts were in fact continuing to provide the same sort of summary trial for treason which had operated before the accession of Edward III not only in the case of levying war against the king but for other types of treason as well.[4] The use of the king's record in trials of treason survived after 1327 only where the crime was

---

[1] *Polychronicon Higden*, IX, 47–8.
[2] *Calendar of Inquisitions Miscellaneous, 1377–88*, no. 275; *Polychronicon Higden*, IX, 48; *Cal. Close Rolls, 1381–5*, p. 465; *Cal. Pat. Rolls, 1381–5*, p. 470; Bird, *Turbulent London of Richard II*, p. 141; *Calendar of Letter Books, Letter Book H*, ed. R. R. Sharpe (London, 1907), pp. 305–7.
[3] Keen, 'Treason Trials', *Trans. Roy. Hist. Soc.*, 5th ser., XII, 85–103.
[4] See chapter 3.

one of fighting against the king in open war. The legal argument for the continuation of an obsolete practice may well have been that to oppose the king in battle was the most notorious and manifest of crimes since there was bound to be a very large number of witnesses. Therefore indictment was not required. This idea was probably supported by the belief that when the king was present in person with his army or without it for that matter his inherent ability to record a crime did away with the need for an extended trial and allowed summary conviction.[1]

In the reigns of Edward I and Edward II the constable was only one amongst many justices who were commissioned for dealing with traitors taken in open insurrection. The first time he presided in a trial where conviction was by the king's record was at Tutbury on 13 March 1322 when the victim was Roger Damory.[2] When civil strife broke out again, in the reign of Henry IV, the constable's authority was paramount. Quite possibly this was because of the development of the jurisdiction of the court of chivalry during the war with France. Thus in 1406 proceedings were started against the rebellious earl of Northumberland and Thomas, Lord Bardolf, not in the common law courts but in the court of chivalry: articles of treason were laid against them and their confederates according to the law and custom of arms but nothing further could be done since the accused were at large in the north.[3] Later the case was transferred to parliament. More successful were the accusations made against Richard II's advisers Scrope, Green and Bussy in a court which claimed to be that of the constable, at Bristol in 1399. They were convicted 'de proditione et mala gubernatione regis et regni' by the constable and the marshal at Bolingbroke's camp.[4] Much clearer from the legal viewpoint is the evidence concerning the trial of Sir Henry Boynton at Berwick on 13 July 1405. Boynton, who had waged open war against the king, was tried in a session of the court of chivalry presided over by John of Bedford, constable of England. There was no indictment or appeal, merely the rehearsal of his crimes and his

---

[1] This argument I have developed in chapter 7.
[2] See chapter 3; Harcourt, *His Grace the Steward*, pp. 399–400, prints the trial from P.R.O., K.B. 27/259 Rex m. 34.   [3] *Rot. Parl.*, III, 604–7.
[4] *Historia Vitae et Regni Ricardi Secundi*, ed. T. Hearne (Oxford, 1729), p. 153: 'primo quidem arrestati sunt, deinde in crastino coram judicibus viz Constabulario et Marescallo judicio sistuntur. Et de proditione et mala gubernatione Regis et Regni convicti, dampnati et decollati'.

conviction of notorious treason on the king's record 'selon les leys et usages darmes de la Court de Chevalerie en Angleterre'. With these and other similar trials in mind it has been argued that the use of the constable's jurisdiction in the reign of Edward IV was not new but had been in operation more than fifty years before.[1] Stubbs on the other hand believed the powers which were given to John Tiptoft, earl of Worcester as constable were unparalleled since they involved 'the extension of the jurisdiction of the high constable of England to cases of high treason'.[2] In the matter of novelty he was incorrect and the examples of appeal of treason which came before the constable in the first half of the fifteenth century are additional proof of his error. Stubbs also emphasized the ability of Tiptoft to hear, examine and conclude all cases of treason summarily, plainly, and without noise and show of judgement on simple inspection of fact, but this was a normal rubric of the canon and civil law and was used frequently in commissions of ecclesiastical jurisdiction. His theory that Tiptoft's powers as constable were a novel usurpation Stubbs based largely on the letters patent of August 1467 which conferred the office of constable on Earl Rivers for life with remainder to his son for his life.[3] At a later date Vernon Harcourt came to the same conclusion.[4] The power awarded they condemned as fraudulent and completely without precedent despite the letters purporting to be a recital of a similar grant to Tiptoft in 1462.[5] The earlier letters were much more concise but in no way contradictory. The recital of 1467 rather than being a deceitful novelty gives the appearance of a realistic exposition of the powers which by that time were inherent in the constable's office. Possibly because of the opposition of the common law courts these had hitherto not been set down with precision but now there was to be a remedy. Tiptoft's own activities probably infused new life into an institution which for fifty years had lacked the opportunity of dealing with rebels taken in battle even if there had been plenty of lesser cases. Edward IV, who was persistently harried by insurrection, can have had little doubt about the value of a court which did away with the necessity of prompting or labouring juries. By granting the letters patent of

[1] Keen, 'Treason Trials', *Trans. Roy. Hist. Soc.*, 5th ser., XII, 85–6.
[2] Stubbs, *Constitutional History of England*, III, 289–90.
[3] *Ibid.*
[4] Harcourt, *His Grace the Steward*, p. 392. The letters patent are printed pp. 407–11.   [5] *Ibid.*, p. 407.

1467 he was making sure there should be no doubt as to the proper and legal nature of the constable's judicial powers. The spurious antiquarianism by way of introduction, while in no way invalidating the genuine nature of the constable's jurisdiction, is proof of the crown's desire to ensure its future operation.

If there was any novelty in the powers exercised by the constable in the reign of Edward IV it did not lie in his dealing with the treason of levying war within the realm but with certain treasonable crimes which hitherto had always been dealt with at common law. These were offences which involved imagining the king's destruction and death, perhaps by corresponding with his enemies.[1] The earl of Oxford, De Vere his son and Sir Thomas Tudenham were arrested in February 1462 for such an offence and tried by Tiptoft.[2] Investigation, however, reveals that the accused had probably committed not one but three crimes.[3] They had conspired to receive a Lancastrian army under the duke of Somerset and were guilty of receiving letters from Margaret of Anjou. They intended also, when travelling north with King Edward and his army, to try to murder him.[4] The last crime may well have been construed as coming within the military jurisdiction of the constable since the plotters had joined the royal banner. Amongst those learned in the law some doubts may have been entertained about the legality of this trial. The chronicler John Warkworth commented that the prisoners were tried according to the law of Padua, apparently feeling that Tiptoft had been persuaded by his foreign studies into extending the constable's powers.[5] Very likely he was not failing to recognize a trial under the law of arms but rather taking note of an exceptional one. There was no such critical comment made about the trial of Richard Steres, a London skinner, in 1468 yet the crime committed was similar to one of those attributed to Oxford and his friends. Steres had been instrumental in

---

[1] *Gregory's Chronicle*, ed. J. Gairdner (Camden Soc., 1876), p. 218.

[2] *Letters and Papers illustrative of the Wars in France*, ed. Stevenson, II, II, 779.

[3] *Three Fifteenth Century Chronicles*, ed. J. Gairdner (Camden Soc., 1880), p. 175.

[4] *Calendar of Milanese Papers, 1385–1618*, pp. 106–7.

[5] John Warkworth, *A Chronicle of the First Thirteen Years of the Reign of King Edward the Fourth*, ed. J. O. Halliwell (Camden Soc., 1839), p. 5. Warkworth's criticism of Tiptoft for impaling a number of Lancastrians taken aboard ship at Southampton in 1470 as being 'contrarye to the lawe of the londe' has less weight. Simon Redyng was impaled in 1336 as an ally of Hugh Despenser: *Chronicles of Edward I and Edward II*, I, 320.

keeping a number of Lancastrians in communication with Queen Margaret. It was presumably on this account that he was tried before the constable and sentenced to death.[1] Although the details of the case are not sufficiently clear for it to be argued conclusively that the court of chivalry had assumed a new competence, a strong suspicion must remain.[2]

Even after Tiptoft's death the court of chivalry continued to play an important role in the suppression of insurrection. There were several indications of the crown's interest and reliance. In July 1471 a commission headed by the earl of Essex was instructed, as we have seen, to enquire into several insurrections in Essex, to arrest offenders and to punish them or deliver them for punishment to the constable of England.[3] The only previous example of referring traitors for punishment from one law to another had occurred in the reign of Richard II and was in the reverse direction. In 1398 the court of chivalry had feared to inflict sentence of blood itself:[4] seventy years later its presiding judge and his officers were regarded as qualified supervisors of executions. At the end of the reign of Edward IV, in October 1482, the government appointed during pleasure the king's servant Robert Rydon to the office of the king's promoter of all causes civil and criminal or concerning crimes of lese-majesty before the king's judges of the constableship and admiralty of England. Rydon was not the first to hold this position since a reference was made to his having all the accustomed profits of office as well as 20 marks a year from the receipt of the exchequer.[5] An enrolment dated 10 December 1483 shows the office was given to Master William Biller, notary, at about that time.[6] In contrast with Rydon, Biller's appointment was for life. In November 1482 the office of constable was put into commission when the occupant Richard, duke of Gloucester, was about to set out for Scotland.[7] A different solution was tried in

---

[1] *Cal. Pat. Rolls, 1467–77*, p. 123.
[2] What form of trial Tiptoft himself suffered is not known. He was 'brought to London at parliament arrestede and condemned to death by Sir John Vere, earle of Oxford and beheaded at the Tower-hill and after buried at the Blacke-Friers': Stow, p. 423. According to one London chronicle Tiptoft was 'Rayned at Westmynster in the Whytehalle and there Endited of treason': *Chronicles of London*, p. 182. Warkworth says he was 'juged be suche lawe as he dyde to other menne': *Chronicle*, p. 13.
[3] *Cal. Pat. Rolls, 1467–77*, p. 287.   [4] *Cal. Pat. Rolls, 1396–9*, p. 433.
[5] *Cal Pat. Rolls, 1476–85*, p. 343.   [6] *Ibid.* p. 411.
[7] *Foedera*, ed. Rymer (original edn.), XII, 169.

October 1483 when the duke of Buckingham, the next holder of the office, turned traitor himself. Instead of appointing as in the previous year three knights and four civilians as commissioners, Sir Robert Assheton was made vice-constable for the time being in order to proceed against certain persons guilty of lese-majesty.[1] One of these was Buckingham.

There were other courts with jurisdiction over matters pertaining to arms in addition to the court of chivalry presided over by the constable of England and military courts convened on campaigns. The evidence is not extensive but it is quite clear. Sir John Annesley, who at the time of the Good Parliament had appealed Thomas Caterton of treacherously selling the castle of St Sauveur to the French, was unable to get any satisfaction for four years. Walsingham gives the information that men who feared similar charges against themselves managed to stop the appeal on the grounds that it was against the law of the land for 'aliquem de ipso regno pro ulla causa tali lege (armorum) in regno pugnare'. Eventually, so he says, 'coactis juridicis et senioribus militibus regionis diffinitum est pro causa extrinseca, sicuti pro praesenti causa, quae non infra regni limites orta est e pro possessione rerum transmarinarum, bene licere quemquam duello confligere'.[2] Here is a reference to a court of chivalry with local authority existing at a time of peace. The assessors, jurors or judges were senior knights and they were apparently selected from a single region. Since Annesley and Caterton had the bulk of their lands in Nottinghamshire and Yorkshire respectively, it is possible that the area in question was England north of the Trent. The other piece of evidence suggests in contrast a county community of chivalry keen to enforce a proper standard of behaviour in military matters on its members. On 30 April 1450 the duke of Suffolk 'postquam coram militibus et generosis patriae Suffolchiae, recipiendo sacramentum Corporis Christi, juravit excusandum se fore immunem de proditionibus sibi impositis et de venditione Normanniae . . .'[3] Why Suffolk should feel obliged to purge himself in this manner is not easily explained unless it was to secure the loyalty of his well-wishers and feed men whilst he was in exile.

[1] *Cal. Pat. Rolls, 1476–85*, p. 368.   [2] *Historia Anglicana*, I, 431.
[3] *Letters and Papers illustrative of the Wars in France*, ed. Stevenson, II, II, 767. A chivalric court of sorts met at the end of April 1398 at Windsor. The dukes of Hereford and Norfolk appeared before an assembly of English chivalry and battle was technically joined between them: *Rot. Parl.* III, 383 a.

There were a number of occasions when suspected traitors, either before or after they were arraigned, were taken into the king's presence. Usually the purpose was examination. In 1402 Henry IV cross-questioned a Franciscan lay brother from Aylesbury about his belief that Richard II still lived and about his loyalty to that monarch. Very likely only when Henry was satisfied was the friar taken before the justices at Westminster for trial.[1] In June 1405 when the revolt in the north had failed the king spoke personally to Archbishop Scrope, one of the leaders. He pointed out to him that he was responsible for the plight of the citizens of York and he called him a traitor.[2] The conspirators in the Southampton plot in 1415, when their secret had been revealed by the earl of March, were brought before the king and confessed to him. The next day, according to Stow, they were arraigned in the king's presence.[3] Edward IV supervised the suppression of treason very closely. In 1461 Sir Baldwin Fulford, who had been captured while fleeing to Brittany, was brought before him before being put on trial.[4] In August 1474 the duke of Clarence, the sheriff of Cornwall and a number of knights and esquires were instructed to proclaim in every town in Cornwall the acts of parliament by which Henry Bodrugan esquire had been attainted of treasons, felonies and riots, to arrest him and his confederates and bring them before the king in person without bail or mainprise.[5] In a more sinister vein was the interview in 1468 between King Edward and Cornelius 'Sutor', the servant of Sir Robert Whittingham. This man was arrested by Sir Richard Wydvile in London and presented to the king at Stratford Langthorne on suspicion of carrying letters from Queen Margaret to various Lancastrian sympathizers in England. Three days later he was committed to the Tower, put to torture and persuaded to incriminate those whom he knew were communicating illegally.[6] Sometimes the king was present in court in person during a treason trial. Henry IV attended the session at Oxford castle on 12 January 1400 when Blount, Buxhill, Sely and other participants in the recent rebellion were arraigned and tried.[7] The trial of Sir

---

[1] *Eulogium Historiarum*, III, 390.
[2] *Historians of the Church of York*, ed. J. Raine (R.S., 1894), III, 290.
[3] Stow, p. 346.
[4] C. L. Scofield, *The Life and Reign of Edward IV* (London, 1923), I, 200.
[5] *Cal. Pat. Rolls, 1467-77*, p. 491.
[6] *Letters and Papers illustrative of the Wars in France*, ed. Stevenson, II, II, 789.   [7] P.R.O., E. 37/28.

Thomas Hungerford and Henry Courtenay at Salisbury was delayed from November 1468 to January 1469 because Edward IV wished to be present when the verdict was pronounced.[1] Presumably both monarchs believed that in this way the jurors would feel obliged to find the accused men guilty.

Although the king might attend treason trials in the courts of common law he did not dare accuse the suspects himself once the session had begun. The practice of the king recording a man's guilt in a writ to the justices ceased in the early fourteenth century. In other courts the device was much longer lived. It became a part of many attainder acts, especially those directed against men who stood against the king in open battle or figured in trials under the law of arms held before the constable or his deputies. In another case the king in person accused his brother of treason before parliament and the conviction was set down in an act.[2] At common law if in a case of felony the king wished to support the accusations of the jury or answer the response of the accused he had to use his attorney. The office of king's attorney had its origins in the thirteenth century and although during the next hundred years the occupant could be found at work in the king's bench prosecuting and defending the king's business when lesser crimes were involved, there is no evidence of him suing in a case of high treason. In the fifteenth century in his capacity as king's coroner in the king's bench he certainly heard appeals of treason but there is only a single example before 1485 of his acting as public prosecutor against suspected traitors. In the session before Richard, duke of Gloucester and other justices at Salisbury in January 1469 Sir Thomas Hungerford and Henry Courtenay were indicted of having conspired to aid Queen Margaret and her son Edward to enter the kingdom and depose Edward IV. The two accused were brought to the bar of the court by the sheriff of Wiltshire. Hungerford said he was not guilty and put himself on the country: Courtenay pleaded a pardon and also put himself on the country. At this point according to the record Henry Sotehill, who sued for the king, said they were guilty. Thereupon a jury was summoned before the justices and it found the accused guilty: sentence followed.[3]

Most cases involving high treason were dealt with in sessions held by commissioners of oyer and terminer. Only rarely were

---

[1] Scofield, *Reign of Edward IV*, I, 482.   [2] Above, p. 147; below, p. 170.
[3] *Cal. Pat. Rolls, 1485-94*, p. 149.

they handled from the outset by the king's bench although when as sometimes happened those who were accused could not be got before a lesser court and outlawry resulted, the criminal might on capture be taken into the king's bench for sentence: he might on the other hand present a pardon there. Very probably the actual trial process in these courts will never be known in its entirety, yet the details which have survived are instructive. On the first occasion the accused was brought into court the indictment was read out to him. In the fifteenth century it was in English. It seems certain that the prisoner was not given a copy of the indictment in writing nor was he allowed to retain counsel, give evidence or call witnesses. Unless fortuitously skilled in the law he was usually unable to challenge the indictment and thereby profit from the rigid rules concerning its form and wording.[1] Certainly the plea rolls offer negligible evidence of action on these lines. Those who were accused of treason or felony were allowed to challenge up to thirty-five petty jurors and Fortescue implies they would commonly do so.[2] There is little evidence in the plea rolls that the accused made any statement in court at all except to enter a plea of guilty or not guilty or perhaps to plead his clergy. His legal rights apparently extended merely to the making of this response to the charges which were put to him. It was inevitable since the laws of evidence were so rudimentary that a strong emphasis should be laid on the confessions of accomplices. The judges were not passive hearers of evidence but as in all criminal cases active protagonists for the crown. They seem to have tried to cajole the accused into admitting his guilt or to have browbeaten him for the same reason. They put questions so as to elicit the part played by accomplices and to discover the motives, although no doubt in treason cases these had usually been discovered by prior examination. On occasion, though infrequently, witnesses testified on the king's behalf. The cases in question often concerned the possession and illicit use of royal seals.

The petty juries which were summoned to these treason trials quite often found their task distasteful. The jury which tried Kirkby and Algor for the murder of the Genoese ambassador John Imperial swore Kirkby committed the deed while defending him-

---

[1] Holdsworth, *History of English Law*, III, 610–20.
[2] J. Fortescue, *De Laudibus Legum Anglie*, ed. S. B. Chrimes (Cambridge, 1942), p. 65.

self. The justices, an impressive array comprising Cavendish, Bealknap, Tresilian, Skipwith and Fulthorp, asked them how this could be. They said they were wholly ignorant. Questioned further they stubbornly offered the same answer. Kirkby was eventually sentenced to be drawn and hanged but only because his associate in the crime turned approver.[1] In a trial at Westminster in 1402 a number of friars who were involved in the affair of the false Richard were told by the judge they should put themselves on the king's mercy. Instead they asked for trial by jury. No Londoners or men of Holborn wanted to serve and so the jurors were drawn from Islington and Highgate. The jury found the accused guilty but after the execution its members came weeping to those friars who were collecting the corpses. They explained that unless they returned a verdict of guilty they would have been put to death themselves.[2] Quite obviously the crown did not hesitate from putting pressure on petty juries as well as juries of indictment. In September 1384 when John Northampton, Richard Norbury and John More were produced for trial before Montagu, Tresilian and Bealknap they confessed all the charges against them were true and put themselves completely on the king's grace: 'et hoc ideo fecerunt quia propter subornationem in hominibus patriae confidere non audebant'.[3] The device operated in 1381 of asking a second and a third jury to acknowledge the truth of the charges brought by a jury of presentment and then using the second jury as a petty jury is further evidence and has already been mentioned.[4] Although the justices of the bench permitted these practices and perhaps even helped to devise them, there were two occasions at least when they found the king's determination to secure conviction unpalatable. In 1405 William Gascoigne, the chief justice of the king's bench, refused to adjudge the archbishop of York to death for treason because he was a prelate, and left the court. Two other judges had to be commissioned for the task.[5] Another example of judicial dissatisfaction supposedly occurred in the reign of Edward IV. According to the chronicler Stow, when

---

[1] P.R.O., K.B. 27/476 Rex m. 31d; P.R.O., C. 47/68/12/358. There is evidence to suggest that when in the fourteenth century petty juries acquitted the accused they might be forced to say who had in fact done the deed: *Year Books, Liver des Assises*, 37 Edward III pl. 13.

[2] *Eulogium Historiarum*, III, 392–3.   [3] *Polychronicon Higden*, IX, 48.

[4] *Historia Anglicana*, II, 35–6; above, pp. 139–40.

[5] *Historians of the Church of York*, III, 290.

Sir Thomas Cook was accused in the king's bench in 1468 of sheltering Lancastrian messengers and of promising to raise funds for Queen Margaret Chief Justice Markham determined against the king's pleasure that the offence was not treason but misprision 'the which was no desert of death but to be fined'.[1] For this decision it was said the earl Rivers and his wife, who were anxious to procure Cook's fall, saw to it that the judge lost office. Certainly he had been replaced by June 1471.[2]

Procedure in treason trials held in parliament during this period has been a persistent problem for historians. If it was not just a matter of declaring an offence as treason under the act of 1352 then process was not according to the common law entirely nor yet a copy of the civil law, although some use was made of both. In the Merciless Parliament which met in February 1388 and where appeals of treason made against five royal favourites were heard, it was apparently decided that judicially at least parliament did not need to follow the rules of other laws but should act according to its own procedures.[3] Quite possibly these were derived from earlier trials in parliament. At the outset of the reign of Richard II procedure was uncertain. When in 1376 he was brought to answer in parliament to certain charges of a seditious nature Lord Latimer was probably not allowed counsel to assist his pleadings nor was he given the charges in writing: but he was allowed time to consider his answer. In 1377 Weston and Gomeniz, who had surrendered the fortresses in their charge to the French under suspicious circumstances, were arraigned as for treason and had to answer orally

---

[1] Stow, p. 420.

[2] *The Great Chronicle of London*, p. 207.

[3] The lords of parliament declared that in cases of so high a crime as was mentioned in the appeal, one which touched the king's person and the realm and some of whose alleged perpetrators were peers, the matter must be tried in parliament and by the procedure of parliament, not by civil or common law or by the law of any inferior court: *Rot. Parl.*, III, 236. How great an influence on parliamentary trial procedures was had by the common law is still uncertain. Miss Clarke argued that the appeals of treason of 1388 were completely different from appeals of treason at common law but offered no convincing evidence in support: Clarke, *Fourteenth Century Studies*, pp. 134–5. Stephens, Wilkinson, and Plucknett have each implied that in 1388 appeal of treason in parliament was merely an extension of common law processes but their evidence is not compelling either. Very likely trial procedure in parliament at this time was not yet fixed although parliament was probably already recognized as the proper tribunal for state trials. By 1388 there existed a number of precedents about trial proceedings: these, under discussion, simply crystallized into 'the law and course of parliament' and assumed an independent existence.

forthwith without the benefit of legal advice.[1] When Sir Ralph Ferrers was brought into parliament in 1381 to explain certain letters sealed with his seal which were addressed to the French king, it was decreed that counsel was not to be permitted in cases of treason.[2] In contrast with common law procedure Weston and Gomeniz were not given the opportunity to enter a plea of guilty or not guilty: the charges were read out and they were asked to offer any defence they could. This had been the method used when Latimer and Lyons were tried in 1376 and was to reoccur in the trials of Bishop Despenser in 1383 and the earl of Suffolk in 1386. Unlike Weston and Gomeniz the crimes of these men were not construed as treason however. In 1388 the procedure was changed for when Sir Nicholas Brembre had been accused of treason he was asked how he would plead.[3] It was the Lords Appellant also who reintroduced into the *Lex parliamenti* the concept of conviction in absence, that is by default.[4] This was more a process of the civil law than the common law and it was a factor in the rise of attainder. The trial of Brembre, which offered the accused a chance to plead, deprived him on the other hand of the right to respond, that is to refute the allegations of treason laid against him. In 1397 John of Gaunt, lord high steward for the trial of Gloucester, Warwick and Arundel, apparently taunted Arundel with denying the victims of 1388 a hearing.[5] Since Brembre was the only one of the five favourites who had been accused to appear in parliament at the time of the trial the reference was probably to him. Public opinion in favour of allowing suspect traitors to answer was strong. In the parliament of 1399 the commons petitioned that anyone who was impeached or accused in parliament or any other court should be allowed a defence and not be condemned unheard. They were unsuccessful, for Henry IV found it politic not to accede to the request.[6] Early in its history the act of attainder, if it was directed against men who were alive but at large, was usually accompanied by a statement to the effect that it should not operate if the accused

---

[1] *Anonimalle Chronicle*, ed. V. H. Galbraith (Manchester, 1926), p. 93; *Rot. Parl.*, III, 10–11.

[2] *Rot. Parl.*, III, 91–2,

[3] *Polychronicon Higden*, IX, 149.

[4] *Rot. Parl.*, III, 236–7.

[5] *Eulogium Historiarum*, III, 374. Gaunt's words were: 'Quia parliamentum te accusavit, meruisti damnari sine responsione secundum legem tuam'.

[6] *Rot. Parl.*, III, 442.

presented himself in the king's court within a certain period.[1] But in 1459 the Yorkist leaders were allowed no opportunity to come and explain their conduct and were condemned unheard. This caused a considerable outcry but it was to no avail and the practice became a common one.[2]

Appeal of treason in parliament disappeared at the beginning of the fifteenth century and the other mode of trial which attainder superseded, impeachment, occurred for the last time for 171 years in 1450. The victim was the duke of Suffolk. He was treated much better than those who had stood trial in parliament in the later years of the fourteenth century. He was given a copy of the commons' charges against him and allowed time to compile his reply. When he had explained his conduct he ingeniously put himself or was allowed to put himself on the king's mercy, without departing from his answers. He refused to put himself on his peerage and thereby escaped with a sentence of exile.[3] There can be little doubt that the procedure of the trial was fashioned to Suffolk's benefit and that the king's lawyers applied themselves not to his prosecution but to secure an acquittal or the next best thing. His opponents failed because they could not carry all the lords with them and therefore the pressure on the king was not so great he had to forsake his supporter completely. Nearly thirty years later there occurred what in the matter of legal procedure was the most mysterious parliamentary trial of the later middle ages. The case concerned the treason of George, duke of Clarence and started when he appeared before King Edward, his brother, in the royal palace at Westminster to answer to certain charges, 'upon which in the presence of the Mayor and aldermen of the city of London the king began with his own lips . . . to inveigh against the conduct of the . . . duke'. Clarence was placed in custody and later appeared for trial in the parliamentary session of 1478.[4] He does not seem to have been allowed counsel or given time to answer. The charges were made orally by the king himself, a mode of accusation which was

---

[1] For example see *Cal. Close Rolls, 1392–6*, p. 294 (Sir Thomas Talbot), *Rot. Parl.*, III, 351 b, 374, 380–1 (Sir Thomas Mortimer), *ibid.*, III, 604–7 (the earl of Northumberland and Lord Bardolf), *ibid.*, IV, 497 a (William Pulle of Wirral), *ibid.*, V, 14 b, 15, 17, 18 a (Lewis Leyson of Glamorgan and Philip Eggerton of Spondesley).
[2] *Rot. Parl.*, V, 346–9; *English Chronicle*, ed. Davies, p. 83.
[3] *Rot. Parl.*, V, 176–83.
[4] *Chronicle of the Abbey of Croyland*, p. 479.

entirely novel but which had the attribute of being irrefutable since from the time of Edward I it had been a maxim of the lawyers that the king's word, as long as it was based on his own personal knowledge of the fact, was the most perfect of records.[1] Having pointed out that 'no one said anything against the duke but the king' the chronicler provocatively adds that 'some parties were introduced however as to whom it was greatly doubted by many, whether they filled the office of accusers rather, or of witnesses: these two offices not being exactly suited to the same person in the same cause'.[2] It is very likely that they were in fact witnesses and that the intention was to stop the wager of battle which Clarence made. The duke was able to deny the accusations even if he was unable to say much more. Almost certainly he was never given the charges in writing since the crimes imputed to him at the palace of Westminster involved embracery and were different from the charges of treason which were produced in parliament.[3] Whether it was parliament as a whole or perhaps the lords by themselves who gave judgement on his guilt is not known. The Croyland chronicler states that parliament was of the opinion that the informations it had heard were established and therefore passed sentence. This was formally pronounced by the duke of Buckingham, who had been appointed steward of England for the occasion just as Richard, earl of Warwick was in December 1461 for the act of attainder against Henry VI.[4]

A trial of a different sort was that of Sir John Oldcastle, in the parliament which met in November 1417. Oldcastle had originally

[1] *Cal. Chanc. Rolls, 1277–1326*, pp. 343–4; Plucknett, 'Origin of Impeachment', *Trans. Roy. Hist. Soc.*, 4th ser. XXIV, 56. See above, p. 42, n. 1.

[2] *Chronicle of the Abbey of Croyland*, p. 479.

[3] *Ibid.*, p. 480. Clarence, who was outraged by the execution of Stacey and Burdet, entered the council chamber when King Edward was at Windsor and affirmed their innocence. The king, on his return, accused his brother of violating the laws of the kingdom by menacing judges and jurors, that is to say of the crime of embracery. The question is whether the reference was to Clarence's attempt to reopen the Stacey–Burdet case in council or to the way the duke had secured the condemnation and death of Ankarette Twynho at Warwick the previous year for her supposed poisoning of his wife: see *Cal. Pat. Rolls, 1476–85*, p. 72. The charges of treason which were made against Clarence in parliament are in *Rot. Parl.*, VI, 193–5.

[4] *Cal. Pat. Rolls, 1461–7*, pp. 63, 89, 451. Peerage treason cases and the jurisdiction of the steward of England I have not treated as a separate field. This was done by Vernon Harcourt in his excellent monograph *His Grace the Steward*. The use of the steward of England as president of the court of parliament had its origins in 1397 when Gaunt took the office: *Rot. Parl.*, III, 377 a.

been indicted for treason on 10 January 1414 before a commission of oyer and terminer with competence in London and Middlesex, and was subsequently outlawed on 7 June 1414.[1] Oldcastle had inherited through his wife the title Lord Cobham and although it had been taken from him while he was in hiding it was apparently decided on his capture to bring him before parliament to answer to his former peers. When he appeared the original indictment was read out and he was asked what excuses he could offer to save himself from execution. Instead of answering directly he took the opportunity to preach of the mercies of God, arguing that vengeance was His alone. 'The chiefe Justice' we are told 'admonished the Regent not to suffer the time so vatnely in molesting the nobles of the Realme' and so Bedford ordered the prisoner to answer properly the matter laid to his charge. Oldcastle quite regardless continued to speak of other things until warned a second time, when he answered that the lords could not judge him as long as his liege lord King Richard was alive in Scotland.[2] This was considered to be open admission of his guilt and he was sentenced to be drawn, hanged and burned hanging. There was no thought of an act of attainder. He was allowed to answer but to charges made orally and he was not permitted legal counsel. What had happened was that Oldcastle was treated as any Lollard traitor would have been when captured as an outlaw, but had been brought before his peers in parliament rather than put to answer in the king's bench. Another odd sort of legal process and one which cannot properly be called a trial occurred in the parliament of 1424. Sir John Mortimer, who had been imprisoned on suspicion of treason, escaped from the Tower of London for a second time, and was recaptured and then indicted before a commission of oyer and terminer at the London Guildhall. The record was sent *coram ipso Rege in Cancellaria* and on the following day Mortimer was brought before the duke of Gloucester, the lords temporal and the commons in parliament and the indictment was read out to him. The commons told the duke and the lords they wished to affirm it as the truth, acting so it seems as a grand jury finding a true bill. The duke on the advice of the lords and at the request of the commonalty then ordained it so and pronounced sentence. Mortimer was given no chance to reply to the charge and was not

---

[1] *Cal. Pat. Rolls, 1422–9*, p. 547; *Rot. Parl.*, IV, 108, 109.
[2] Stow, p. 349; *Cal. Pat. Rolls, 1422–9*, p. 547.

allowed to make a plea.[1] The combination of indictment in a common law court and affirmation of the indictment in parliament was unique, being apparently devised to avoid having recourse to a petty jury.

When a man had been duly found guilty of high treason the punishment to which he was sentenced was for the king to decide. So also was whether he should be pardoned. Jack Cade was quite wrong in thinking that a pardon for treason, in order to be effective, must be issued under the authority of parliament, although it was true that until the reign of Henry VII an act of attainder could only be completely annulled by a subsequent parliamentary act.[2] When the crown commissioned its officers to suppress insurrection the ability to grant pardon to the rebels was given but rarely. Most often it was conceded at a time of crisis to a man whose influence in the realm was very great. In August 1382 John of Gaunt was given a commission of oyer and terminer in Yorkshire to receive fines and ransoms in respect of treasons and insurrections before as well as after conviction. The duke and his fellow commissioners were empowered to respite execution of judgement at their discretion and all the people they fined were to receive charters of pardon under the seal of Lancaster.[3] In the reign of Edward IV when insurrection was endemic, power to pardon was only granted infrequently and might not be used on convicted traitors. One of those who was given such authority was Sir Ralph Percy. In March 1463 he was allowed to receive into the king's grace repentant rebels who had not yet been attainted and to grant their

---

[1] *Year Books of Henry VI, 1 Henry VI*, pp. xxiv–xxvii; *Rot. Parl.*, IV, 202 a. Mortimer's imprisonment, as has been pointed out above, had been particularly grievous. A petty jury, conceivably, might have been swayed by this.

[2] Stow, p. 392. Letters patent of pardon or pardons under the great seal usually 'enabled' men at law without restoring their livelihood; basically they resurrected the recipients from legal death and made them capable of participating in contracts: see *Rot. Parl.*, VI, 230 b. Lander has suggested that to be sure of getting back his lands a man in the fifteenth century needed an act of parliament reversing his conviction: J. R. Lander, 'Attainder and Forfeiture, 1453 to 1509', *Historical Journal*, IV (1961), 123. A pardon even if it claimed to annul a particular act of attainder was usually insufficient to restore livelihood unless accompanied by a grant of the lands which the accused had possessed previously: see for example *Cal. Pat. Rolls, 1461–7*, p. 269. A king who was attainted by parliament did not need, if he managed to gain the throne once more, to annul the offending act. This was decided at the outset of Henry VII's reign using the readeption of Henry VI as the precedent: *Year Books*, 1 Henry VII Mich. pl. 5.

[3] *Cal. Pat. Rolls, 1381–5*, p. 157.

lives or licence to leave the realm to such as had been attainted.[1] Another man entrusted with this power was Lord Herbert. He was permitted by letters under the privy seal dated 13 May 1472 'to resceyve, accept and admytte to his grace and pardone all such persones in Wales as shuld be thought to me the said William acceptable, taking of theym an othe to be from thensforward true Liegemen to oure said Sovereigne Lord'.[2] In commissioning magnates to suppress rebellion the crown on occasion found it necessary specifically to retain for itself all power to grant grace and pardon. This was done for example by Henry VI and his advisers in 1460 when the duke of York was given authority to put down insurrection throughout the realm.[3] The reason for the reservation must have been the anomalous constitutional and political position of the duke, rather than the common desire to supervise closely the setting and collecting of fines.

In the mid-fourteenth century there was a popular feeling that there should be no pardon for treason at all. A petition was put forward in the parliament of 1347 to this effect and it was requested that if any had been granted they should be disallowed.[4] This attitude was changed little by the insurrections and state trials in the last quarter of the century. In the first parliament of 1390 the crown was asked to limit the awarding of pardon for murder done by waylaying, assault or of malice prepense, for rape or for treason.[5] In its overall effect the statute which resulted was of little avail and by the mid-fifteenth century pardons were being dispensed with great liberality. One of the few exceptions was the crime of treason: traitors never found them easy to obtain. There was some legislation to restrict royal liberality in this respect. In the parliament of 1453–4 it was enacted that no pardon for treason should be allowed to any offender under the statute of 29 Henry VI against breakers of truces and safe conducts (a confirmation of the act 2 Henry V st. 1, c. 6), and in the first parliament of Edward IV (1461) it was ordained that no pardon for treason should be extended to a rebel a second time.[6] Pardon for treason was most easily

---

[1] *Cal. Pat. Rolls, 1461–7*, p. 262.
[2] *Rot. Parl.*, VI, 30 b.   [3] *Ibid.*, V, 383 a.
[4] *Ibid.*, II, 167. An interesting pardon of treason was granted to the earl of Desmond in 1349. It was conditional on his bearing himself faithfully in the future. If he did not and was convicted of other treasons the deeds which had been forgiven were also to be taken into account: *Cal. Pat. Rolls, 1348–50*, p. 434.
[5] *Ibid.*, III, 268 a.   [6] *Ibid.*, V, 224–5; *ibid.*, V, 488 a.

obtained when, on rare occasions, the crown decided to pardon all criminals including rebels at once. This was done by Henry IV in the parliaments of 1399 and January 1404.[1] Once a king had given a pardon he usually stood by his word. One notable occasion when he did not occurred in 1397 when Richard II through parliament revoked the pardons awarded to Arundel, Gloucester and Warwick for their deeds in 1388.[2] Another instance is referred to by the chronicler Warkworth. He recounts that the Bastard Fauconberg, who had been a great cause of worry to Edward IV, was captured at Southampton in 1471 and conveyed north to the duke of Gloucester at Middleham. The duke put him to death notwithstanding a charter of pardon which he was reputed to have.[3] Quite often a pardon was given in return for a sizeable fine. The Yorkist kings were particularly fond of this 'punishment by the purse'. When Edward IV after Tewkesbury went in person to Kent, Sussex and Essex to deal with those who had aided Fauconberg, he commissioned Lord Denham, Sir John Fog and others who 'satt uppone all Kent, Sussex and Essex that were at the Blakhethe and uppone many othere that were not there'. To obtain pardon fines had to be paid:

for some manne payed CC marke, some a C pounde, and some more and some lesse, so that it cost the porest manne VII s which was not worthe so myche but was fayne to selle suche clothinge as thei hade, and borrowede the remanent and laborede for it aftyrwarde; and so the Kynge hade out of Kent myche goode and lytelle luff.[4]

In retrospect it is obvious that cases of treason although of vital and personal concern to the king were subject to the same legal process as any other felony. There is no evidence of a deliberate attempt on the part of the crown to bring all those accused of treason before one particular court. Such cases were in fact heard and terminated in a variety of courts. These included the king's bench, courts held under special commissions, the court of the steward of the household, chancery, the king's council, various

---

[1] *Rot. Parl.*, III, 544 b.

[2] *Ibid.*, III, 350 b. In March 1351 a general pardon which had been granted to Richard, bishop of Ossory, was revoked on the grounds that he had obtained it by giving misleading information. Had the king known, so it was said, that he was guilty of enormous seditions it would never have been granted: *Cal. Pat. Rolls, 1350-4*, p. 55.

[3] Warkworth, *Chronicle*, p. 21.   [4] *Ibid.*; Stow, p. 425.

types of courts of chivalry, and parliament. In addition parliament, quite properly under the 1352 statute, and council, less properly, took upon themselves to declare which crimes amounted to treason.

Naturally enough the crown was particularly eager to secure the conviction of suspected traitors and this resulted in some sharp practice. At some trials the king appeared in person, no doubt hoping that his presence would intimidate the jurors. Attempts were made to elicit suitable charges from juries of presentment and inquest. The use of the jury of inquest in itself and the manner in which questions were put to it are suggestive of incipient crown prosecution. It is possible that the submission of charges originating at an inquest or in a bill of indictment for the approval of a grand jury was intended to influence the petty jury. There were also less sophisticated methods of influencing used. We hear occasionally of grand juries being 'laboured' and of petty juries being too frightened to follow the dictates of their own consciences. The prevalence of these practices is hard to assess but since they were commented on in a disapproving manner and with surprise by chroniclers we may assume that they were relatively uncommon. When the crown did bring pressure to bear it acted covertly: there was no open contravention or alteration of common or statute law. Another notable feature of procedure in matters of treason concerned parliament. Impeachment disappeared after 1459,[1] appeal of treason in parliament had been forbidden in 1399 and bill of attainder except in a single instance was never part of an actual trial in parliament. Sensibly the king realized that the days of parliament as the scene of the state trial were over. Despite certain drawbacks the courts in which important traitors were to be tried in future were primarily those of the common law.

[1] In the parliament of 1459 the commons attempted unsuccessfully to impeach Lord Stanley for his behaviour in the Bloreheath campaign: *Rot. Parl.*, v, 369 b.

7

THE ORIGINS AND THE EARLY HISTORY OF
THE ACT OF ATTAINDER

PARLIAMENT was the scene of most of the state trials and faction battles of the fourteenth century. It was natural that this should be so since on the one hand any magnate accused of activity against the crown usually had the right to be tried by his peers, while on the other any successful baronial insurrection needed the aura of a parliamentary settlement, both to remove the stigma of its treasonable origins and to provide for suitable government in the future. Whoever the victor of any political confrontation, once the royalists had adjudged the contrariants or vice versa, the need was felt to pronounce penalties on the hard core of the vanquished. Initially the punishment was part of the judgement in parliament but after Richard II's revenge against Gloucester, Arundel and Warwick in the session of 1397–8 the judicial process almost disappeared and the pronouncement of penalty came to stand by itself. This was the act of attainder. The period of evolution came to an end in 1459 when the Yorkist leaders were proscribed by act of parliament without, or so it seems, any previous judicial process. Those who were the victims were not given the opportunity to answer but had to watch from afar while they were condemned as traitors and their heirs disinherited. A fashion was set and until the end of the century the king *de facto* periodically proscribed his enemies in this way. The opinion of historians has been that it was nothing less than judgement by legislation and as such one of the most unsavoury features of English medieval government.[1]

To pronounce a man a traitor in a parliamentary act was not the only method of attainder. By the second decade of the fourteenth century the word *atteindre* was being used generically to describe any case in which final legal judgement had been made and the accused found guilty. This was of course usually by verdict of a court of common law, but it could also refer to guilt established by battle, by outlawry, or under the ancient prerogative power of

[1] For a statement of the generally-accepted view of attainder see Lyon, *Constitutional and Legal History*, p. 606.

178 THE LAW OF TREASON IN ENGLAND

the crown, that is, by record or by notoriety. By 1350 the word *atteint* was being used in the records of parliament and of the courts to denote the legal consequences to the person and property of his being convicted: particularly to the extinction of civil rights resulting from treason and felony, for the crime which was the cause of the attainder could of course be the latter as well as the former.[1] As *atteint* took on a new meaning the word *convictus* was used increasingly to denote the fact of being found guilty without any reference to the consequences. There is therefore no reason why the examination of parliamentary attainder should be befouled or impeded by questions of terminology.

Few aspects of constitutional law have been neglected as much as attainder in parliament. Although its obvious importance has been readily acknowledged very few historians have been led to investigate and we are still served by the brief and guarded assessments of Stubbs, Maitland and Holdsworth.[2] The only reasoned exposition of political attainder is to be found in a monograph by Vernon Harcourt, and then only incidentally to a central theme of trial by peers.[3] Recent legal and constitutional research has been concentrated on the state trial of the fourteenth century rather than that of the fifteenth. Many features of parliamentary justice have been clarified, yet a direct and immediate connexion between impeachment and appeal on the one hand and the act of attainder on the other has not yet been established.[4] To suggest that fifteenth century attainder grew simply from the appeal against the dead Gloucester or the impeachment of the absent Sir Thomas Mortimer in the parliament of 1397–8, is, I believe, quite erroneous. Even a superficial examination reveals that until the end of the Lancastrian era acts of attainder differed very much one from another and that there was more than one line of development. Not until 1459 did the different varieties fuse into a standard type of act, one which was to prove extremely serviceable for the proscription of defeated rebels and the forfeiture of their lands until

---

[1] *Year Books, 12 Edward II*, ed. J. P. Collas (Seld. Soc., 1953), pp. xxi–xxxiv.
[2] Stubbs, *Constitutional History of England* (5th edn, Oxford, 1903), III, 273, 480; F. W. Maitland, *Constitutional History of England* (Cambridge, 1908), p. 215; Holdsworth, *History of English Law*, I, 381, II, 451.
[3] Harcourt, *His Grace the Steward*, pp. 388–90.
[4] In his 'Impeachment and Attainder', in *Trans. Roy. Hist. Soc.*, 5th ser., III (1953), 145–58, Plucknett looked for such a connexion but concluded that attainder was basically a fifteenth-century development (*ibid.* 157).

the end of the Wars of the Roses. In contrast, the period 1400 to
1459 suggests a variety of purposes behind the use of attainder, a
confused tradition and an evolution which owed as much to
chance as to deliberate governmental policy.

To find the roots of parliamentary attainder we must go back
some way. Vernon Harcourt believed the origins were to be
discovered in 1308 and 1321, when first Gaveston and then the
Despensers were ordered into exile by parliament.[1] In both cases
there was lacking any mention of judicial process or judgement
inside parliament itself. Quite rightly Vernon Harcourt took this
to be the essential element in any act of attainder. Investigation of the
circumstances of these acts shows very clearly that they were made
by a frustrated baronage which could see no accepted constitutional
method of removing three hated favourites from the king's side. In
both cases the victims were 'awarded', that is, simply sentenced, not
adjudged: Gaveston by the 'people' as a traitor and robber of the
people,[2] the Despensers by the lords as disheritors of the crown.[3]
Gaveston, we are told, was to stand as a man attainted and judged.
On both occasions the king's consent was exacted from him. It is
well known that at the outset of Edward II's reign there was some
debate amongst the magnates as to how they should act when they
believed the king had gone against his coronation oath or when he
barred legal redress against the misdeeds of his minions. Around
1308, when still one of the opposition, the younger Despenser, it
seems, went so far as to write down a defence of the use of force in
such circumstances so that the king might be led into doing his
duty.[4] In 1308 the baronial opposition did not base its attainder
solely on a political philosophy: it adapted for its use a process from
the common law, namely judgement by notoriety. A notorious
criminal or a common criminal was a man with a bad name in his
own locality. Against him there was no need for a formal indictment: popular clamour alone would suffice. Furthermore, as Plucknett demonstrated, there were occasions when mere notoriety
operated as an instant conviction.[5] It seems that in 1308 and 1321

[1] Harcourt, *His Grace the Steward*, p. 388, note 3.
[2] British Museum, Burney MS. 277, fo. 5D: there is a translation in Wilkinson,
Constitutional History, III, 364–5.   [3] *Stat. Realm*, I, 181.
[4] *Cal. Close Rolls, 1318–23*, pp. 292–3; *Chronicles of Edward I and Edward II*,
I, 153–4; *Stat. Realm*, I, 182.
[5] Plucknett, 'Origin of Impeachment', *Trans. Roy. Hist. Soc.*, 4th ser.,
XXIV, 60–1.

these common law practices were being introduced into parliament and that very early parliamentary attainder was in this way associated with them. There was however little connexion between these awards and the attainder acts of the fifteenth century. Plucknett has shown how from the outcry against Justice Willoughby in 1341 notoriety entered on a new role, that of serving instead of indictment as the basis for a common law trial.[1] No longer was it to work an instant conviction. In the state trials at the end of Edward III's reign and in that of his grandson notoriety was sometimes used in parliament as the basis of accusation and an added ground for conviction of both royal favourites and humbled magnates.[2] But with the arrival of the act of attainder in the fifteenth century notoriety disappears. One act alone, that against Northumberland and Bardolph in 1406, makes use of the term 'notorious', and this rarity in appearance is matched in legal records as a whole.[3] The principles behind attainder must be looked for in other directions.

The statute of treasons of 1352 provided that when a future case involved a crime not covered under the act but which seemed to be treason, the justices should not proceed to judgement until the case had been shown and declared before the king in parliament: there it would be decided as either treason or felony.[4] Under this provision, as Rezneck has shown, a fair number of cases were dealt with in the subsequent 150 years.[5] It seems to have been quickly recognized by interested parties, usually by the king, that here was a way of circumventing the narrow definition of treason laid down by the statute. The first case involving declaration arose in 1379 when a London mercer and grocer were indicted by a coroner's jury for the murder of John Imperial, an accredited Genoese ambassador in London.[6] The crown ordered the indictment to be sent into chancery. The crime was then declared as

---

[1] Plucknett, 'Origin of Impeachment', *Trans. Roy. Hist. Soc.*, 4th ser., XXIV, 64–8.
[2] *Ibid.*, 70–1; *Rot. Parl.*, III, 237 b, 377 b–80.
[3] *Rot. Parl.*, III, 606 a.   [4] *Stat. Realm*, I, 319.
[5] Rezneck, 'Early History of the Parliamentary Declaration of Treason', *Eng. Hist. Rev.*, XLII, 497–513. Unfortunately Rezneck failed to realize that many attainder acts contained a declaration of treason within them.
[6] P.R.O., K.B. 27/476 Rex m. 31. Imperial had apparently brought an action against Richard Preston and John Philipot for capturing one of his ships: P.R.O., C. 47/68/12/358. This probably caused the feud which resulted in his death.

treason in the parliament which was being held at Westminster and the declaration recorded in a commission to four justices who were to hold the trial.[1] In court the jury had to be bullied and one of the accused persuaded to turn approver for the crown before his partner's guilt was held as proven. The pair were finally brought into the king's bench at Northampton and asked if they could give any reason why sentence should not be carried out. It is difficult to find any fault in all this. It seems to provide a model illustration of how declaration of treason was supposed to work. Yet most remarkably it was the only case in which the declaration of treason in parliament was followed by a proper trial in a court of common law as the statute seemed to intend. Instead of being a corollary to the working of the common law the procedure was to develop within a quarter of a century into the parliamentary act of attainder.

Responsible for this change to a considerable degree was the rise of parliamentary appeal of treason. The Lords Appellant in the parliament of February 1388 asked for and obtained from the lords of parliament the conviction in absence of four appellees.[2] This was after many of their alleged crimes had been declared treason by the same lords. The grounds for the judgement was notoriety. There had been no accusation in a lower court and therefore parliament after declaration need not refer the matter back but could proceed to judgement. The position was the same in the Talbot case of 1394. Sir Thomas Talbot was a war veteran and an ex-captain of the fortress of Guînes who suspected that the dukes of Lancaster and Gloucester, when acting as the English plenipotentiaries at the Lelighem truce talks, had misbehaved and acted against the king's best interests.[3] On this account he had instigated a rebellion against them in Lancashire and Cheshire. In retaliation the two dukes appear to have appealed Talbot of treason in the parliament of 1394. There the crime was declared as undoubted treason, but instead of there following an immediate conviction against a man who was still at large, Talbot was allowed three months to appear in the king's bench: if he failed to turn up he was to be held convicted and lose all his possessions, lands held

---

[1] *Rot. Parl.*, III, 75 b; P.R.O., K.B. 27/476 Rex m. 31d.

[2] *Rot. Parl.*, III, 237.

[3] For Talbot's career and the reasons for the revolt see my 'The Northern Rebellions', *Bulletin of the John Rylands Library*, XLVII, 254–74.

to his use included.[1] The process adopted was a development of the method used in 1388 and analogous to a form of parliamentary outlawry for treason. The king probably did not wish at this stage to ape his hated foes and adjudge forthwith. The two dukes on the other hand must have wanted Talbot's deeds pronounced treasonable without delay so as to save their reputations and make men think twice before joining the rebel. Mere outlawry would have taken too much time and would fail both to display the magnitude of the crime or to touch some of Talbot's properties. When Richard II revenged himself on the Lords Appellant in 1397–8 one of those appealed (and impeached too, incidentally), Sir Thomas Mortimer, could not be found. As with Talbot, a proclamation was issued for his appearance in the king's bench within three months. If he defaulted he was to stand convicted and attainted of all the treasons laid against him.[2] His chief crime was the same as that of Warwick and Gloucester, namely the levying of war against the king at Harringay on 13 November 1388. The king did not ask for any declaration of the crime by parliament. The appearances are that declaration, which had combined with parliamentary appeal to crystallize rudimentary attainder, was the element in the partnership which was most likely to be jettisoned. However, the deposition of Richard II and the successful commons' petition in the parliament of 1399 whereby all future appeals were barred destroyed a most useful constitutional tool and one which had of necessity to be replaced.[3]

One device which was utilized was the lodging of an appeal in the court of chivalry whence it was removed into parliament by means of a declaration that it was treason. This at least was what happened in 1406. The earl of Northumberland and Lord Bardolf were the objects of what must have been an appeal of treason or felony in the court of chivalry on the part of the constable.[4] The lords of parliament were asked to advise what subsequent process

---

[1] P.R.O., K.B. 27/532 Rex m. 16; also to be found in *Cal. Close Rolls, 1392–6*, p. 294.

[2] *Rot. Parl.*, III, 380–1. Slightly differently Sir Robert Plesyngton, who had assisted and counselled Gloucester in 1388, was 'awarded' by the king as being guilty of the same crimes as his master. Plesyngton, like Gloucester, was dead: *Rot. Parl.*, III, 384 b.

[3] *Ibid.*, III, 442.

[4] *Ibid.*, III, 604 a. The appeal may have been made initially before council, which awarded it to the court of chivalry.

should be used against the miscreants. In response they declared three alleged crimes as treason and suggested the issue of writs of proclamation to command the appellees to appear in parliament. A time limit of just under three months was set but the device failed and a second writ was issued five months after the first, allowing one more day. Then a third proclamation was made allowing another two days but still no one appeared, and therefore the lords with the king's assent sentenced Northumberland and Bardolf for treason.[1] The period allowed for the culprits to answer by the first proclamation was of the same duration as had been conceded to Talbot and Mortimer but in this case there was no threat of conviction for non-attendance. Only in a second and a third writ of proclamation was this included. The whole procedure was cumbersome and improvised. It owed its creation to the fact that when parliamentary appeal was abolished the king was left without any practical weapon to deal with the noble rebel who was at large or in flight. The reversion of the judgement against Sir John Maltravers in 1351 had ended the feasibility of an actual parliamentary trial in absence.[2] Perhaps the period of five months allowed to the rebels to put in an appearance was connected with the common law process of outlawry, which required exaction in five county courts. There is however no reference to outlawry in the records, nor any hint of an indictment.

If the declaration of treason and its allied act of attainder enjoyed only a laborious success in dealing with the king's enemies in flight, it was far more efficient against rebels who had already been killed. Thus in a parliamentary session of 1383 or 1384 the peasant leaders who had been put to death during the revolt of 1381 without due process of law were, at the request of the commons, declared by parliament to be convicted felons. At the beginning of the next reign the device was used for treason. In March 1400 the former earls of Kent, Huntingdon and Salisbury, Thomas lord Despenser and Sir Ralph Lumley, who two months earlier had attempted a military coup against the king and who had been executed without due process of law, the earl of Huntingdon by the men of Essex and the others by the townsmen of Circencester, were all declared and adjudged by the king and lords in parliament as traitors and as such held to have forfeited all their

---

[1] *Rot. Parl.*, III, 606 b. [2] *Ibid.*, II, 173, 243.

lands in fee simple.[1] The crown was concerned with giving itself a sound title to the rebels' possessions so that the heirs of the traitors would be barred from winning restitution in the way so many others had done in the earlier years of Edward III's reign. The act of attainder carefully specified the exact degree of forfeiture involved. The king, as befitted one who had only recently revoked Richard II's 1397 law on treason, settled for the lands the rebels had held in fee simple alone. In his cautious behaviour there is more than a suggestion that Henry was acting as an avowedly constitutional monarch, possibly in deliberate contrast to his predecessor. In the later years of Edward III's reign there had been some pressure against the crown not to seize as forfeit the lands of men who had not been 'attainted' of treason or felony in their own lifetime. In 1361 the king, though making some minor concessions, had stood firm on the main issue: he would not exclude himself from any forfeiture of war, that is to say for levying war against the crown or adhering to its enemies, regardless of whether the traitor was alive or dead.[2] Henry IV was apparently nowhere near so sure of himself and because of this he introduced

---

[1] *Rot. Parl.*, III, 175 a, 459 b. When in the Leicester parliament of 1414 John Montagu petitioned for the annulment of the attainder act of 1400 against his father, Thomas earl of Salisbury, he referred to the act as a 'judicium et declaratio'. He pointed out that parliamentary attainder of the dead allowed no response and no trial by peers and that this went against Magna Carta. He also challenged the act on the grounds that its passage through parliament as a bill was defective. The points raised were not particularly compelling ones and it seems as if the exact nature of an attainder act had not yet been grasped. The official reply which was given in the next parliament was equally unsure and said that the judgement and declaration were good, just, and legal, and that the case was dissimilar to those of Thomas of Lancaster and Roger Mortimer in Edward III's reign. This was the only occasion the legality of an attainder act was tested: *Rot. Parl.*, IV, 35 b, 36 a, 141 b.

The illegal execution even of an outlawed felon could cause considerable outcry. In 1352 king and council in parliament decided Adam Peshale's lands should go to his son and heir. Peshale had been executed by those sent to bring him before the council: *Cal. Close Rolls, 1349–54*, p. 406.

It is worth while remembering that in classical Rome trials for lese-majesty could continue after the death of the accused and even begin then: Lear, *Treason*, p. 55.

[2] *Stat. Realm*, I, 367–8; there were further complaints in 1372 and 1376: see *Rot. Parl.*, II, 311–12, 335, where the petitioners were referred to the statute of 1361. From about 1358 Edward III had pursued a consistent policy of seeking out and seizing the lands of men who had been guilty of treason of war either in his reign or that of his father. Usually they had aided the Scots. Hitherto such 'forfeiture of war' has escaped the attention of historians, although its great importance is evident.

declaration of treason and an associated act of attainder into a new field. It is a paradox of history that the much abused act of attainder owed its early development to a king who was particularly careful not to proceed unconstitutionally.

Henry IV acted in the same cautious way again in 1404. In the parliament of January of that year the lords declared that the levying of war by Henry Percy and his uncle Sir Thomas Percy in 1403 should be held as treason, and the whole of their possessions were forfeited.[1] That the king should have felt the need for a parliamentary declaration of so obvious and manifest a treason as offering pitched battle against the king's person at Shrewsbury suggests not caution but timidity, for there were no dubious circumstances to regularize like the Circencester executions. Whether the formal defiance which the chronicler Harding says was offered to the king by the two Percys was at all responsible is difficult to say. Certainly evidence from the preceding reign suggests that by this time the very act of renouncing homage was considered treasonable. An inspection of the background to this attainder however provides the most likely reasons for its enaction. Henry Percy's father, the earl of Northumberland, had only recently been declared and adjudged by his peers in the same parliament for his 'gederyng of Power and ... gevyng of Liveries' to have committed in the same rebellion not treason but trespass.[2] On this account there was probably some pressure from parliament as a whole for a definitive statement about the position of the two Percys and their former adherents: the titles of many lands were at stake.

---

[1] *Rot. Parl.*, III, 525 a; *Stat. Realm*, II, 143. The commons asked that since all the lands of Henry and Sir Thomas Percy were about to be forfeited the lands they held to the use of others should be protected (*Rot. Parl.*, III, 538 b–9 a).

[2] Harding, *Chronicle*, ed. H. Ellis (London, 1812), pp. 352–3; *Stat. Realm*, II, 94; *Rot. Parl.*, III, 524 a.

Rezneck believed the Northumberland declaration to be 'almost the last recorded instance of declared treason coming approximately within the scope of the proviso of 1352'. He was perplexed that no longer on the parliamentary record were there to appear 'the reports of individual cases calling either for a declaration of treason or for a verdict of guilt. With this lapsing of the records there disappears for almost two hundred years virtually every trace of the proviso.' Because he failed to realize the declaration of treason was to be found within quite a few acts of attainder, Rezneck was led to assert that declaration only reappeared with 'the ingenious elaboration of the doctrine of constructive treason' by the judges of the sixteenth century: 'Early History of the Parliamentary Declaration of Treason', *Eng. Hist. Rev.*, XLII, 507–8.

To this end Henry IV used the tool of declaration for a second time in the same session. It must have seemed the obvious thing to do at the time, though we may suspect that any previous monarch would have used a royal ordinance at the very most. As yet declaration and attainder were not so closely bound together that the former could not be used without the latter.

Not until 1450 did attainder of the dead develop further. In that year the elected commons petitioned that Jack Cade should be posthumously attainted of treason by authority of parliament 'to putte such Traytours in doubte so to doo in tyme commyng'.[1] Although the rebel leader was physically dead the need was felt for him to be punished by the law of the land, that is to say for the proper extinction of his civil rights. There was no request in this instance for the crimes, which were imagining the king's death and the traitorous levying of men, to be declared as treason. It was simply assumed that they were. Certainly the former was classified as treason in the statute of 1352. Declaration had been dropped and parliamentary judgement against a dead traitor remained alone. It took the form of an act of pains and penalties whereby all his lands and goods were forfeited and his blood corrupted and disabled for ever. It is worthy of note that because one half of the usual formula was missing the attainder was 'ordained'. In other attainders the crimes and their perpetrators had been 'declared and adjudged', 'declared and awarded', but 'ordained' only in the act against Henry and Sir Thomas Percy. In their case the declaration and the attainder had been separate processes.[2] The formula to ordain by advice of the lords and with the king's consent was to become accepted practice in future bills of attainder.

The petition against Cade which the commons presented in the parliament of 1453 demonstrates that the act of 1450 was later found to be insufficient. As we have seen, there had been no declaration of treason either within or adjoining the bill of pains and penalties. Three years later declaration was being specifically asked for. There was no reference to the earlier act, merely a statement of Cade's crimes. It was requested he should 'be take, hadde, named and declared a traitor' and all his acts, deeds and false opinions to be made void, annulled and forgotten. For as virtual master of London Cade had given orders, made legal decisions and

[1] Rot. Parl., V, 224 b.   [2] Stat. Realm, II, 143.

generally administered as though he was the proper government.[1] The attainder act of 1450, though it rendered him a traitor personally, was not thought to have annulled or pronounced judgement on his quasi-official deeds. This now had to be done by declaration pure and simple.

Between the two different processes against Cade came the bill of attainder proposed in the parliament of 1450–1. It was easily the most sophisticated so far. The aim was to do to the dead duke of Suffolk as had already been done to Cade. The royal favourite had recently been impeached without the commons getting any real satisfaction. Doubtless on some secret prompting, the duke had put himself on the king's grace. He escaped the death penalty, being ordered into exile. It profited him little, for while crossing the Channel he was murdered by a band of Sussex pirates: his brutal death did little to abate the popular hatred he had brought upon himself. The commons were determined to press for posthumous legal penalties, claiming that to the impeachment he had failed to make sufficient answer.[2] Therefore 'Jugement of Atteyndre of the said Treasons' ought to have been given against him. As the duke had escaped the commons asked that it should be ordained and established with the advice of the lords spiritual and temporal in parliament that he should stand 'adjudged, demed, declared, published and reputed' as a traitor, his blood corrupted, his issue disabled at law and to inherit none of his lands.[3] The petition was abortive but the crown took note of the formula and was happy to use it for its own purposes in 1459. The Yorkist leaders who that year had raised war against King Henry at Bloreheath and Ludford bridge were to be 'reputed, taken, declared, adjugged, demed and atteynted of high treason'.[4] In the wording of the act there was nothing that was entirely novel, for even the verb 'attainted' had been used before. What was important was that the

---

[1] *Rot. Parl.*, v, 265 a. To deal with those whom he particularly disliked Cade made use of an oyer and terminer commission which was already sitting. The attainder act of 1453 was probably intended to clear Thomas Daniel and Thomas Kent.

[2] *Ibid.*, v, 177–83.

[3] *Ibid.*, v, 226.

[4] *Ibid.*, v, 349 a. Not all the victims had their crimes declared as treason. Three were merely 'to be reputed, taken, demed, adjugged and atteinted': apparently they had not been involved at either Bloreheath or Ludford bridge. The use of the term 'reputed' is suggestive of the methods used by Edward I and Edward II to deal with rebels who had levied war against them. See chapter 3.

victims were not dead but in flight, and that unlike Northumberland and Bardolf in 1406 they were not given time to appear, at least not by parliament. It was also in 1459 that the declaration of treason, an obvious and important factor in the development of parliamentary attainder as a whole, realized its final form as one element in the new concise yet flexible process of public proscription.

Some reference has already been made to those acts of attainder which were promulgated in suspension, so to speak, against men whom the crown classed as traitors. They display another feature of the general development of attainder: the intent to bring the suspect before parliament or some lesser court. If within a certain time he had not put in an appearance he might suffer forfeiture of all his possessions and his heirs be disinherited. The process suggests the utilization of parliament to afforce the normal penalties of outlawry and perhaps to reduce the period of time that county court exaction normally required. Thus in 1393 Talbot was allowed three months in which to appear in the king's bench or lose all the lands he held in fee simple and others held to his use.[1] Northumberland and Bardolf were proclaimed by writ on three different occasions and were allowed a period of grace extending to five months before their failure to appear resulted in their attainder by the parliament of 1406.[2] In the parliament which met in January 1410 the commons petitioned for and obtained a suspended attainder act against Hugh Erdeswick of Sandon, Staffordshire, and his fellow rioters. It was ordained the sheriff of Staffordshire should try to arrest the miscreants once more but that if he failed and they did not appear in the king's bench they were to stand convicted nonetheless of both trespass and felony and lose all their lands, including those which other men held to their use.[3] The problem which the crown faced here was not the punishment of a handful of notorious traitors in hiding or in flight, but the maintenance of law and order in general. The crime was not treason but only felony at the worst, yet so feeble were

---

[1] P.R.O., K.B. 27/532 Rex m. 16.
[2] *Rot. Parl.*, III, 606.
[3] *Ibid.*, III, 630–2. Erdeswick and his friends failed to appear. Their subsequent conviction in the king's bench was said to be by virtue of an act and ordinance in the parliament of 20 January 1410 against which they had defaulted on 1 June 1410. The judges recorded the act against them: *Cal. Pat. Rolls, 1413–16*, p. 242.

the everyday instruments of the government that it had to resort to attainder. This example is the only one from the earlier part of the Lancastrian era, but later on, when conditions got worse and the basic elements of satisfactory government began to disappear, ordinary men sought to use the penalties and form of parliamentary attainder against their own enemies. The parliament roll of 1439 provides three interesting examples. A bill presented by John Stucche of Shropshire asked that one Philip Eggerton, who had been indicted and outlawed for the felony of waging private war and who had failed to answer to letters under the privy seal, should be held attaint of treason if he failed to answer to writ of proclamation within a further eleven months.[1] Similarly Margaret, relict of Sir Thomas Malefaut, who claimed to have been abducted and forced to marry Lewis Leyson of Glamorgan, petitioned that if Lewis failed to answer one of the next eleven county courts to charges of felony and rape he should stand attaint of high treason done against the king's estate, crown and dignity.[2] To both of these petitions and to another which was similar the king gave his assent. The third petition, although not as sensational as the first two, is equally informative. William atte Lowe and other tenants of Tutbury, a parcel of the duchy of Lancaster, complained they had been threatened, attacked and oppressed by one Peter Venables of Aston and his followers, who periodically made a raid from the woods where they lived in the manner of 'Robyn hode and his meyne'.[3] They could not 'be take to be justefied by the lawe but ryde and gone as outelaws'. Therefore the tenants asked the king to ordain by assent of the lords in parliament for the sheriff to fix a day on which the depredators should answer. If they failed to appear the justices who had been appointed to hear the case were to have power to give judgement as if Venables and his men were attaint of felony by due process of law. They were also to forfeit all their lands and goods as for felony. In this instance the intent of the petitioners may have been to shorten the period of five months which was necessary before outlawry was established, or to circumvent the unhelpfulness of local law officers. The first two cases, on the other hand, suggest private attempts to secure the penalties associated with treason as a new punishment for felony.

---

[1] *Rot. Parl.*, v, 17, 18 a.
[2] *Ibid.*, v, 14 b, 15. There was also the case of William Pulle, who was accused of the rape of Isabel, relict of Sir John Boteler: *ibid.*, IV, 497 a.   [3] *Ibid.*, v, 16.

Stucche's quarry had already been outlawed but had suffered little by it. Margaret Malefaut was merely trying to get her abductor into court and she may have hoped that the threat of attainder for treason would suffice. How it was that both petitioners hit on a period of eleven months for this novel type of exaction and how their suggestions were so readily accepted by the crown is not easy to explain, except by the hypothesis that the government was ready to experiment with any device which might help maintain law and order.

Two of the cases concerned riot, which was becoming the most persistent of the government's problems. All three displayed the unsatisfactory nature of the normal common law process of outlawry, taking as it did over five months to become effective, and then assuring no proper result. As an alternative the king could only offer the writ *quibusdam certis de causis* whereby the recipient was summoned to explain his conduct before council or in chancery.[1] Because they gave the defendant no indication of the charge against him the writs were unpopular and their legality questioned. In 1453 therefore the crown decided to regularize their use by means of a covering statute and at the same time strengthen the rather feeble sanctions available to council and chancery for the operation of the writs. The contemporary title of the 1453 act was the statute of riots, and the procedure laid down for the issue of the writs and the penalties for failing to answer indicate a connexion with the attainders of 1439 and 1459. If in the future a man disobeyed a writ summoning him before the council or into chancery the local sheriff was to proclaim in the county court that the culprit should appear where he had been summoned within a month. A man who defaulted then, if of baronial rank, would lose all the lands and posts he held of the king. The procedure would be repeated again and if he failed to turn up this time he would lose his titles and all his other lands, although his heirs would not be penalized after his death. Lesser men were to suffer penalties which were similar, if not quite as sweeping. The procedure was to operate in riot cases only, and for the limited period of seven years from 1 May 1454.[2]

---

[1] See J. F. Baldwin, *The King's Council in England during the Middle Ages* (Oxford, 1913), pp. 288–92.

In 1451 the duke of York tried to get these writs extended to cases of suspected treason: Stow, p. 395.

[2] *Rot. Parl.*, v, 266 b; *Stat. Realm*, II, 361. Very possibly the act was inspired

The definite use to which the statute was put is demonstrated by a series of cases involving men of all stations.[1] Writs of proclamation against a group of twenty-five rioters mostly of relatively humble rank were commanded for example in the parliament of 1459.[2] The act itself was produced at a vital time in the development of attainder. The parliament in which it had its birth was the scene of the attainder acts against an unreachable Sir William Oldhall and the deeds of the dead traitor Cade.[3] It also came within three years of the important bills against Cade's person and the duke of Suffolk. The penalties awarded hitherto on a particular case by a particular parliament were to be available in future, in a form that was only slightly less severe, for processes under either the common law or the royal prerogative. Far from being a punishment reserved to deal with exceptional dangers to the king, attainder could be observed in everyday use against relatively trivial offences, so lightly were held the sanctions of state in the last years of the Lancastrian dynasty. In terms of law a real novelty had been created. The law of parliament in the shape of attainder was being incorporated within the common law, the reverse of the fate of notoriety and appeal in the century before.

A feature common to all the great attainder acts of the fifteenth century was the inclusion of provision for the victim's forfeitures. It was quite usual for the degree and type of forfeiture to be carefully specified, and the greatest attention was given to the traitor's lands. Fee simple was always forfeit: fee tail and lands held to the victim's use might also come within the act, either singly or together. Lands held by those attainted to the use of someone else were often specifically protected. Sir Thomas Talbot was threatened with the loss of all his lands, chattels and goods and such as others had to his use by his gift or feoffment.[4] Most of the rebels of 1400

by the non-appearance before council of Thomas Percy: for the summons see *Procs. and Ords.*, VI, 191.
  [1] See for example Baldwin, *King's Council*, pp. 531–3 and *Cal. Pat. Rolls, 1452–61*, pp. 347, 493.
  [2] *Rot. Parl.*, V, 367 b.
  [3] Sir William Oldhall, against whom there were at least three indictments for treason, was in sanctuary at the royal chapel of St Martin's-le-Grand, London, from 1451–5. For an outline of his career see J. S. Roskell, 'Sir William Oldhall, Speaker in the Parliament of 1450–1', *Nottingham Medieval Studies*, V, (1961), 87–112: also below, pp. 195–7.
  [4] P.R.O., K.B. 27/532 Rex m. 16.

lost only their fee simple.[1] Henry Percy and the earl of Worcester and all those who fought alongside them at Shrewsbury lost fee simple, fee tail and uses, although those lands which an insurgent held to the use of anyone else were protected.[2] Northumberland and Bardolf in 1406 eventually suffered the forfeiture of fee simple in demesne and in reversion, together with the lands held by others to their use.[3] In 1450 the act against Cade and in 1451 the petition against Suffolk introduced a novel feature by specifically asking that their heirs should be declared corrupt of blood and unable to inherit.[4] The whole of Cade's goods and lands were forfeit, but Suffolk was to suffer to only the degree of Northumberland and Bardolf. The act against Sir William Oldhall in 1453 also struck at fee simple and uses, but it had the peculiarity of carrying a clause which exempted from forfeiture any heir who held in fee tail.[5] In 1459 total forfeiture of the type imposed on Henry and Sir Thomas Percy was the lot of the Yorkists, and it remained the fashion for the whole of the civil war period. From such evidence we may conclude that the crown could impose any degree of forfeiture that it desired. So much is obvious. The important question, one which reflects on the very nature of attainder, concerns the necessity of a parliamentary act in order to reach the fees tail and the lands held to a traitor's use.

Historians have commonly held that the reversionary nature of a fee tail barred automatic forfeiture for treason and that the common law courts protected these interests. 'De donis condicionalibus', it has been said, 'confirmed implicitly by the treason statute of 1352, had protected entailed estates from the scope of forfeiture'.[6] A case in the Year Book for 14 Edward III shows that this was indeed the normal common law doctrine.[7] It has also been presumed that lands held to a traitor's use could only be forfeited by act of parliament. Yet at the outset of the fifteenth century the crown was ready to demonstrate that treason could mean immediate and total forfeiture as long as its perpetrators had not come under the

[1] Rot. Parl., III, 459 b; Salisbury and Sir Thomas Blount alone lost the lands which others held to their use: Stat. Realm, II, 154.
In November 1400 Salisbury's wife sued for the lands she held in jointure and was partially successful: P.R.O., E. 175/File 6/f. 21, mm. 1–8.
[2] Rot. Parl., III, 538 b, 539 a; Stat. Realm, II, 143.
[3] Rot. Parl., III, 606 b.
[4] Ibid., v, 224 b, 226.   [5] Ibid., v, 265 b.
[6] Ross, 'Forfeiture for Treason', Eng. Hist. Rev., LXXI, 560.
[7] Year Books, 14 Edward III, ed. L. O. Pike (R.S., 1888), p. 314.

common law by appearance in court or by outlawry. Fee simple and fee tail, as well as lands held to the rebels' use, had been seized as forfeit from the insurgents of Shrewsbury and granted away again before parliament enacted a bill of attainder.[1] The rolls of chancery declare that the rebels' possessions went to the crown by reason of rebellion, not by reason of rebellion and by act of parliament as we find later in the century.[2] The possessions of the men who fought against Edward IV at Barnet and Tewkesbury, including those of the earl of Warwick, were in the hands of the crown or its grantees for almost four years before there was any act of attainder at all.[3] Even then the figure of those attainted was strikingly small, as Lander has pointed out.[4] Several examples can be taken from the civil war period to demonstrate that the crown did not base its claim to any type of land belonging to those who had opposed it in battle solely or even mainly on the relevant act of attainder. Sometimes there was a forfeiture but no act of attainder at all, as in the case of Warwick himself.[5] Quite often the legal records assume that forfeiture took place at the time of battle. William Findern esquire is mentioned as having made forfeiture actually on Barnet field.[6] The executors of Sir Hugh Courtenay lost their right to his goods, chattels and debts because he fought against the king at the battle of Tewkesbury and accordingly they belonged to the king by reason of his rebellion.[7]

---

[1] See for example *Cal. Pat. Rolls, 1401–5*, pp. 252, 257, 316. In a case in 7 Henry IV, which was mainly concerned with the procedure the earl of Kent should adopt when seeking livery of his traitor father's fees tail, Justice Markham declared 'Quant un homme fait haut Treason, tout sa terre en fee simple ou en fee taile est seisable, et par tiel seisin le Roy ad fee et inheritance'; one of the justices pointed out that in his writ the king had recorded he was seised of Kent's fees tail by cause of forfeiture but the other judges held the writ to be mere common form without any such implication. There may well have been a difference of opinion between the king and his bench on the issue: *Year Books*, 7 Henry IV, Mich. pl. 19, Trin. pl. 6.

[2] *Cal. Pat. Rolls, 1401–5*, pp. 252, 253, 255, 256, 257. As Vernon Harcourt pointed out, the expression 'ratione rebellionis suae' is the stock phrase for when there had been no judgement which the escheator could use as his root of title: Harcourt, *His Grace the Steward*, p. 376 n.

[3] *Cal. Pat. Rolls, 1467–77*, pp. 266, 274, 297.

[4] Lander, 'Attainder and Forfeiture', *Historical Journal*, IV, 128–9.

[5] Dr R. L. Storey has pointed out to me that Warwick, after his death at Barnet, was indicted before commissions of oyer and terminer and thereafter exacted: see P.R.O., K.B. 9/41 and 76.

[6] *Cal. Pat. Rolls, 1467–77*, p. 336.

[7] *Ibid.*, p. 374.

Similarly earlier in the century Thomas Bradshagh of Halgh was held to have committed treason and felony by being armed against the king at the battle of Shrewsbury, thereby suffering forfeiture.[1] The example of Sir John Massy on the same occasion can be used to show that the rebels forfeited both fee simple and fee tail in such circumstances.[2] This reference is dated August 1403, five months at least before there was any act of attainder. When open insurrection had to be suppressed on the battlefield there can be little doubt that the crown claimed forfeiture of war. In 1361 Edward III had stated categorically that he intended to retain this privilege, and although in 1376 the commons petitioned against forfeiture in cases of felony and treason which was not based on proper conviction during lifetime there is nothing to indicate that it was subsequently surrendered. It mattered not at all that the rebel was dead: why should it indeed? In all these cases it must have been the word of the king which decided who was a traitor, just as it did with men who adhered to the crown's enemies. The king was relying on his prerogative as he had done since Saxon times. In this way neither the rebel nor his forfeitures were touched by the common law and therefore the whole of his possessions could be forfeit and not just his fee simple.

Why then have an act of attainder at all where the treason was one of levying war against the king? In 1400 the rebels had been put to death without due process of law and therefore their position had to be defined for both the crown's purpose and that of the heirs. Either because of the illegal circumstances or because he was attempting to conciliate, Henry IV decided that in nearly every case only fee simple should be forfeit. In 1404 the act of attainder acknowledged that the whole of the Shrewsbury rebels' estates were forfeit but exempted from confiscation those lands which an insurgent might hold to the use of anyone else. The aim was probably to clarify matters of title for those who sought after or who already held a traitor's lands.[3] The act of 1459 and several of its successors were carefully designed to protect interests which might have been forfeited, had they not been specially excepted. In cases which involved armed insurrection the act of attainder seems to have been used to advertise the size of the forfeiture the crown intended to exact. The acts were not intended

[1] *Cal. Pat. Rolls, 1401–5*, p. 256.   [2] *Ibid.*, p. 253.
[3] *Rot. Parl.*, III, 538 b, 539 a.

primarily to enable the king to reach fees tail or lands held to a traitor's use, since these were forfeit already.

On at least one occasion the prime purpose of an act of attainder was not to declare treason, compel attendance or fix the degree of forfeiture, but to affirm and supplement a conviction in a court of law. The commons in the parliament of 1415 asked the regent Bedford that the judgement awarded before royal commissioners against the earl of Cambridge, Henry, lord Scrope of Masham and Sir Thomas Grey should be affirmed as good and legal and held in perpetuity.[1] This was done by an act which ordained that forfeiture should be as the common law demanded. In 1424 an act of parliament ordained and decreed that the indictment against Sir John Mortimer, whose crime was that as a prisoner suspected of treason he had managed to escape, was affirmed as good and true.[2] Mortimer was to be executed as a traitor and his lands in both fee simple and fee tail forfeited to the crown. This affirmation by act of attainder followed a previous affirmation of the same indictment on the part of the commons in the same parliament which looks very much like impeachment. Similar to this use of attainder to support conviction in a court of law was the affirmation and supplementation of the common law process of outlawry. Thus in the parliament at Reading in 1453 the indictment and attainder by outlawry of Sir William Oldhall were put on record before the extent of his forfeiture was set down in an act.[3] The special reasons for such action are instructive and involve Oldhall's traitorous machinations over an extended period.

Between March 1451 and approximately June 1455 Sir William

---

[1] *Rot. Parl.*, III, 64-7. There may also have been some doubt as to whether, Lord Scrope's crime of having knowledge of treason was in fact treasonable. The parliament which met in October 1399 was used by Henry IV to affirm the judgement on Sir Henry Green, who had been sentenced and executed with doubtful legality at Bristol on 29 July 1399. In the same parliament the king declared he held Green's lands by way of conquest: see *Cal. Pat. Rolls, 1408–13*, p. 281. The comparable judgement on the earl of Wiltshire was also affirmed: *Rot. Parl.*, III, 453.

[2] *Rot. Parl.*, IV, 202 a. Everything to do with the imprisonment, trial and condemnation of Mortimer is complex. Some of the intricacies are explained in *Year Books of Henry VI, 1 Henry VI*, pp. xxiv-xxvii. The most controversial point is the date and intent of the 'statute of escapes' and whether it was passed retroactively to deal with the second of Mortimer's attempted escapes. It is not to be confused with the act of attainder against him. Treason was not of course replevisable: see the statute of Westminster I (1275) (*Stat. Realm*, I, 30-1).

[3] *Rot. Parl.*, V. 265 b.

was in sanctuary at the royal chapel of St Martin's-le-Grand in London. Whilst he was there he was indicted in several counties. All the charges related to his conspiracies in the years 1451 and 1452, two of the plots having apparently been concocted while he was actually in sanctuary. The nefarious deeds he had either intended or performed ranged from seizing the king's own person to devising an insurrection in the Welsh march. He was outlawed for the first time probably at the end of March 1452 but this was annulled before 26 August: however, a new writ of exigent was issued in November.[1] On Oldhall's second outlawry the earl of Pembroke was granted the whole of his landed estate, having failed to acquire it for what must have been technical reasons during the previous year. Three months later on 22 June 1453, during the second session of the Reading parliament, a bill which the commons presented formally rehearsed that Sir William was attaint of high treason by means of outlawry. Say the rolls of parliament 'he of divers treasons stondeth endited and atteynted by uttlawrie after the cours of youre lawe for the which his Goodes and Catailles, Londes and Tenementes . . . be . . . forfeited and seised'. Then followed the attainder act.

One reason for the act was probably to advertise both Oldhall's outlawry and the nature of his crime. Another reason concerned his stay in sanctuary. At a later date he was to claim, and the plea was accepted, that he was not technically in sanctuary but in prison, since there were two yeomen watching the chapel to prevent his escape.[2] The law was that a felon who was in gaol at the time of his outlawry could lose only his moveables.[3] The crown's awareness that such a provision applied in Oldhall's case is suggested by the fact that it withheld a grant which was intended for the earl of Pembroke at the time of Sir William's first outlawry. So as to remove the doubt concerning any limitation of the forfeiture occasioned by the second outlawry, a parliamentary act of attainder was passed. Another reason for the bill is suggested by the nature of outlawry itself. A man attainted of high treason by that process could not be made to forfeit either his fees tail

---

[1] Roskell, 'Sir William Oldhall', *Nottingham Medieval Studies*, v, 104–5.

[2] *Ibid.*, 105. Only from 1486 was there a limitation of the sanctuaries which might receive fugitive traitors.

[3] See *Year Books, 19 Edward III*, (R.S.), pp. 338–40. The particular relevance of this decision to Oldhall's case is shown by its rehearsal in the year book of 1453.

or the land held to his use. This was actually stated in one act of attainder.[1] The bill against Oldhall in fact, while declaring forfeit the lands held to his use, protected any tail commenced or taking effect before the treasons had been committed. In 1453 therefore, because of the doubtful position of a traitor under surveillance in sanctuary, outlawry had to be affirmed and placed on the record by act of attainder in parliament: at the same time the act was used to strike at the lands which were held to the victim's use.

An examination of the various types of attainder act from 1394 to 1453 and the elucidation of the principles behind them does not unfortunately in itself explain every aspect of those acts which parliament passed from 1459. So much we might expect, since each of the earlier acts drew some feature from the situation it was designed to remedy. The acts of the later fifteenth century however had much in common and were apparently based on the example of 1459, which therefore merits special consideration.

The Coventry Parliament which sat from 20 November to 20 December 1459 has acquired an evil reputation. There seems little doubt that it was packed with men nominated by the Lancastrian household. Undoubtedly the passing of the bill of attainder was the main business of the session and parliament was dismissed when the process of compilation was completed. The evidence suggests that the bill was drafted by the king's official legal advisers, that is to say by Richard Choke, Thomas Lyttelton and Thomas Billing, who were his serjeants at law, and by William Nottingham, his attorney.[2] Expert advice may also have been forthcoming from the chief justice of the king's bench, Sir John Fortescue.[3] That the reputation of these men of law remained unsullied in the subsequent decades suggests they went about their business in a legal enough way. Neither the royal lawyers, the king, nor the Lancastrian courtiers who probably set things in motion were taxed by the Yorkists with abusing the law or with unfair practice within parliament. The statute of 1460 (39 Henry

---

[1] Rot. Parl., VI, 503 b. The act was that of 1495.

[2] P.R.O., E. 404 71/4/20. These four men of law were paid 13s. 4d. a day from 10 November to 16 December 'in recompense of the grete coste and labour' of coming to London to give 'thaire diligent attendaunce aboute oure matiers.' I owe this reference to Dr R. L. Storey. For evidence of the packing of the parliament see Rot. Parl., V, 367.

[3] Paston Letters, ed. J. Gairdner (Edinburgh, 1910), I, 479. John Bocking wrote to John Paston that 'the Chief Justice is right herty.'

VI c. 1), passed when the duke of York was in control of the government, yet a full year before the Yorkists got round to their own act of attainder, condemned the acts of the Coventry Parliament as malicious. It affirmed that the forfeiture of the Yorkist lands had been inspired by covetousness and rancour, with no thought for the 'weal of the king nor of the said realm'. The only feature which was condemned as illegal was the lack of due and free election of the knights and burgesses.[1] Most of the fifteenth-century chronicles which touch on this problem do so but briefly. One London chronicler says that the rebel lords 'indictati sunt . . . super grand prodicione et declarati pro *ateyntid traytours*'.[2] The *Great Chronicle of London*, displaying the general tenor, states that the Yorkist magnates together with many knights and esquires were attaint of high treason and the acts of the parliament of 1455 annulled.[3] The reports of 'William Worcester' and Robert Fabyan are just as uninformative.[4] Whethamstede, who was impressed by the king's desire to mitigate justice with mercy, did not question that the proceedings were of a proper and lawful nature.[5] There is however one statement by a chronicler which hints at some dissatisfaction with the proceedings in parliament. The *English Chronicle* complains that the Yorkists 'withoute any answere as traytours and rebelles to the kyng were atteynt of treson'.[6] This was a complaint which had been made at the time of the trial of Richard, earl of Arundel in 1397. The crime for which he was sentenced was as with the Yorkists that of levying war against the king.

In the bill of attainder itself the first section rehearsed the misdeeds of the duke of York himself from as far back as 1450.[7] Cade had intended to make York king; the duke had come from Ireland in manner of war and forced an entry into the king's chamber. He had broken the oath of loyalty taken in St Paul's in 1452 and he was guilty of levying war against the king at St Albans and Bloreheath. After the first of those battles he had forced the king and parliament to pass an act for the exoneration of the Yorkists and

---

[1] *Stat. Realm*, II, 378.
[2] *Three Fifteenth Century Chronicles*, p. 169.
[3] *The Great Chronicle of London*, p. 191.
[4] *Letters and Papers illustrative of the Wars in France*, ed. Stevenson, II, II, 771; Robert Fabyan, *Newe Chronycles of England and of France*, ed. H. Ellis (London, 1811), p. 635.
[5] *Registrum Abbatiae Johannis Whethamstede*, ed. H. T. Riley (R.S., 1872), I, 537.   [6] *English Chronicle*, ed. Davies, p. 83.
[7] *Rot. Parl.*, v, 346 a–48 a.

had personally sworn never again to resort to arms even if provoked. He had also attempted to surprise the king's army at Ludford, intending to seize both the crown and the duchy of Lancaster. Those of the Yorkist faction who were 'atteynted of high treson as fals traitours' at the same time as their leader were divided into three groups. Last in the actual bill was a trio comprising Alice, countess of Salisbury, Sir William Oldhall and Thomas Vaughan, esquire. They were each held to have imagined and encompassed the king's death during the summer of 1459, the countess at Middleham and the two gentlemen at 'Garlickhithe' in London. Furthermore it was claimed they had 'labored, abetted procured, stered and provoked' York, Warwick and Salisbury to commit their treasons. The two other larger groups consisted of the nobles and gentry who had fought at Bloreheath or been in the camp at Ludford. In view of the crimes attributed to York at the beginning of the bill of attainder it is interesting to find that he was actually attainted for the crime of levying war against the king's person at Ludford. Why the government should decide to rest its case solely on the most recent of the duke's misdeeds is surely worthy of consideration. Any pardon for earlier misdeeds could easily have been revoked, but the crown in York's case was interested only in the episode near Ludlow and not even in Bloreheath.

At Bloreheath there had been a chance encounter in which the earl of Salisbury defeated Lord Audley. Neither York nor the king was present in person but we know that the royal standard had already been erected.[1] Soon after the battle Henry and the main body of the royal army set off in pursuit, apparently intending to bring the Yorkists to a general action. In view of his personal qualities and his medical history the king's energy was remarkable. The commons in their bill of attainder stated

youre Highnes ever as hastely as it coude be thought folowed, not sparyng for eny ympedyment or difficulte of way, nor of intemporance of wedders, jupartie of youre moost Roiall persone and contynuance of labours XXX dayes or thereaboutes not to rest eny oon day where ye were another sauf oonly on the Sondayes, and somtyme as the case required logged in bare feld somtyme two nyghts togider with all your Host in the colde season of the yere.[2]

As he moved forward the king despatched the bishop of Salisbury to offer to nearly all the Yorkist leaders a general pardon on the

---

[1] *Registrum Whethamstede*, p. 338.   [2] *Rot. Parl.*, v, 348 a.

dismissal of their troops.[1] After some deliberation the dissidents made answer through the earl of Warwick that they had no faith in the king's pardons, even those confirmed in parliament. They would however appear before the king if a way could be devised to ensure their personal safety.[2] Ignoring this response Henry advanced his standards again, but before he came into contact with his quarry he received another letter, dated 10 October, wherein the Yorkist lords explained how in order to avoid a battle they had continually retreated before him. This time they asked him for a safe conduct so as to be able to present him with certain articles: they added that they were now at Ludlow and could retreat no further. 'We here', they wrote, 'that we be proclamed and defamed in oure name unryghtfully, unlawfully and saving your high reverence untrewely and otherwyse (as God knoweth) than we have given cause.' They also bitterly denounced those persons 'as intend of extreme malice to proceed ... for such inordinate covetise ... as they have to our lands, offices and goods ...'[3] The impression is given that the king, urged on by the court party, was doing everything possible to get the Yorkists onto a battle-field: furthermore it seems that until he actually proclaimed them as traitors the dissidents had persistently refused to fight. Judging by the letter they despatched to the king this proclamation must have been made at about the same time that Henry ordered the writs to be issued for the summoning of a parliament, that is to say 9 October 1459. Then the Yorkists notified him they intended to stand and fight. This resolve was not in fact put into practice, since on the night of 12 October the rebel leaders discovered that many of their men had deserted and therefore they abandoned the fortified camp and fled.[4] Their banners, we are told, they left standing. When on the morn Henry discovered what had happened he

---

[1] *Registrum Whethamstede*, p. 339.
[2] *Ibid.*, p. 340.
[3] *English Chronicle*, ed. Davies, pp. 81–3; see also Holinshed, *Chronicles*, III, 254–6. In the parliament of 1455 after the first battle of St Albans the Yorkist leaders claimed that one of their letters had been deliberately kept from the king. Because of this they argued that the battle of St Albans was justified: Stow, p. 400.
[4] However, one chronicler says 'The seid dukes and erles left the ffeld because the king was in the vaward and displaied his banner to fight therfor': see *Six Town Chronicles*, ed. R. Flenley (Oxford, 1911), p. 148. None of the Yorkist leaders appears to have been summoned officially to the Coventry Parliament: see *A ... Summons of the Nobility to the Great Councils and Parliaments*, ed. W. Dugdale (London, 1685), pp. 452–3.

pardoned nearly all the remaining Yorkist soldiery except for a few ringleaders: of these some were only fined but others were hanged and quartered. Finally the king again pronounced and proclaimed the rebel lords as traitors and announced that their lands, goods and offices were forfeit.[1]

This pattern of events has more than a mere antiquarian interest. The raising of standards and banners by both the royalists and the rebels and the significance of the king's actual presence at Ludford bridge are best explained in terms of what may be called the legal aspect of war. These laws or usages owed nothing to the common law, being in fact international. There were stringent rules governing the use of banners: to display them was the sign of declaring open war. As Keen has said, 'A liegeman appearing against his king in arms under banners displayed was clearly levying war upon him and could be taken as a traitor.'[2] Certainly it was common at this period for treason to be alleged in court against any group of rioters which displayed a banner. However, for the crime to be manifest treason which needed no proving, the king himself must be present with his own banner displayed.[3] No doubt the desire of the Lancastrian courtiers to get King Henry on to a battlefield against the Yorkists stemmed from this knowledge. When the two factors of rebel banners and royal presence were in conjunction the crown was able forthwith to assume all the rebel possessions as forfeit and there was no need for legal process against the owners. Judgement, or rather conviction, was given by the king's record, that is to say by the prerogative inherent in his position. The defamatory proclamation to which the Yorkists took exception was possibly meant to summon the rebel leaders before the king, perhaps under the procedure laid down in the statute of riots of 1453.

[1] Hall, *Chronicle*, p. 242.

[2] Keen, 'Treason Trials', *Trans. Roy. Hist. Soc.*, 5th ser., XII, 95.

[3] The crime would need no proving because the king, the enemy being within his own view, could work an instant conviction by his own record: see Plucknett, 'Origin of Impeachment', *Trans. Roy. Hist. Soc.*, 4th ser., XXIV, 56-9, 61-4. *Rot. Parl.*, II, 3-5 seems to suggest that in the earlier fourteenth century at least, the king could only record in time of war. See also *Cal. Pat. Rolls, 1327-30*, p. 141.

Even in Tudor times it was accepted that the king had absolute power in war time. In 1565 Sir Thomas Smith wrote 'In war time and in the field the prince hath also absolute power, so that his word is law; he may put to death or to other bodily punishment whom he shall think to deserve without process of law or form of judgment . . .': *De Republica Anglorum*, ed. L. Alston (Cambridge, 1906), p. 58.

It may equally well have been intended as a form of outlawry under the royal prerogative as had been decreed by Edward II and the earls of his council against the rebels of 1322. There is also the third possibility that the government's intent was to summon the rebel leaders to answer in parliament, as in the case of Northumberland and Bardolf in 1406. This might explain the parliamentary writs.

Keen has offered evidence to show that the usages of war relating to banners and the royal power to 'record' were still in operation in the early years of Edward IV, and we may therefore take it they were available to his predecessor.[1] With such proscriptive powers available why, it may be asked, was there need for an act of attainder? The answer is, I believe, connected with the medieval fear of legal irregularity and lack of due process. Medieval men watched very carefully for any legal flaw. In 1327 Henry of Lancaster had won back the lands of his dead brother Thomas on the technicality that in 1322 Edward II had failed to display his royal banner at Burton-on-Trent and thereby failed to declare it a time of open war.[2] In addition he pointed out, and this was probably the case in 1459, that the courts of common law had remained open and the chancellor continued to hear cases. Both were signs there was no open war. There is certainly no record of a suspension of the courts in 1459, although such a thing was not unheard of in the fifteenth century: it was proposed by Henry IV in 1403 and actually occurred in 1470 and 1481.[3] Another factor may have been the controvertible position of the Yorkists who had fought against Audley at Bloreheath. They had not borne arms against the king himself and if he were to record judgement against them it would have been open to challenge. When the king recorded of his own view, that is to say when he was present in person, the record could not be annulled: but a challenge at law might be successful if he recorded

---

[1] Keen, 'Treason Trials', *Trans. Roy. Hist. Soc.*, 5th ser., XII, 88–92.

[2] *Rot. Parl.*, II, 3–5.

[3] Henry IV wrote 'consideranz qa cause de guere move contre nous dedeins nostre reaume nous pourrons fere toutez nos courtez cesser, en sauvacion de noz et nostre reaume' (letter to his council, 23 Oct. 1403: H. C. M. Lyte, *The Great Seal* (London, 1926), p. 130). On the arrival in England of Warwick and Queen Margaret on 13 September 1470 the council ordered the suspension of the courts during the time of war: Scofield, *Reign of Edward IV*, I, 536.

On 22 June 1481 Edward IV ordered the justices to adjourn their courts till Michaelmas for the purpose of resisting the Scots (*Foedera*, ed. Rymer (original edn) XII, 141).

a crime which he did not see. Such was the implication of Justice Willoughby's judgement in the Marshall case of 1338-9.[1] The king and his advisers must also have been aware of the growing tradition of attainder and its several uses for dealing with different causes involving treason. As we have seen, attainder by parliamentary act was in the air.

Yet another reason for the 1459 attainder act, and one which underlines its multipurposed character, is provided by an examination of the small third group of victims. Alice, countess of Salisbury, Sir William Oldhall and Thomas Vaughan esquire were probably never on a battlefield. Their crime was that they had conspired to accomplish the king's death and had given advice and encouragement to York and the earls.[2] The only further information we have concerning these crimes lies in the important fact that Oldhall was actually indicted on a charge of treason and thereby had come within the common law.[3] Presumably this was between 4 July 1459, when he was supposed to have committed his misdeed at 'Garlickhithe', London, and the end of the Coventry parliament. Since he survived the Yorkist nadir it is very possible that he was never brought into court, though he may well have been outlawed. His fellow victims may have been in the same position. If Oldhall's crime was the one in London then the five county courts necessary to complete the process of outlawry could have been fitted in between July and December, when the bill of attainder became an act. If the act of attainder completed a judicial process which had only progressed as far as indictment, that is to say took the place of a trial, it was only the second time this had ever happened, the previous occasion being in 1424 when Sir John Mortimer's indictment was confirmed in parliament. It seems far more likely that in their case the act affirmed and supplemented the outlawry which had already occurred, and was intended to define the degree of penalty involved. If in fact the trio had been convicted under the common law then, unlike the rebels of Ludford bridge at least, a parliamentary act was essential in order to reach their fees tail and the lands held to their use.

---

[1] Plucknett, 'Origin of Impeachment', *Trans. Roy. Hist. Soc.*, 4th ser., XXIV, 63.

[2] *Rot. Parl.*, V, 349. The countess of Salisbury was an heiress in her own right and therefore an attractive victim for attainder.

[3] *Cal. Pat. Rolls, 1452–61*, p. 535.

Thus the act of 1459 was designed to answer not one but a number of legal problems, and it did so neatly and concisely. The criticism directed against it at the time was probably founded on the Yorkists' complaint that they had not been able to appear before Henry in order to answer to writ of proclamation. In reality they had been offered the chance but had feared to take it. The criticism of later centuries arose from a complete misunderstanding of the nature of this attainder. It was not the act which supplied the crown with its right to the rebels' possessions but the ancient royal prerogative which operated in time of open war. Attainder merely regularized any legal difficulties as it had done in 1400. It settled any doubts about the position of the rebels who had been at Bloreheath. It was also intended to set down the degree of forfeiture the government intended to exact and to protect interests which might otherwise have been the subject of interminable wrangles in the courts. Lastly it affirmed and supplemented the outlawry of a small group of Yorkists, one of whom, Sir William Oldhall, had been the subject of a similar act six years previously.

Attainder by parliamentary act developed slowly, case by case, over a period of seventy years. Each stage of the development was as legal as it was logical. There was no introduction of a revolutionary instrument for use against political opponents, as has often been implied. Nothing could be further from the truth than the verdict that it was judgement by means of legislation. Parliamentary attainder, which nearly always dealt with treason, owed much to the great statute of treason of 1352 wherein the means had been provided for the declaration of doubtful crimes in parliament. It was influenced by the desire for a form of parliamentary exaction and outlawry: also the need to affirm and supplement judgements made in courts of common law and to set penalties which were beyond the powers of those courts. In 1404 and 1459 acts of attainder imposed punishment on those convicted by the king's own record: their forfeiture was forfeiture of war.[1] Despite the seminal nature of the 1352 act of treasons and the parliamentary experiments in accusation of treason during the reign of Richard II a large part of the responsibility for the development of the act of

---

[1] The term 'forfeiture of war' does not appear very often in legal records. For one example see *Cal. Close Rolls, 1327–30,* p. 55: at issue was the prerogative of the bishop of Durham.

attainder lies with the Lancastrians. In 1400 Henry IV found it necessary to use such an act against the dead rebel earls and there was another four years later against the two Percys. A king more sure of himself and less worried about placating public opinion would not have bothered.

8

TREASON AND THE CONSTITUTION

WHAT was the role of the law of treason in English medieval history as a whole? The success of English medieval constitutionalism hinged on the balance of power between the king and the estates of the realm. After 1215 no king, however capable and powerful, was able to become a tyrant. The barons on the other hand, although they tried many times, were unable to transform the government into an oligarchy. The commons had no chance of changing the government into a democracy, but from 1300 they could not be ignored by either of the other two powers. The late medieval English law of treason was both a cause and a result of this balance and when it was tampered with, as for example in Richard II's reign, there was serious danger to constitutional government.

During most of the period under review the law of treason, because they held it so important, was subject to the watchful scrutiny of the barons and commons. On the interpretation of what constituted treason there generally prevailed between the king and his subjects a compromise, one which is well demonstrated by the fairly common use made in accusations of the phrase 'treason against the realm'. This shows that many men believed more than the royal dignity was at stake. Quite obviously the king was mindful of his own duty to the crown, that is to the conceptual union of the monarch and his people. The first examples appeared at the end of the thirteenth century. In 1300 in a letter to Boniface VIII Edward I wrote about his quarrel with the Scots.[1] He said that John Balliol and his subjects had invaded England and pillaged the countryside, crimes which were to his own and his people's traitorous destruction. The letter was intended for perusal by canon lawyers and its terminology might conceivably have been influenced by Roman maxims, but in 1305 the sentence on William Wallace referred quite distinctly to the nation as a whole: the traitor's corpse was to be dismembered because of his sedition not only to the king but also to the people of England and

---

[1] *Chronicles of Edward I and Edward II*, I, 119.

Scotland.[1] In the next reign and during Edward III's minority the notion began to flourish. A writ from Edward II dated 4 June 1320 to the sheriff of Norfolk referred to the forging of coin as a special form of treason done to the king and the people of his realm [*sedicionem nobis et populo regni nostri*].[2] The term appeared again two years later. When Edward II was busy dealing with Thomas of Lancaster and other dissident barons in March 1322 he issued a list of rebels who were to be arrested and gaoled until they could be dealt with as traitors to the king and the kingdom.[3] In 1330 Edmund, earl of Kent, who had acknowledged his guilt, was condemned as a traitor for falsely and maliciously making confederations contrary to his fealty and allegiance, to the destruction of the king and the subversion of the realm. Later the same year Roger Mortimer, for a variety of crimes most of which were accroachments of the royal power, was adjudged in parliament a traitor and enemy of the realm.[4] The sources of at least four of these six examples were royal ones and the other two were parliamentary.

From the time when Edward III seized the reins of government until the year of the Peasants' Revolt references to treason against the kingdom did not figure in the records at all. This did not mean that Edward was pursuing a treason policy which was purely royal in its sympathies, for it was in the period from the beginning of the Hundred Years War to 1352 that the government, in order to aggravate accusations of treason, made use of the charge of accroaching the royal power, which being suggestive of the doctrine of capacities and the possibility of a division between the king and his people was much the same thing. Despite these indications of the existence of a concept of treason which sanctified more than the person of the king, those who designed the statute of 1352 failed to give it recognition. Very probably they did so because of the popular pressure for a new, narrower definition, which in turn was created by the king's efforts to extend the penalties for treason to lesser crimes, so as to suppress riot and disorder the more effectively.

In 1381 'treason against the realm' reappeared. A number of

[1] *Chronicles of Edward I and Edward II*, I, 142.
[2] *Select Cases in the Court of the King's Bench*, ed. Sayles (Seld. Soc., 1955), p. 102.
[3] *Parl. Writs*, II, I, 283.
[4] *Cal. Close Rolls, 1330–3*, p. 17; *Rot. Parl.*, II, 53.

15

local juries described the peasant rebels of their regions as seeking the destruction of the kingdom. Some of the Kent presentments of that year spoke of treasonable insurrection against not only the king but also his people.[1] In 1388 the magnates who appealed the king's friends of treason in the Merciless Parliament referred to the high treason 'par eaux fait encountre le roi et soun realme come traitours et enemys du roi et de roialme'.[2] In 1394, at the prompting of the dukes of Lancaster and Gloucester, Sir Thomas Talbot, who had recently been in rebellion in Lancashire and Cheshire, was declared by parliament to have committed an offence which was manifest high treason against the king's person and the realm.[3] In the new statute of treason devised by Richard II in 1397 for purposes of revenge on his baronial opponents, there was mention of treason against the crown [encontre la corone].[4] In this case, as in the previous two, treason was given the description in the rolls of parliament of 'haute traisoun'. Even in the records of lesser courts there figured treasons said to have been committed against the kingdom.[5]

If the autocratic King Richard in his moment of triumph had decided it was a useful practice to talk of treason as being against the kingdom as well as the prince, the Lancastrians might be expected to employ the phrase even more enthusiastically. This seems to have been the case. The indictment against the Tottenham highway robbers and 'depopulatores agrorum' of 1401 referred to them as common felons and traitors who intended to destroy the king and his kingdom.[6] The friars involved in the affair of the 'false Richard' were adjudged in the king's bench to be traitors to the king and the kingdom, having intended by their speech to excite the people against their king, to the final destruction of the realm.[7] Two of the chief conspirators in the plot against the life of Henry V in 1415 and the Lollard leader Sir John Oldcastle two years later were each condemned as traitors against the realm as well as the king.[8] When large-scale insurrection occurred later

---

[1] Réville, Soulèvement des Travailleurs, pp. 182, 185.
[2] Rot. Parl., III, 229 b.
[3] P.R.O., K.B. 27/532 Rex m. 16; Cal. Pat. Rolls, 1391–6, p. 294.
[4] Stat. Realm, II, 98–9.
[5] See, for example, P.R.O., K.B. 27/550 Rex. m. 23 (the Oxfordshire rebellion of Henry Pope in 1398).   [6] P.R.O., K.B. 9/189/10.
[7] Thornley, 'Treason by words', Eng. Hist. Rev., XXXII, 560–1; P.R.O., K.B. 27/564 Rex m. 12.
[8] Rot. Parl., IV, 66, 108 b.

in the century, treason against the kingdom as well as the king was mentioned in most of the relevant indictments and parliamentary bills of attainder. In a commons' bill of attainder Jack Cade was held to have traitorously imagined the destruction of the king and the subversion of the realm.[1] His adherents in Kent were found by local inquests to have been guilty of imagining or planning the death of King Henry and the destruction of the kingdom of England.[2] Since very probably these indictments were framed in accordance with official instructions their formulae demonstrate that 'treason against the kingdom' was a phrase accepted by the king's lawyers. The Yorkist period has often been regarded as one of absolutist trends in kingship, yet Yorkist attainder acts showed the same tendency as the Lancastrian. Edward IV held that his brother George, duke of Clarence intended falsely and traitorously 'th'extreme distruction and disherityng of the Kyng and his Issue' and planned to 'subverte all the polityk rule of the Royaulme'.[3] The attainder act against the dead duke of Buckingham and his supporters in 1484 stated that in Brecknock castle they had conspired, imagined and compassed the death of the king and the destruction of the realm.[4]

The terms 'subverting the realm', 'destroying the realm' or 'traitor to the realm' were never the sole basis of an accusation of treason. They were used only to aggravate charges of treason which were acceptable at common law, that is to say compassing the king's death, levying war against him, adhering to his enemies and the like. Some rebels, for example those of 1381 and the Lollards in 1414, may have deliberately intended the destruction of the kingdom or at least the overthrow of the social order, but in many cases to describe an attempted political coup or a local insurrection as seeking the destruction of the realm was partly recognition of the cooperative nature of English late medieval government and partly propaganda aimed at securing the support of barons and commons for the condemnation of rebels and the forfeiture of their property.

In England during the later middle ages there existed not one but two doctrines of treason side by side. One doctrine was the one which has been the concern of this volume, the law of treason as seen through the eyes of the king and his legal advisers. The

---

[1] *Rot. Parl.*, v, 265 a.
[2] Virgoe, 'Some ancient indictments', *Kent Records*, xviii, nos. 7, 30, 36.
[3] *Rot. Parl.*, vi, 193 b.   [4] *Ibid.*, vi, 244–9.

other was the theory of treason of the barons and to a lesser extent of the people. Its main features were revealed in petitions to the king, in indictments, in parliamentary appeals of treason, impeachments and bills of attainder, but especially in actual definition of treason, and action taken against supposed traitors when for a time the magnates had been able to seize power from the king. The philosophy underlying the baronial *dicta* has already been mentioned. It was founded on the idea of a difference between the king's person and his office: loyalty, so it was argued, was owed to the latter rather than the former. Treason was held to lie particularly in causing a division between the king and his people, thereby endangering the union which was the basis of the late medieval English state. These notions were first expressed in about 1308, were still entertained in some quarters in the mid-fifteenth century, and were used by Henry VIII as the basis of treason charges against Empson and Dudley at the outset of his reign and against the Nun of Kent and her confederates over twenty years later.[1] In 1388 the magnates had a rare opportunity to turn their concepts of treason into actual law by using parliament, which they controlled, to declare the misdeeds of the king's ministers as traitorous. Significantly, of the fourteen offences found to be treason by the lords of parliament eight were some form of accroachment of the royal power.[2]

The barons and people also had a part to play in the formulation of the law of treason through participation in criminal procedure. Their role was an accusatory one. There was firstly the laying of charges by means of appeal, often the resort of those who had suffered personal hurt. This has usually been associated with the centuries before the fourteenth and fifteenth, but appeal of treason, at least, was surprisingly long lived, both in the courts of common law, where appeals often came from approvers, and in parliament. A second form of popular accusation tended to arise at times of public outrage over notorious misdeeds. It found expression simply in public outcry. In turn this clamour might serve as an indictment, but only as long as the king was willing. Only on rare occasions and in parliament does it seem to have worked an instant conviction without the need for trial. A third form of popular accusation was impeachment, a complaint initially to the king or

[1] *D.K.R.: Third Report*, Appendix II, pp. 226–7.
[2] *Rot. Parl.*, III, 237.

his council by a number of people, which lacked surety for prosecution. Impeachment in general may not have been confined solely to parliament, but impeachment of treason most certainly was. As with public clamour, royal support was necessary for success. The occasions when impeachment of treason occurred in parliament were very few, perhaps no more than four, and on two of these, in 1388 and 1397, it was closely associated with appeal. In another case, the one which occurred in 1450, the parliamentary commons impeached the duke of Suffolk to a number of lords and asked that their bill of impeachment be the basis of an act of attainder.[1] This was virtually the end of accusations by the commons or lords of parliament against the king's ministers for over 170 years. A fourth method of accusation of treason which involved popular participation was the parliamentary act of attainder. Such acts might be based on bills proposed or sponsored by the commons or lords, and those introduced on the king's behalf needed the commons' and the lords' assent. Bills of attainder initiated by the commons were not always successful: two notable failures were those directed against the duke of Suffolk in 1451 and against Sir William Oldhall in 1453.[2] During the fifteenth century, from about 1433–45, there were a number of attainder bills proposed by the commons not for the condemnation of traitorous ministers or magnates but for the conviction for treason of men guilty only of felony or trespass.[3] This was because of the shortcomings of exaction and outlawry, and the need to compel appearance in court by the threat of heavier sanctions.

Despite these examples of popular participation in the passing of bills of attainder, even to the extent of interfering with the procedures of the common law, the royal power was paramount. Apart from one instance in 1414 there is no evidence of opposition by the commons and lords to any attainder bill proposed by the king or his ministers, much less of successful resistance.[4] Outside parliament there was complaint in 1459 that the attainted Yorkist lords had not been given the chance to answer the charges against them, but this also was unique.[5] Step by step the uses of the act of attainder increased. Initially it gave the king title to the land of traitors who had died before they could be put on trial. Later it

---

[1] Rot. Parl., v, 176–83.　　　　[2] Ibid., v, 226, 265 b.
[3] Ibid., iv, 447 b, 497 a; v, 14 b, 15, 17, 18 a.
[4] Ibid., iv, 35 b, 36 a, 141 b.　　　[5] English Chronicle, ed. Davies, p. 83.

set the degree of forfeiture for those who had been tried and found guilty or outlawed. Later still it was used to condemn suspected traitors in their absence, and after that, as in the case of the duke of Clarence in 1478, to convict them in their presence or after arraignment.[1] Lastly it was used to convict them in their absence although they were in royal custody at the time when the bill was proposed in parliament. This was what happened in the case of Elizabeth Barton and her confederates in 1534, and Thomas Cromwell in 1540.[2]

Attainder acts were the products of parliament and thus in theory the shared responsibility of the king and his people. In practice, because the king's final approval was essential and because of his ability from 1461 to dominate completely the lords and commons in parliament, his control over attainder was virtually complete. That conviction of suspected traitors by attainder act did not supplant trials before commissions of oyer and terminer suggests that despite the lack of overt opposition public opinion was not very sympathetic to the device. Perhaps also the king valued the propaganda to be made from an actual trial in court. The early development of attainder by act was influenced greatly by the king's power to 'record' the treason of those of his subjects who had fought against him on a battlefield, a most important weapon in the king's arsenal of prerogative. His power to record other types of treason, never extensive, disappeared in the early fourteenth century, but summary conviction for treasonable military acts survived into the sixteenth century in the form of martial law. It was openly acknowledged as a much surer way of getting conviction for treason than by the common law and for this reason was used as often as possible.[3] It was a form of accusation and conviction in which the magnates and the people played no part except when they were the victims.

Another way the king was able to further his own doctrine of treason was through his judges construing borderline offences as treason. This was most easily done under the clause of the 1352 act which referred to compassing or imagining the king's death. A large number of offences were capable of being held as causing

---

[1] *Rot. Parl.*, VI, 193 b.
[2] *Stat. Realm*, III, 446–51; *Calendar of Letters and Papers, Foreign and Domestic, Henry VIII*, xv, no. 498.
[3] *Letters and Papers, Henry VIII*, XII, no. 468.

the king such concern that his health and thus his life was jeopardized. Sometimes the king's legal advisers argued that the misdeed in question had caused the people to withdraw their love from the king, thereby causing him to worry, which again endangered his health. Paradoxically, this offence of causing a division between the king and his people was very reminiscent of accroaching the royal power, and thus suggestive of a popular influence. It was first put into those words in the reign of Henry IV. Whatever the origins, later kings turned it very much to their own profit. Compassing and imagining the king's death as a category of treason seems to have surpassed all its rivals in popularity from 1352 until the treason act of Henry VIII in 1534. The wide and ingenious constructions the government was able to employ suggests a most amenable bench of judges well endowed with royalist sympathies. This was in fact the case, but even sympathetic judges had their principles. Henry VIII, for example, was rebuffed in the Elizabeth Barton case. The king and Thomas Cromwell had hoped to charge the nun with concealing treason but the judges would not have it, pointing out rather tartly that she had provided an excess of revelation rather than insufficient.[1] The frequent conferences which the fifteenth- and sixteenth-century kings called with the judges about treason suggest that the monarch's power in the matter of obtaining convictions was not absolute. He usually got his way in the end, it is true, but he must appear to observe legal convention: he was never able to flout openly the procedures of the common law.

What the late medieval and early Tudor kings did was to tamper with legal process in areas where there were no proper rules, particularly with the actual machinery of indictment and trial. The framing of indictments became increasingly the business not of local juries, although they must pronounce on their veracity, but of the king's legal advisers.[2] Thomas Cromwell spent a great deal of time at this and thought it essential to do so. A prosecution strategy was an obvious by-product, and the king held discussions with his ministers and judges for the purpose.[3] Treason charges were compiled not only from the holding of inquests or from information received from private sources, but also, and

---

[1] *Letters and Papers, Henry VIII*, vi, no. 1445.
[2] For example, *ibid.*, vi, no. 1382; xii, no. 1106, 1156.
[3] As in *ibid.*, vi, no. 1381.

increasingly, as a result of the extensive interrogation of prisoners, the questions for which were often provided by the king's council.[1] The answers received from fellow conspirators would be compared, to discover any discrepancies, and then a new set of questions put to the prisoners, and so on. If memories were weak the rack or the threat of it may have been used. Confessions were greatly prized by the king's lawyers and few traitors were put on trial until they had admitted some degree of involvement and all their plans were known. The information acquired was drafted into indictment form and sent to a grand jury for verification. Before the trial commenced the petty jury was picked or packed and then 'laboured', that is, told of the king's view of the offence, an operation which was sometimes used on presenting juries as well. From about 1469 a royal prosecutor, usually the king's attorney, appeared in treason trials. A part of his duties was to introduce such sophistications as confessions already made by the accused or his confederates, the results of examinations and the evidence of witnesses. Trials, particularly treason trials, became less concerned with the character of the accused and much more with the evidence against him. The act 33 Henry VIII c. 23, under which trial for treason was to be in any shire designated by the government, was no gross iniquity, since by that time there was much less need for a jury to have knowledge of the locality and the circumstances of the crime.[2] The significance of all these developments was not just the increase of the part played by the king in trial procedure, but the corresponding decline in the importance of the role of the people.

Although the English king could sometimes turn the laws of treason to his own advantage by interpreting them in a way which was not originally intended, and although he could implement them as he thought fit, he dared not go openly against them. He had little chance of achieving the position Richard II had aimed at in 1387, when he persuaded the judges to class as treason any interference with the king's regality, the continuance of parliamentary business against his command and the impeaching of his ministers without his consent.[3] The kings from Edward I to Edward IV, Richard II apart (and even he for the greater part of his reign) observed the laws of treason remarkably well. Edward I

---

[1] *Letters and Papers, Henry VIII*, XII (pt. I), no. 201.
[2] *Stat. Realm*, III, 863–4.   [3] *Ibid.*, II, 102–4.

convicted traitors by means of his record, but only those of his subjects who had fought against him on the battlefield: for this there were ancient precedents, as there no doubt were for his inclusion within the treason laws of the crime of levying war against the king. Edward III was guilty of efforts to extend the penalties for treason to lesser crimes, intending thereby to suppress lawlessness the more effectively, but he eventually desisted, allowed treason to be defined exactly, and modified his policies to obey the act. It is difficult to see how in 1381 some misdeeds called treasons by local juries came within the definitions of the act of 1352, but this was the greatest of popular medieval rebellions and some extreme repressive measures were to be expected. At the end of the century there were three cases of ambush on the highway which were classified as treason. So in the reign of Henry VI was a case of illegal purveyance for the royal household, and in the time of Edward IV the robbery of a church.[1] There were also two or three minor cases which may have infringed the law but concerning which the information is too exiguous to allow a confident verdict. Only in the reign of Richard III was there what appears to have been gross abuse of the law. In 1483 there does not seem to have been any legal process at all, proper or improper, before the execution of William Lord Hastings, and there seems to have been very little before the deaths of Earl Rivers, Sir Richard Grey, Sir Thomas Vaughan and Sir Richard Hawte. That examples like these were so rare is to the credit of the English governmental system of the later middle ages and the essentially moderate law of treason which was a vital part of it.

[1] Above, pp. 95 n. 2, 116 n. 4, 136.

MISPRISION

No STUDY of late medieval treason would be complete without an investigation of that class of offences which was referred to contemporaneously as misprision. The treatment of this topic by modern historians has been at once both exiguous and unfortunate, more so even than that of treason itself. One error has been to hold misprision as almost the equivalent of treason,[1] another has been to take the Tudor usage of the word and apply it to the crimes of the fourteenth and fifteenth centuries.[2] Initially the word misprision had no strong or special connexion with treason. Tudor statutes may refer to 'misprision of treason'[3] but the records of the later middle ages contain not a single example of the phrase: in them it is always misprision *tout court*. The popularizer of 'misprision of treason' was probably Sir Edward Coke. In the *Institutes of the Laws of England* he separated 'misprision of treason' from 'misprisions divers and severall' and awarded it a separate if slender chapter.[4]

Coke was led into error in both chapters by his unsound critical apparatus. He elected to commence his investigations by means of etymology. 'Misprisio', he wrote, 'cometh of the French word *mespris* which properly signifieth neglect or contempt: for *mes* in composition in the French signifieth *mal* as *mis* doth in the English tongue: as mischance for an ill chance and so *mesprise* is ill apprehended or known. In legall understanding it signifieth when one knoweth of any treason or felony and concealeth it'.[5] In fact the proper meaning of the word was not a neglect or contempt but a mistaken or wrongful action. It derived not from the Old French *mespris* but from *mesprison*, a mistake. This can be easily demonstrated by an examination of the record evidence of the fourteenth and fifteenth centuries. Furthermore it is obvious that the word took on additional meanings as the years passed.

---

[1] See Keen, 'Treason Trials', *Trans. Roy. Hist. Soc.*, 5th ser., XII, 98, n. 6.
[2] As done, for example, by C. Oman, *History of England, 1377–1485* (London, 1920), p. 246 and recently by A. Rogers, 'Parliamentary Appeals of Treason in the Reign of Richard II', *American Journal of Legal History*, VIII (1964), 115.
[3] For example, the statutes 1 Edward VI c. 12 and 1 Mary st. 1, c. 1.
[4] Coke, pp. 36–7.   [5] *Ibid.*, p. 36.

At the beginning of the fourteenth century the word misprision had the meaning default. An example is to be found in a petition on the parliament roll of the sessions of 1308–9: 'le Eschetor e ad pris le manere avauntdite en la mayne le Roy, par le resun qe le avauntdite Huwe ne fit pas gre pur le entre, e pur ceo prie Estene de Tedemers a nostre seigneur le Roy qi il de sa grace ly voyle pardoner cel meprision'.[1] By 1341 misprision was being used in reference to the failure of the king's officers and ministers to perform official duties in a satisfactory manner. In parliament that year the commons, when referring to an investigation of the conduct of the chancellor, the treasurer and other great officers, drew attention to the fact that 'les ditz Justicz en les dites Commissions assignez ont mys divers Officers atteintz devant eux a si grevouses Fyns, nient eant regard a la quantite de lours mesprisions'.[2] Another petition of the same year stated 'Et si pleint soit faite de queconqe Ministre de nulle mesprision et de ce soit atteint en Parlement . . .'[3]

In the later fourteenth century the word often took on a stronger meaning. A misprision referred to in the Good Parliament of 1376 was wilful misbehaviour in office rather than omission of duty: 'ascuns novelx Enquestes d'Office prises par voz Eschetours et autres Ministres purportantz ascuns Terres estre tenuz de vous en chief, par ont mesmes les Terres et plusours autres ovesqe ont este seisez en votre main'.[4] In the same parliament Richard Lyons was accused of 'plusours disceites, extorsions et autres malx faitz par luy au Roy notre Seigneur et a son poeple' when he was one of the king's council and as a farmer of the subsidy and the customs.[5] He had procured the imposition on wool, skins and other merchandise of certain taxes not assented to by parliament: he had purchased the king's debts at a discount and then arranged for their total repayment. He had also procured licences to carry abroad wools and skins, thereby avoiding the Calais staple. His misdeeds were achieved 'par preignant sur luy notoirement en toutes les dites choses poair Roial' and although they were not called misprisions in the roll of the parliament of 1376 they were in that of the subsequent session.[6] There was probably a deliberate policy by the king at this time to use 'misprision' where perhaps the charge of

[1] *Rot. Parl.*, I, 276.
[2] *Ibid.*, II, 128 b.
[3] *Ibid.*, II, 131 a.
[4] *Ibid.*, II, 342 a.
[5] *Ibid.*, II, 323–4.
[6] See *Ibid.*, III, 12 b.

usurping or accroaching the royal power would have been used before 1352. Quite remarkably between 1376 and 1387 the baronial opposition tended to use the same phrase when it accused the king's ministers and officers of grave misconduct. In 1386 Michael de la Pole, earl of Suffolk and chancellor of England, was impeached in parliament by the commons largely on the grounds that he had profited himself financially during his period as chancellor. He had, so it was said, purchased royal lands at low prices and was responsible for mis-spending taxation intended to provide for the keeping of the seas and the defence of Ghent. He had defrauded the king out of his due profits in two notorious cases. He had also granted an unsatisfactorily large number of pardons for treasons and felonies and had given certain franchises to Dover castle 'en disheritison de la Corone et subversion des toutes les Places et Courtes du Roi et de ses Lois'.[1] At the time of the impeachment these offences were referred to collectively as 'defautes et mes-prisions', and in the next parliament simply as 'certeins mes-prisions'.[2]

The term misprision did not always refer to misdeeds com-mitted by those who held office under the crown. Sometime before July 1347 a large confederacy of evildoers in the port of Lynn, assuming to themselves royal power, boarded ships which were laden with corn for Gascony. They seized the cargo and offered it for sale ashore. They arrested men who were bringing corn to the town for purposes of sale and adjudged some to the pillory. They also arrested the mayor of the town and many good men and compelled them by means of threats to maintain their misprisions and unlawful quarrels.[3] In this case the word misprision seems to have been used because the miscreants usurped office and then acted in a *quasi* official capacity. Another category of misprision not involving ministerial default or misbehaviour and one which seems to have first arisen at the end of the fourteenth century concerned illicit communication with the Roman curia. In April 1388 Master William Menasse obtained a pardon for misprision in prosecuting a cause overseas contrary to the laws and customs of the realm and for which a writ of *praemunire facias* had been issued against him.[4] In February 1402 Henry Chichele, the future archbishop of Canterbury, who had been provided to a canonry and

---

[1] *Rot. Parl.*, III, 216–20.   [2] *Ibid.*, III, 242 a.
[3] *Cal. Pat. Rolls, 1345–8*, p. 388.   [4] *Cal. Pat. Rolls, 1385–9*, p. 430.

prebend in the cathedral church of Salisbury, was pardoned the contempts, trespasses and misprisions involved and was given licence for the execution of the papal bulls notwithstanding the second statute of *provisors* of 1390.[1] None of the four fourteenth-century statutes of *provisors* and *praemunire* introduces the word misprision, nor does it seem to have been in common use in the English courts. Another case, one which was more notorious, where offences were construed as misprision involved Edward III's mistress Alice Perrers.[2] In the parliament of January 1377 the favourite was found guilty of maintaining quarrels in the courts against the king's wishes, of persuading the king to pardon Richard Lyons his forfeiture and inducing him not to send Sir Nicholas Dagworth to Ireland.[3] The second and third offences were unknown to the common law either as felony or misdemeanour. They were solely political crimes.

One important class of misprisions stemmed from the suspicious behaviour of a number of English captains in France during the early years of Richard II's reign. In the majority of cases they were held to have received money from the king's enemies at the time when they surrendered territory or fortresses. In 1383 during the impeachment in parliament of Sir William Elmham, Sir Thomas Tryvet and three other captains of Henry Despenser's army, the chancellor said that it was 'grant mesprision . . . qe aucun lige du Roi rendroit ou durroit as ditz Enemys Chastel, Forteresce, Vitaille, Armure ou autre Refrechement sanz commandement et auctorite del Roy especial'.[4] It was still worse, he added, 'de vendre et aliener a mesmes les Enemys aucun Fort, Vitaille, Armure ou autre Refrechement par repreignant d'iceulx Enemys Monoie ou autres Biens'. Another offence drew forth this instructive homily: 'il n'est mye lisible chose, einz moelt grant mesprision en la persone de chescun lige Homme du Roi de faire Treitie avec aucun Enemy du Roi sanz la volentee et expresse auctorite du Roi mesmes ou de son lieutenant'.[5] The captains could have rightfully claimed that they were guilty only of accepted military practices. There had been no deliberate adherence to the

---

[1] *Cal. Pat. Rolls, 1401–5*, p. 46.
[2] *Cal. Inquis. Misc., 1377–88*, p. 1; *Cal. Pat. Rolls, 1377–81*, p. 205.
[3] *Rot. Parl.*, III, 12 b.
[4] *Ibid.*, III, 157 a.
[5] *Ibid.*

king's enemies and the crown knew it. The leader of the expedition, Henry Despenser, bishop of Norwich, was impeached because he had failed to fulfil the indenture he had made with the king. He had not served the crown for the stipulated period nor mustered the proper number of men at Calais. He had also refused to take a royal lieutenant with him.[1] These misdeeds were described as 'certeines mesprisions'.

The importance of this series of parliamentary trials lies in the fact that several of the crimes, although termed misprisions, stood quite close to treason. In 1377 William Weston had been sentenced to be drawn and hanged for offences which were quite similar.[2] In 1383 at one point in the trial the chancellor warned that no soldier should accept gold from the king's enemies 'Qar autrement chescun Treitour qe desore dorroit ou vendroit les Chastelx et autres Forteresces du Roi a tieux Enemys pur or ou autre avoir, se purroit excuser del treison en mesme le manere'.[3] Another indication was that Sir Thomas Tryvet, who on one occasion had granted safe conduct under his own seal, was accused of accroaching the royal power, a charge which had hardly been used since the 1352 statute of treason but which must have revived fading memories.[4] That misprision came so close to treason at this time was not accidental. Very likely the king started to popularize the word misprision in an attempt to remove the sting from charges of accroaching the royal power made in parliament against ministers and royal servants. Five years after these trials in parliament the word misprision was used to describe the misdeeds of an Italian merchant who had exported gold and silver plate from England and had betrayed the secrets of the realm to the French.[5] Had these offences been the work of an Englishman they would have been undoubted treason.

To Coke, as we have seen, misprision of treason meant basically the concealment of treason. Later writers, when referring to medieval cases involving knowledge of treason not reported to the king, have mistakenly used the same term. Certainly Bracton, writing in the thirteenth century, implied that to refrain from passing on to the king a knowledge that his life was in danger was tantamount to treason, but the word misprision was unknown

[1] *Rot. Parl.*, III, 153–4, 156 b.   [2] *Ibid.*, III, 10–12.
[3] *Ibid.*, III, 153 a.   [4] *Ibid.*, III, 157 b.
[5] *Cal. Pat. Rolls, 1385–9*, p. 501.

to him.[1] The first indication in the period under review that the concealed knowledge of treason might be held as the committing of treason, presumably by imagining or compassing the king's death, occurred at the time of the Merciless Parliament in 1388. Sir Nicholas Brembre, one of the five principal accused, was charged with the others with a long list of crimes. Fourteen of the articles of accusation were declared by the Lords Appellant to be treason and Brembre was involved in five of the fourteen. He was allowed to plead not guilty and then first a committee of twelve lords and later the representatives of the London guilds were appointed as petty jurors. The lords failed to return the desired verdict and at first the guildsmen gave the vaguest of answers. Therefore the Lords Appellant asked the mayor of London, certain aldermen and the recorder whether they believed Brembre had knowledge of the treasons laid against him or not. Their answer was that he was more likely to have known than to have been ignorant.[2] Seemingly the Lords Appellant had changed the charges to concealment of treason. The London citizens recognized the uncertain nature of the crime for when they had given their verdict they asked the recorder 'quid dicit lex tua in casu isto?'. The answer was given that 'ille qui scivit talia atque celavit et non detexit merito puniretur vitae privatione et cetera' but there was no suggestion that the matter touched on treason.[3] The parliament rolls conceal both the dubious nature of the charge and the type of legal process involved, simply stating that Brembre was found guilty of high treason as contained in the articles.[4] To the Lords Appellant the mere knowledge or concealment of treason was treason and there was no need to declare it as such. Yet there was one gross inconsistency. The tenth article charged against the household knights Simon Burley, John Beauchamp, John Salesbury and James Berners, said they 'avoient conusance de les Tresons faitz par les Ercevesqes et autres Traitours atteintz'.[5] They should have given notice to the 'good lords' of the realm of these treasons traitorously imagined but did not, preferring to counsel and sustain the traitors. Each of the four knights was found guilty of treason but none of them on account of the tenth article. Therefore it cannot be said that any victim of the Appellants was

---

[1] Bracton, *De Legibus Angliae*, ed. Twiss, II, 265.
[2] *Polychronicon Higden*, IX, 166–8.   [3] *Ibid.*, IX, 168.
[4] *Rot. Parl.*, III, 238.   [5] *Ibid.*, III, 242 b.

definitely condemned for treason because he did not reveal his knowledge of treason.

A more probable example of the crown holding the knowledge and concealment of treason as treason is to be found in the trial of the Southampton plotters of 1415. Two of those accused, the earl of Cambridge and Sir Thomas Grey, pleaded guilty to the charge of conspiring to kill Henry V and make the earl of March king. Henry Lord Scrope of Masham, the third accused, answered that Grey had told him of the plot and he had discussed with the other two their plan for the killing of the king and his brothers. His intention in doing this, so he avowed, was to impede their design. He admitted concealing the treason but on the charge of imagining the king's death he pleaded not guilty. A commission composed of a number of important magnates decided that Scrope 'conscius et sepius cum eisdem Proditoribus communicans et ad communicandum sepius consentiens nec Proditionem illam interim Domino Regi seu eius consilio discoperavit set illud a dicto Domino Rege et eius Consilio totaliter concelavit'.[1] Therefore they adjudged he had committed high treason [altam ceditionem], deciding that Cambridge and he as traitors for imagining, consenting to, conspiring and concealing the death of the king should be drawn, hanged and beheaded. Thus in 1415 to know of yet to conceal treason was treason since the purpose could only be malicious, but it was not yet referred to by the term misprision.

The next relevant case occurred in 1468. Sir Thomas Cook, a London mercer and an ex-mayor, was accused by one John Hawkins, who had himself been accused by a servant of Sir Robert Whittingham. According to a jury of presentment Hawkins and an associate called Hugo Mulle had visited Cook and told him that Queen Margaret was about to invade England with a large army and that Sir Richard Tunstall, the Lancastrian commander of Harlech castle, intended raising Cheshire and Lancashire and then marching on London. Cook was accused of sheltering and hiding Hawkins and Mulle: furthermore it was claimed he had promised Margaret money from himself and his friends. He had confessed himself to be one of her supporters and had sent her words of comfort. The jury which found him guilty of receiving and sheltering Hawkins and Mulle acquitted him of the other crimes.[2] Cook was able eventually to present a pardon covering

[1] *Rot. Parl.*, IV, 65–6.   [2] P.R.O., K.B. 27/830 Rex m. 41.

all treasons, murders, rapes, insurrections, rebellions, congregations, embraceries and maintenances, but he still had to pay a fine. The *coram rege* rolls make no allusion to the nature or category of the crime of which he was found guilty: the statement that it was adjudged misprision comes from a contemporary chronicler.[1] John Stow, writing over a century after the event, adds the information that Chief Justice Markham, who presumably was the chairman of the session, 'determined somewhat against the king's pleasure that the offence done by Sir Thomas Cooke was no treason but misprision, the which was no desert of death but to be fined at the king's pleasure . . .'[2]

By the end of the fifteenth century it was possible for a man to be attainted by act of parliament for misprision just as it was for treason or felony. In the parliament of 1491–2 a bill of attainder was submitted which stated that in November 1491 John Hayes, late of Tiverton, Devon, had received and presumably sheltered the bearer of a letter from John Tailour, a traitor, who was at that time in Normandy in the service of the king of France. Hayes had allowed the messenger to depart 'without any arrest or trouble to him therefore made and also caste the said Writing in the fire and concealed all the matier' failing to show it to the king before he was arrested. The implication was that the letter contained treasonable material. The bill asked for it to be ordained that Hayes should be 'convicted and atteynted of misprision . . . by hym committed and doon ayenst the kings mooste Royall Persone, of and for his unlawfull demeanyng and concealement'.[3] The crown accepted the bill without amendment. In this case misprision undoubtedly meant concealment and the crime concealed was very likely treason. Yet there was no use of the phrase 'misprision of treason'.

The punishment which the act ordained for Hayes was the forfeiture of all his goods, fees, offices and annuities and imprisonment until he made a fine and ransom with the king. This was the normal penalty for misprision as a petition presented by the commons in parliament in 1384 shows. It asked for pardon and release for all escapes of felons, trespasses, negligences, misprisions, ignorances and all other things 'dont le punisement

---

[1] *Letters and Papers illustrative of the Wars in France,* ed. Stevenson, II, II, 789–90.   [2] Stow, p. 420.
[3] *Rot. Parl.,* VI, 455.

16

cherroit en fyn ou en ranceon ou en autres peynes pecunieres ou en emprisonment des corps . . .'[1] Such crimes were deliberately separated from treason, murder, robbery, rape and felony, which carried penalties of life and limb. The same formula was rehearsed in a general pardon in the parliamentary session at Shrewsbury in 1398 and can be found in other pardons.[2]

[1] *Rot. Parl.*, III, 202 b.   [2] *Ibid.*, III, 369 a.

PETTY TREASON

TREASON could be committed against a man's immediate lord as well as the monarch, and indeed in the Germanic law codes infidelity towards one's lord was much more prominent. In the twelfth century, probably owing to the wave of Romanism, the king's legal advisers began to emphasize the gravity of the crime while seeking to distinguish between the king and lesser lords as offended parties. Maitland suggested that the distinction was not readily accepted and that petty treason perpetrated against a lord was but slowly marked off from high treason perpetrated against the king.[1] Certainly those who wrote on matters of law in the later thirteenth century made no great effort to separate one type of treason from the other and with a single exception avoided direct reference to the less heinous kind.

Bracton implies there were crimes of lese-majesty which might be directed against persons other than the monarch and, making an adaptation from the *Digest* (48, 19, 28, 11 *De Poenis*), stated that those who plot against the lives of their lords should be burned with fire.[2] *Fleta*, who wrote as if lese-majesty was an offence only against the king, stated in his chapter 'De Crimine Falsi' that any man who forged the seal of the lord to whose household he belonged and authenticated therewith any writs or sealed any charter or letter to the disherison of his lord or the loss of another should on conviction be drawn and hanged, the same penalty as for treason against the king.[3] The author of the *Mirror of Justices* made reference to treasons committed against others than the king but only incidentally when dealing with appeal of treason. He mentioned a category of treason where a man defiled the wife of his ally [*allie*], or falsified his seal, or killed his father or other

---

[1] Pollock and Maitland, II, 504.

[2] Bracton, II, 334: '... publicorum quaedam (crimina) majorem poenam inferunt propter personam contra quam praesumitur, sicut est crimen lacsae majestatis ut si contra personam ipsius regis sit praesumptum ... Habet enim crimen laesae majestatis sub se multas species, quorum una est ut si quis ausu temerario machinatus sit in mortem domini regis vel aliquid egerit vel agi procuraverit ad seditionem domini regis vel exercitus sui vel procurantibus auxilium et consilium praebuerit vel consensum licet id quod in voluntate habuerit non perduxit ad effectum': *ibid.*, II, 299.　　　　[3] *Fleta*, p. 58.

kinsman or his lord or ally, or gave aid or counsel to his ally's adversary in a plea concerning life or member or earthly worship, or disclosed his counsel or confession or acted badly or carelessly as his attorney.[1] For this author, to appeal a man of these crimes was to appeal him of treason. This was quite distinct from appeal of lese-majesty, which concerned only the king and was dealt with in another chapter. Of the men who wrote legal treatises at the turn of the fourteenth century *Britton* alone referred categorically to two types of treason. He called them great treason and little treason and they were classes which hardly tallied with high and petty treason of the fifteenth century.[2] Great treason was to compass the king's death, to disinherit him of his kingdom, to falsify his seal or to counterfeit his coin, but, said *Britton*, a person might likewise commit great treason against others in several ways as for example by procuring the death of anyone who had given him their trust. Treason in general *Britton* defined as any mischief which a man did knowingly or procured to be done to one to whom he pretended to be a friend. Thus under little treason were apparently included lesser crimes against one's lord such as counterfeiting his seal, committing adultery with his wife, or violating his daughter or the nurse of his children. How far these distinctions of *Britton* were based on the legal practice then current is not clear, there being very few cases of treason before the courts whose reports survive. All we may state with any certainty is that at the end of the thirteenth century there was more than one type of treason, one kind being an offence committed against a man's immediate lord rather than the king.

In the first half of the fourteenth century the number of cases involving the offence later called petty treason which appeared before the courts was small. Nor are they well documented. In the fifteenth year of the reign of Edward II a woman was tried for attempting unsuccessfully to kill her husband and was sentenced to be burned. Although there was no reference to petty treason in as many words the penalty exacted showed that the offence was not treated as an ordinary felony.[3] 'If a woman be attainted of any treason', said *Britton*, 'let her be burnt'.[4] In the twelfth year of

---

[1] *Mirror*, p. 54.   [2] *Britton*, I, 40–1.   [3] Hale, I, 380.
[4] *Britton*, I, 40–1; A. Fitzherbert, *La Graunde Abridgement* (London, 1516), I, f. 259 has a case 46 Mich. 1 Richard III before Sir Guy Fairfax and his fellow justices of assize in which burning was specifically stated to be the punishment for a woman guilty of petty treason.

Edward III a servant girl aged thirteen was burned for murdering her mistress. The writer who reported the case called the crime treason *tout court*, there being no epithet appended.[1] A more notorious murder which occurred only a few years later must have drawn attention to the lesser type of treason. This was the killing in his house near Ware of John de Shoreditch, one of the king's council and a trusted ambassador, on 10 July 1345. He was done to death by suffocation by four of his household servants.[2] On capture the miscreants confessed their guilt and were sentenced to the traitor's death of being drawn, hanged and beheaded. The only other case of significance in this period is very badly documented. Sir Matthew Hale, apparently following Coke, held that for a son to kill his father was likewise petty treason and quoted a case from the twenty-first year of Edward III's reign.[3]

Quite often the only indication for the historian that a man was found guilty of the lesser species of treason lies in the sentence of drawing and hanging or in the case of a woman, burning. The land owned by the convicted man escheated to his immediate lord as in the case of any other felony. This was in contrast to the custom in high treason whereby the lands were forfeited to the crown. The position was clearly demonstrated by the Hill case of 1347. Chief Justice Thorpe said that the crown would have both the chattels and the lands of the convicted man only where the treason touched the king or when it was a matter of adhering to his enemies. Otherwise the lands would escheat to the immediate lord.[4] How long this had been royal practice is difficult to determine but the phraseology of the *Liver des Assises* suggests that in that respect the Hill decision was no new departure. All this was mentioned incidentally to the main point at issue, which was charters of privilege in general form and their bearing on forfeiture. As has already been shown the issue of forfeiture was a major reason for the enactment of the treason statute of 1352. Petty treason was only an incidental cause although it figured quite bulkily in the final form of the act because of the commons' demand for a definition of treason in

---

[1] *Year Books, 11 and 12 Edward III* (R.S., 1883), p. 627.
[2] Murimuth and Avesbury, *Chronica*, p. 171.
[3] Hale, I, 378; Coke, p. 20. Matthew Paris refers to a case of parricide in 1255. He says that on conviction the accused man 'Londoniis tractus ad patibulum suspensus est': *Chronica Majora*, v, 490.
[4] *Year Books, Liver des Assises*, 22 Edward III, pl. 49.

general. This had arisen from a tendency on the part of the judges to construe various serious felonies as high treason.[1]

The statute 25 Edward III st. 5, c. 2 carefully distinguished between treason which concerned the king and that which did not, although no use was made of the words 'high' and 'petty'. The lesser type of treason was defined as when a servant killed his master, a woman her baron or 'home seculer ou de religion tue son prelat'.[2] As Maitland pointed out 'master' did not mean lord or 'servant' vassal. The 1352 definition seems to have been a narrowing of the existing category. There was no mention of the crime of a servant who falsified the seal of his lord or who committed adultery with his wife or daughter or the nurse of his children. The precedents for calling these crimes treason were ignored, as was the example from Edward II's reign of a woman being burned for an unsuccessful attempt to murder her husband, and the example of parricide from the twenty-first year of the reign of Edward III.

In the remainder of the fourteenth century there were only minor developments in the history of petty treason. In the thirty-third year of Edward III's reign Chief Justice Shareshull decided that a servant who had left his master had killed him on a grudge conceived while in his service over a year before and that therefore the crime was petty treason.[3] Seven years later one particular case seems to have given rise to the dictum that if a servant and the wife of his master plotted the master's death and the servant committed the murder in her absence, then he alone was guilty of petty treason as a principal: the wife was an accessory.[4] She was, however, to be burned. More important for the history of treason in general was the new practice of referring to the two types of treason as high and petty. The words 'high treason' came into common use

---

[1] Above: chapter 4 in general.   [2] *Stat. Realm*, I, 319–20.

[3] *Year Books, Liver des Assises*, 33 Edward III, pl. 7: 'Un home fuit arraine devant Shard. sur un endictment de ceo qe il avoit felonisement occis son Maister. Qui plede de rien culpable. Et trove fuit qe il occist: mes fuit trove qe il ne fuit pas son maistre a cel temps mes un an devant. *Shard.* Avoit il nul mal voilant del servant vs son Maistre; issint qe per cest ceo qe il avoit son Maistre en agait: Trove fuit per Enquest qe oyl. Purcque fuit trahy et pendu'. The case was referred to in 19 Henry VI by Justice Hody: see Fitzherbert, *La Graunde Abridgement*, I, f. 257. Hody also made the point that a servant who murdered his master's wife was committing petty treason since he must have been obedient to her as well as her husband.

[4] *Year Books, Liver des Assises*, 40 Edward III, pl. 25.

in the reign of Richard II possibly because of the political strife. It is perhaps not too fanciful to see in the usage an aspiration to theocratic monarchy on the part of the king and a fear of the same thing among the baronial opposition. In the Merciless Parliament of 1388 the archbishop of York, Robert de Vere, duke of Ireland, Michael de la Pole, earl of Suffolk, Robert Tresilian C.J.K.B. and Nicholas Brembre, the ex-mayor of London, were all appealed 'de hautes tresons par eux faitz encountre le roi et soun realme'.[1] In the parliamentary session of September 1397 when the commission of government of 1386 was annulled as a usurpation of royal power, it was declared that anyone who procured to be made a similar commission in time to come or made use of the power of such a commission and was duly convicted of it in parliament 'soit adjugge pur traitour et ceo de haut traisoun fait encontre le roy et sa corone'.[2] The new statute of treason which Richard II and his parliament promulgated in the same session also made use of the word 'high'. Those who committed any one of four listed offences 'et de ceo soit duement atteint et adjuggez en parlement soit adjuggez come traitour de haute traisoun encontre la Corone'.[3] These references to high treason, it may be noted, appear in records written in Norman-French, in the parliament rolls in fact. There are very few such references in Latin, even in the fifteenth century. The earliest example dates from 1402, when the judges conferred with the king's council about certain words spoken by John Sperhauk. They were found to amount to 'alta et maxima proditio'.[4] Such phraseology was rare. Usually in court records of the late middle ages the type of treason was implied by the context alone.

The first time the adjective 'petty' was used to describe treason was probably in 1423. In the parliamentary session of that year the commons petitioned successfully that since the statute of 1352 had said nothing about those who were indicted, appealed or taken on suspicion of great [graunde] treason and then when imprisoned made their escape, the deed should be declared treason.[5] There was also a rider to the effect that the lands of those attainted should go to their immediate lord and not necessarily to the king. It was the penalty 'come de ceux qe sount atteintz de petite Treison'. The

---

[1] Rot. Parl., III, 229 b.
[2] Ibid., III, 349–50.
[3] Stat. Realm, II, 98–9.
[4] P.R.O., K.B. 27/564 Rex m. 12.
[5] Rot. Parl., IV, 260 b.

appearance of the term 'petty treason' in 1423 did not lead to its common adoption. The rolls of parliament tended increasingly to refer to treason which concerned the royal majesty as high treason, while using no adjective at all in cases of petty treason.[1] In the records of other courts the type of treason continued to be revealed more by the context than anything else.

The process of trial in cases of petty treason was like that for any other felony. Unlike high treason it could be tried before the justices of the peace.[2] The statute *Pro Clero* which supplemented the treason act of 1352 confirmed that benefit of clergy still applied. It stated 'Touz maneres des clercs, auxibien seculars come religiouses qi serront desore convictz devant les justices seculers pur qecomqes felonies ou tresons touchantes autres persones qe le roi meismes ou sa roiale majeste, eient et enjoient franchement desore privilege de Seinte Eglise et soient saunz nule empeschement ou delai liverez a les ordinaries eux demandantz'.[3] In return for this confirmation the archbishop of Canterbury promised the king that clerks so delivered to the ordinary should be safely kept and properly punished. Possibly the church failed to carry out its part of the bargain, since in the parliament which met in September 1402 the archbishop of Canterbury had to reaffirm his predecessor's promise about safe-keeping and punishment.[4] Henceforth these were to be according to a constitution made by the archbishop and the other bishops of the province based on the arrangements of 1351, although with the addition of certain novel penalties. No clerk convicted of petty treason, so it was stated, or one who was known as a common thief, was to be allowed to purge himself contrary to the intent of the new constitution. This was a revision of existing practice rather than a change in policy. There was no alteration of the law until 1497, when one particular case of the murder of a master by his servant caused parliament to legislate in general terms in a rider to an act of attainder.[5] James Grame, a London yeoman, had wilfully murdered his master Richard Tracy 'to the right perilous ensample of othre ill disposed' and when arraigned had pleaded his clergy. The bill of attainder requested that Grame should be attainted of murder 'as a felon

---

[1] For illustration, see *Rot. Parl.*, IV, 497 b, V, 17 b, 54 a, 451 a, 632 b and *Cal. Pat. Rolls, 1446–52*, pp. 45, 61.
[2] See *Cal. Pat. Rolls, 1476–85*, p. 72.   [3] *Stat. Realm*, I, 325.
[4] *Ibid.*, II, 133; *Rot. Parl.*, III, 494 b–5 a.   [5] *Stat. Realm*, II, 639.

that hath offendid in pety treason' and that he should be drawn
and hanged as a lay man, his privilege notwithstanding. 'Also be it
ordeyned . . .', the act continued, 'that if any laie persone hereaftir
purpensidly murder their Lord, Maistcr or Sovereign immediate
that they hereaftir be not admytted to their Clergie' but on conviction or attainder the guilty party be executed 'as though he
were noe Clerk'.

ILLUSTRATIVE MATERIALS

PROCEDURE against the murderers of John Imperial, a Genoese ambassador, including parliamentary declaration of the crime as treason, 1379: P.R.O., K.B. 27/476 Rex mm. 31, 31d and supplementary.

Dominus rex mandavit justiciariis suis hic breve suum clausum in hec verba:

Ricardus Dei gratia rex Anglie et Francie et dominus Hibernie, dilectis et fidelibus suis Johanni de Cavendissh et sociis suis justiciariis ad placita coram nobis tenenda assignatis, salutem. Indictamentum factum coram vicecomitibus nostris Londoniae et coronatore eiusdem civitatis de morte Johannis Imperial de Jannu super visu corporis eiusdem Johannis unde Johannes Kyrkeby, mercer, et Johannes Algore, grocer, indictati sunt coram nobis in cancellariam nostram de mandato notsro missum vobis mittimus sub pede sigilli nostri mandantes quod eo viso ulterius inde fieri facias quod de iure et secundum leges et consuetudines regni nostri Anglie fuit faciendum. Teste me ipso apud Westmonasterium secundo die martii anno regno nostro tertio.

Breve vicecomitibus Londoniae et coronatori eiusdem civitatis de mittendo indictamentum predictum in cancellaria predicta directum sequitur in hec verba:

... Quia quibusdam certis de causis coram nobis et consilio nostro in presenti parliamento nostro propositis certiorari volumus super indictamento facto coram vobis de morte Johannis Imperial super visu corporis eiusdem iam unde Johannes Kyrkeby serviens Johannis More, et Johannes Algor, serviens Ricardi de Preston indictati sunt ut dicitur, vobis precipimus quod indictamentum predictum cum omnibus illud tangentibus nobis in cancellariam nostram sub sigillis vestris distincte et aperte ac salve et secure sine dilatione aliqua mittatis. Et hoc breve ut nos inde plenius certiorari ulterius inde fieri faciamus quod de iure et secundum leges et consuetudines regni nostri Anglie fuerit faciendum. Teste me ipso apud Westmonasterium xxvi die Februarii anno regni nostri tertio.

Indictamentum de quo in brevibus predictis fuit mentio sequitur in hec verba:

... Et sic dicunt juratores predicti quod predictus Johannes Kyrkeby ipsum Johannem Imperialis felonice interfecit occasione predicta et non ex aliqua malicia precogitata seu discordia inter eos perhabita.

Dicunt etiam juratores predicti quod predictus Johannes Algore, grocer, erat tunc presens in loco predicto quando felonia predicta facta fuit cum uno baselardo extracto in manu sua et quosdam predictorum servientium prefati Johannis Imperialis verberavit et vulneravit ut supradictum est ... Et super hoc dominus rex mandavit justiciariis suis hic breve suum clausum in hec verba:

Ricardus, Dei gratia rex Anglie et Francie et dominus Hibernie dilectis et fidelibus suis Johanni de Cavendissh et sociis suis justiciariis ad placita coram nobis tenenda assignatis, salutem. Transcriptum quarumdam litterarum nostrarum patentium in cancellaria nostra sexto die martii anno regni nostri primo irrotulatarum per quas quidem litteras patentes nuper susceperimus in salvum et securum conductum nostrum ac in protectionem et defensionem nostras speciales Janum Imperial Januensem patronum cuiusdam tarite vocate *La Seinte Marie de Janua* ...

Postea scilicet die sabbati in tertia septimana quadragesime isto eodem termino coram domino rege apud Westmonasterium venerunt predicti Johannes Kyrkeby et Johannes Algore per Alanum de Buxhill constabularium Turris Londonie de mandato domini regis ducti qui alias in custodia sua per consilium ipsius regis commissi fuerunt allocuti sunt separatim qualiter de felonio et seditione predictis se velint acquietare. Dicunt separatim quod ipsi in nullo sunt inde culpabiles et inde de bono et malo ponunt se super patriam ... Et dominus rex mandavit justiciariis suis hic breve suum clausum in hec verba:

Ricardus Dei gratia etc. Johanni de Cavendyssh et sociis suis justiciariis ad placita coram nobis tenenda assignatis, salutem. Transcriptum cuiusdam declarationis proditionis per nos et consilium nostrum de assensu et avisamento procerum magnatum et communitatis regni nostri Anglie in ultimo parliamento nostro apud Westmonasterium tento inter alia facte, concordate et ordinate in rotulis eiusdem parliamenti nostri irrotulate vobis mittimus presentibus interclusum, mandantes quod eo viso eadem facta concordiam et ordinationem super declarationem huiusmodi totiens quotiens casus huiusmodi exigit et requirit coram nobis firmiter observari et teneri ac debito executione demandari faciatis iuxta vim, formam et effectum declarationis eiusdem ...

Et ad eundem crastinum sancti Johannis Baptiste prefatus Johannes Cavendisshe, capitalis justiciarius etc., liberavit hic in curia veredictum iurate predicte coram eo et sociis suis justiciariis etc. Postea die et loco infra contentis coram Johanne Cavendisshe, Roberto Bealknappe, Roberto Tresilian, Willelmo Skypwyth, Rogero de Fulthorp et Henrico Percehay justiciariis infranominatis, venerunt Johannes Kyrkeby, mercer, et Johannes Algor, grocer, infranominatos, per custodem Turris Londoniae de mandato domini regis ducti ac servientes domini regis ad placita venerunt. Et similiter juratores venerunt qui ad hoc electi, triati et jurati, dicunt super sacramentum suum quod predictus Johannes Kyrkeby interfecit prefatum Johannem Imperiall se defendendo. Quesiti iidem juratores qualiter hoc fuit se defendendo qui dicunt quod penitus ignorant. Quesiti sepius iidem juratores per justiciarios quam stricte idem Johannes Kyrkeby in casu predicto positus fuit quod aliter evadere non potuit, qui dicunt ut prius quod penitus inde ignorant. Quesitum ulterius iidem juratores si ipsi aliquid aliud pro veredicto de prefato Johanne Kyrkeby dicere velint nec ne qui dicunt precise quod nichil aliud pro veredictum dicere sciunt seu velint . . . Et quo ad prefatum Johannem Algor iidem juratores dicunt quod idem Johannes in nullo est culpabilis de morte predicta nec ea occasione se retraxit. Et interim predicti Johannes et Johannes committuntur prisone Turris Londonie ad salvo custodiendum etc. . . . Postea scilicet die martis proxime ante festum sancti Nicholai anno regni regis nunc Anglie quarto coram domino rege apud Norhamptoniam venerunt predicti Johannes de Kirkeby et Johannes Algor per Johannem Staple et Thomas atte Mille servientes domini regis ad arma pretextu cuiusdam brevis domini regis de cancellaria ipsius regis eis inde directi quod affilatur inter precepta de anno quarto supradicto ducti qui committuntur marescallie. Et statim per marescallum ducti venerunt. Et quesitum est a prefato Johanne de Kyrkeby si quid pro se habeat vel dicere sciat quare ad iudicium de eo super veredicto predicto procedi non debeat. Qui quidem Johannes de Kyrkeby dicit quod clericus est. Quesitum est ulterius ab eo sepius si quid aliud dicere sciat etc. nec ne qui dicit quod non. Et quia idem Johannes de Kyrkeby privilagio clericali in hoc casu iuxta declarationem et ordinationem predictas gaudere non potest. Ideo idem Johannes de Kyrkeby distrahatur et suspendatur. Et inquiratur de terris et catallis suis etc. Et predictus Johannes Algor devenit probator et fecit appellum quod affilatur inter recorda de anno quarto regis nunc. Et predictus Johannes Algor committitur prisone in custodis Ricardi Imworth marescalli.

Indictment of certain Oxfordshire insurgents, 1398: P.R.O., K.B. 27/550 Rex. m. 23.

Juratores . . . presentant quod Johannes Milford, webbe, de Cogges et alii ut primi et principales insurrectores et capitales ductores et abbettatores quorumdam rebellium ad quemdam insurrectionem contra dominum nostrum regem et ligeanciam suam in comitatu Oxonie nuper subortam faciendam in simul jurati et interligati fuerunt, in mortem ipsius domini regis et magnatum regni sui Anglie destrucionem felonice et proditorie contra ligeantiam suam ymaginando, proponendo et conspirando adiuncta sibi et aggregata quam magna potentia et multitudine diversorum hominum de assensu eorum et falsa interligeancia et covina videlicet Johannis Bedemansone de Wytteney et aliorum . . . felonice et proditorie contra dominum regem et ligeantiam suam de novo insurrexerunt et ibidem hostiliter mustraverunt.

Traitorous use of an old royal seal: *Year Books*, 2 Henry IV. Trin. pl. 25.

En bank le Roy un homme fuit arraigne de ce que il avait fait un commission de part le Roy et l'avait pris un auncient seal d'un auncient patent et par subtilty avait mis a cel commission par quel il avoit cuile money des gentes en pais par colour de cel commission et issint avoit enveigle plusours des subjects le Roy et il (quidant que ce ne ust estre qe trespass) dit que il ce ne poit dedire et pria de faire fine. Et pur ce que il avait son seal et tout en nature d'un commission et l'avait use avant come il ust faux le seale le Roy fuit trahe et pendus.

Indictment of notorious highway robbers as traitors, 1401–2: P.R.O., K.B. 9/189/10

Inquisitio capta apud Westm' coram domino rege termino Pasche anno regni regis Henrici post conquestum Anglie tertio [quarti.] Middlesexia.

Item presentant quod Robertus Twygge, Alexander Forster, Johannes Smyth de Wycombe, David Boteler alias dictus White, Petrus Bernewell, Thomas Betewang, Johannes Meryton alias dictus Meryngton, Ricardus Gryndere alias dictus Shether, Ricardus Messenger alias dictus Webbe, Johannes White de comitatu Glocestria, webbe, Thomas Draper, thefe, Thomas Andrew alias dictus Andrewe Kelsey, die lune proximo post festum sancti Michaelis anno regni regis Henrici post conquestum Anglie tertio apud Totenham in comitatu Middlecestrie sunt cum aliis felonibus ignotis ut communes incidiatores altarum viarum et depopulatores agrorum in alta via inter villam de Totenham predictam et Londinium iacuerunt in insidiis ad communem populum regni regis Anglie et ligeos ipsius domini regis per viam predictam venientes depredandos et ex totis eorum velle et operibus felonice et proditorie murdrandum, interficiendum et destruendum et principaliter homines legum Anglie, ita quod nulla lex in regno predicto uti poterit. Et sic per huiusmodi incidias felonice et proditorie ut communes felones et proditores domini regis et regni sui ad destruendum et deprecandum quoscumque ligeos domini regis per altas vias Anglie pretereuntes die anno locis et comitatu predictis quemdam hominem ignotum de viginti marcis argenti in pecunia numerata felonice et proditorie ibidem depredati fuerunt. Et quod predicti Robertus Twygge, Alexander et omnes alii sunt communes proditores et notarii latrones, depopulatores agrorum et incidiatores altarum viarum ad communem populum domini regis per altas vias ad diversa mercata infra comitatum predictum transeuntem et cultores agrorum circa culturas suas laborantes felonice et proditorie depredandos, interficiendos, murdrandos et destruendos in maximam destruccionem populi domini regis et legis Anglie destruccionem. Et tanquam proditores insurrexerunt causis supradictis die anno loco et comitatu predictis.

Over the names of the first nine accused there appears the interlineation 'ponit se culpabilis'.

An indictment similar to the one above: P.R.O., K.B. 9/189/34.

Juratores presentant quod Robertus Pechell, capellanus de Claxby et Willelmus atte Ree de Herefordstok sunt cum aliis proditoribus et felonibus ignotis ut communes insidiatores viarum et depopulatores agrorum felonice et proditorie machinantes qualiter et quomodo pauperes agricolas circa eorum culturam laborantes ac alios ligeos domini regis per altas vias Anglie transeuntes felonice et proditorie depredari et murdrare ac legem regni regis Anglie ... quantum cum eis est ... destruere, die dominica in festo dominie in Ramispalmarum anno regni domini regis nunc tercio per altam viam iuxta Iseldon felonice et proditorie iacuerunt in insidiis et adventum Nicholai Potter et aliorum ibidem expectancium et ipsum ibidem de uno mazere ... et aliis bonis et catallis ad valenciam xl s. felonice et proditorie depredati fuerunt.

Over the name of Robertus Pechell there appears the interlineation 'ponit se culpabilis' and over that of Willelmus atte Ree the words 'per Nicholam Pitt et socios suos'.

The *Year Books* touch on the law of treason but rarely. This is the only fifteenth-century statement I have found on forfeiture for treason: *Year Books*, 7 Henry IV Mich. pl. 19 (f. 32).

Markham. Quant un home fait haut treason tout sa terre en fee simple ou en fee taile est seisable et par tiel seisin le Roy ad fee et inheritance et si un home eit droit il aver par petition etc. ... *Markham.* En lever de guerre enconter le Roy si cestuy que leva le guerre soit mort en le bataile ses terres sont seisables et einsement si homme apres treason fait ensue ouster le meere son terre serra seisie.

Indictment of those compassing the death of the king by necromancy, 1440: P.R.O., K.B. 9/72/14.

London.
Inquiratur pro domino rege quod ... Rogerus Bultybrok die mercurie proximo post festum nativitatis sancti Johannis Baptiste anno regni

dicti regis decimo octavo supradicto in parochia et warda predictis et continue ab illo die usque diem jovis in tertia septimania quadragesima tunc proximo futurum per assensum et preceptum dictorum Alianore (*ducissa Gloucestrie*) et Thome Southewell eisdem die mercuris et parochia prefata, Rogerus Bultybrok facilis in dictis artibus magicis nigromancie et astronomie, assidue laboravit de nativitate dicti regis et dependenciis eiusdem nativitatis ad sciendum quando idem rex moreret licet iuxta determinationem sacrosancte ecclesie ac doctrinam diversorum doctorum cuilibet ligeo domini regis de intromittendo de regibus et principibus in forma predicta absque eorum voluntate et precepto inhibitum fuit et postquam dictus Rogerus sic fecit. Idem Rogerus Bultybrok vicesimo septimo die octobris anno regni dicti regis decimo novo apud Londoniam in parochia sancti Sepulcri in warda de Faryndon extra per assensum et voluntatem predicti Thome Southewell prefato Rogero adtunc ibidem datos, cuidam Johanni Solers, armigero, et multis aliis de populo domini regis felonice et proditorie manifestavit et detegit quod idem Rogerus Bultybrok per calculationem suam per ipsum in forma predicta factam bene scivit quod idem rex non diu viveret sed infra breve obiret ad intencionem quod per detectionem et huiusmodi manifestationem ... ab ipso rege cordialem amorem retraherent et idem rex per notitiam illarum detectionis et manifestationis caperet talem tristitiam in corde suo iidem per illarum tristitam ac dolorem cicius moreret.

The indictment of William Collingbourne, as Gairdner noted, is not to be found among the records of the king's bench. Croke however was able to offer a version; it may well be authentic:

London, Hillar. 2. Richard III.

Willelmus Collingbourn nuper de Lydyard in comitatu Wiltescirie, armiger, et alii falsi proditores mortem Regis et subjectionem regni proditorie imaginaverunt et compassi fuerunt: Et ad perimplendum excitaverunt etc. quendam Tho. Yate ei offerendo octo libras ad partes transmarinas exire ad loquendum ibidem cum Henrico nuncupante se Comit. Richmundiae et aliis etc. proditorie attincti per Parliamentum etc. Ad dicendum. Quod ipsi cum omni potestate etc. revenirent in Angliam citra festum Sancti Lucae Evangelistae; Et totum integrum redditum totius regni Angliae etc. de Termino Sancti Michaelis etc. in eorum relevamen haberent: Et ulterius ad demonstrandum eis, Quod per concilium ipsius Willelmus Collingbourn sic dictus comes Richmundiae et alii etc. ad terram Angliae apud Poole in Comitatu Dorcestriae arrivare voluerunt. Ipse Willelmus Collingbourn et alii proditores eis associando commotionem populi ipsius Regis insurrectionem et guerram erga ipsum Regem interim levare causarent; et partem ipsorum falsorum proditorum contra Regem in omnibus acciperent; et omnia infra regnum Angliae ad eorum dispositionem essent; Et ulterius ad dicendum et demonstrandum dictis proditoribus etc. ad destinandum Johannem Cheyney usque ad Regem Franciae ad demonstrandum sibi quod ambassiatores sui in Angliam a dicto Rege Franciae venientes defraudari debeant: Et quod Rex Angliae nullum promissum eis custodiret; sed solummodo ad deponendum seu ad respectuandum guerram inter Dominum Regem tempore Hiemali: Eo quod in principio temporis Aestivalis Anglica potestas in omnibus preparari possit ad bellum dicto Domino Regi Franciae praebendum et eundem Regem et terram suam adtunc finaliter distruendo. Et ulterius ad advisandum ipsum Regem Franciae ad auxilium dictorum proditorum pecuniis etc. Ut ipse iter Regis Angliae usque terram Franciae impedire proponet. Et sic praedictus Willelmus Collingbourn et alii fuerunt proditorie adhaerentes etc. Et quod praedictus Willelmus Collingbourn etc. alii falsi proditores Deum praeoculis etc. a diutino tempore intendens per Covinam, assensum et voluntatem diversorum aliorum proditorum eisdem proditoribus adhaerentium etc. associaverunt. Et mortem Regis per guerram, commotionem et discordiam inter Regem et ligeos suos infra regnum Angliae levandum compassi fuerunt etc. Et ad illud perimplendum praedictus Willelmust Collingbourn et alii diversas billas et scripturas in rythmis et balladis de murmurationibus, seditionibus et loquelis et proditoriis excitationibus, falso et proditorie fecerunt, scripserunt et fabricaverunt et illas per ripsos sic factas scriptas et fabricatas die super diversa ostia Ecclesiae Cathedralis sancti Pauli London proditorie posuerunt et publice ibidem fixerunt ad movendum et excitandum ligeos Regis billas et scripturas illas legentes et intelligentes commotionem et guerram erga ipsum Regem facere et levare contra ligeanciae suae debitum et finalem destructionem Regis et subversionem regni etc.

The Third Part of the Reports of Sir George Croke,
ed. H. Grimston (London, 1683), ppl 122–3.

SELECT BIBLIOGRAPHY

PRIMARY SOURCES

C.47   Chancery, Miscellanea.
C.49   Chancery, Parliamentary and Council Proceedings.
C.81   Chancery, Warrants for the Great Seal, Series I.
E.37   Exchequer, Treasury of the Receipt, Marshalsea Court Rolls.
E.175   Exchequer, King's Remembrancer, Parliamentary and Council
      Proceedings.
E.403   Exchequer of Receipt, Issue Rolls.
E.404   Exchequer of Receipt, Warrants for Issues.
J.I.1   Justices Itinerant, Assize Rolls.
J.I.3   Justices Itinerant, Gaol Delivery Rolls.
K.B.9   King's Bench, Ancient Indictments.
K.B.27   King's Bench, Coram Rege Rolls.
K.B.29   King's Bench, Controlment Rolls.
S.C.8   Special Collections, Ancient Petitions.

PRINTED SOURCES

RECORDS

Abbrevatio Placitorum. Richard I to Edward II. Rec. Comm., 1811.
Agarde's Indexes (P.R.O. Literary Search Room).
Annual Reports of the Deputy Keeper of the Public Records.
Calendar of . . . Various Chancery Rolls.
Calendar of . . . Close Rolls.
Calendar of Documents relating to Scotland. Ed. J. Bain. Edinburgh,
    1881–4.
Calendar of . . . Fine Rolls.
Calendarium Inquisitionum post mortem sive Excaetarum. Ed. J. Caley and
    J. Bayley, Rec. Comm., 1806–28.
Calendar of Inquisitions Miscellaneous (Chancery) . . .
Calendar of Inquisitions post mortem *and other Analogous Documents.*
Calendar of Letter Books . . . of the City of London.
Calendar of Letters and Papers, Foreign and Domestic, Henry VIII.
Calendar of . . . Papal Registers.
Calendar of . . . Patent Rolls.
Documents and Records Illustrating the History of Scotland. Ed. F.
    Palgrave. London, 1837.

Documents Illustrative of the History of Scotland. Ed. J. Stevenson. Edinburgh, 1870.

Foedera, Conventiones, Litterae etc. Ed. T. Rymer. Original and Rec. Comm. editions as stated.

Historical Manuscripts Commission, Reports.

Issues of the Exchequer. Henry III–Henry VI. Ed. F. Devon. London, 1837.

Memoranda de Parliamento. Records of the Parliament holden . . . in . . . A.D. 1305. Ed. F. W. Maitland. R.S. 1893.

Monumenta Germaniae Historica, Legum. Ed. A. Boretius. Hanover, 1883.

Parliamentary Writs and Writs of Military Summons. Ed. F. Palgrave. Rec. Comm., 1827–34.

A perfect copy of all summons of the nobility to the Great Councils and Parliaments of the Realm. Ed. W. Dugdale. London, 1685.

Proceedings and Ordinances of the Privy Council. Ed. N. H. Nicolas. Rec. Comm., 1834–7.

Rotuli Parliamentorum. Ed. J. Strachey and others. London, 1767.

Select Cases in the Court of the King's Bench, I–VI. Ed. G. O. Sayles. Seld. Soc., 1936–65.

Statutes of the Realm. Rec. Comm., 1810–28.

The Third Part of the Reports of Sir George Croke. Ed. H. Grimston. London, 1683.

Year Books (a) *Les Reports del Cases en Ley.* References are to the edition of London, 1678–9 unless stated otherwise. (b) R.S. (c) Seld. Soc.

LEGAL TREATISES

Bracton, H. *Henrici de Bracton de Legibus et Consuetudinibus Angliae.* (a) Ed. G. E. Woodbine. New Haven, 1915–42. (b) Ed. T. Twiss. R.S., 1878–83.

    Note Book. Ed. F. W. Maitland. London, 1887.

Britton. Ed. F. M. Nichols. Oxford, 1865.

Coke, E. *The Third Part of the Institutes of the Laws of England.* London, 1797.

Fitzherbert, A. *La Graunde Abridgement.* London, 1516.

Fleta, II, Prologue, Bk. I, Bk. II. Ed. H. G. Richardson and G. O. Sayles. Seld. Soc., 1953.

Fortescue, J. *De Laudibus Legum Anglie.* Ed. S. B. Chrimes. Cambridge, 1942.

Glanvill. (a) *De Legibus et Consuetudinibus Regni Angliae.* Ed. G. E. Woodbine. New Haven, 1922. (b) *Tractatus de Legibus et Consuetudinibus Regni Angliae qui Glanvilla vocatur.* Ed. G. D. G. Hall. London, 1965.

Hale, M. *Historia Placitorum Coronae: the History of the Pleas of the Crown.* Ed. Sollom Emlyn. London, 1736 and 1778.
Hengham, R. *Radulphi de Hengham Summae.* Ed. W. H. Dunham. Cambridge, 1932.
The Mirror of Justices. Ed. W. J. Whittaker. Seld. Soc., 1895.
Smith, T. *De Republica Anglorum.* Ed. L. Alston. Cambridge, 1906.

CHRONICLES

Annales Monastici. Ed. H. R. Luard. R.S., 1864-9.
Anonimalle Chronicle. Ed. V. H. Galbraith. Manchester, 1926.
Baker, Galfridi le. *Chronicon Galfridi le Baker.* Ed. F. M. Thompson. Oxford, 1889.
Brakelond, Jocelin of. *The Chronicle of Jocelin of Brakelond.* Ed. H. E. Butler. London, 1949.
The Brut. Ed. F. W. D. Brie. Early English Text Society, 1906.
Canterbury, Gervase of. *Gervase of Canterbury: Historical Works.* Ed. W. Stubbs. R.S., 1879-80.
Chronicle of the Abbey of Croyland. Ed. H. T. Riley. London, 1854.
Chronicle of the Grey Friars of London. Ed. J. G. Nichols. Camden Soc., 1851.
Chronicles of London. Ed. C. L. Kingsford. London, 1905.
Chronicles of the Reigns of Edward I and Edward II. Ed. W. Stubbs. R.S., 1882-3.
Chronicon Angliae. Ed. E. M. Thompson. R.S., 1874.
Chronicon de Lanercost. Ed. J. Stevenson. Bannatyne Club, 1839.
Continuation of the Chronicle of Florence of Worcester. Ed. B. Thorpe. English Historical Society, 1849.
The English Chronicle from 1377 to 1461. Ed. J. S. Davies. Camden Soc., 1856.
Eulogium Historiarum. Ed. F. S. Haydon. R.S., 1863.
Fabyan, Robert. *Newe Chronycles of England and of France.* Ed. H. Ellis. London, 1811.
Flores Historiarum. Ed. H. R. Luard. R.S., 1890.
Fordun, Johannis de. *Chronica Gentis Scotorum.* Ed. W. F. Skene. Edinburgh, 1871-2.
Gray, Thomas. *Scalacronica of Sir Thomas Gray of Heton, Knight.* The edition is that of the Maitland Club, 1836, unless stated otherwise.
The Great Chronicle of London. Ed. A. H. Thomas and I. D. Thornley. London, 1938.
Gregory, William. *Gregory's Chronicle.* Ed. J. Gairdner. Camden Soc., 1876.
Guisborough, Walter of. *The Chronicle of Walter of Guisborough.* Ed. H. Rothwell. Camden Soc., 1957.

242 SELECT BIBLIOGRAPHY

Hall, Edward. *Chronicle.* Ed. H. Ellis. London, 1809.
Higden, Ranulphus. *Polychronicon Ranulphi Higden.* Ed. C. Babington and J. R. Lumby. R.S., 1865–86.
Historia Anglicana. Ed. H. T. Riley. R.S., 1863–4.
Historia Vitae et Regni Ricardi Secundi. Ed. T. Hearne. Oxford, 1729.
Historians of the Church of York. Ed. J. Raine. R.S., 1894.
Holinshed, Raphael. *Chronicles of England, Scotland and Ireland.* London 1808.
Langtoft, Pierre de. *Chronicle of Pierre de Langtoft.* Ed. T. Wright. R.S., 1866.
Letters and Papers illustrative of the Wars of the English in France. Ed. J. Stevenson. R.S. 1864.
Murimuth, Adam and Avesbury, Robert. *Chronica.* Ed. E. M. Thompson. R.S., 1889.
Paris, Matthew. *Chronica Majora.* Ed. H. R. Luard. R.S., 1872–83.
Rishanger, William. *Wilhelmi Rishanger, Chronica et Annales.* Ed. H. T. Riley. R.S., 1865.
Six Town Chronicles. Ed. R. Flenley. Oxford, 1911.
Song of Lewes. Ed. C. L. Kingsford. Oxford, 1890.
Stow, John. *Annales or a Generall Chronicle of England.* Ed. E. Howes. London, 1631.
Three Fifteenth Century Chronicles. Ed. J. Gairdner. Camden Soc., 1880.
Trivet, Nicholas. *Annales Nicholai Trivet.* Ed. T. Hog. English Historical Society, 1845.
Trokelowe, John de and Blaneforde, Henry de. *Johannis de Trokelowe et Henrici de Blaneforde, Chronica et Annales.* Ed. H. T. Riley. R.S., 1866.
Vita Edwardi Secundi. Ed. N. Denholm-Young. London, 1957.
Warkworth, John. *A Chronicle of the First Thirteen Years of the Reign of King Edward the Fourth.* Ed. J. O. Halliwell. Camden Soc., 1839.
Whethamstede, John. *Registrum Abbatiae Johannis Whethamstede.* Ed. H. T. Riley. R.S., 1872.

SECONDARY SOURCES

Attenborough, F. L. (ed.) *The Laws of the Earliest English Kings.* Cambridge, 1922.
Aubert, F. *Parlement de Paris de l'origine à François I.* Paris, 1894.
Baldwin, J. F. *The King's Council in England during the Middle Ages.* Oxford, 1913.
Barrow, G. W. S. *Robert Bruce and the Community of the Realm of Scotland.* London, 1965.

Bellamy, J. G. 'The Coterel gang: an anatomy of a band of fourteenth century criminals'. *Eng. Hist. Rev.*, LXXIX. 1964.
'The Northern Rebellions in the later years of Richard II'. *Bulletin of the John Rylands Library*, XLVII. 1965.
'Appeal and Impeachment in the Good Parliament'. *Bulletin of the Institute of Historical Research*, XXXIX. 1966.
Bird, R. *The Turbulent London of Richard II.* London, 1949.
Brissaud, J. *Manuel d'histoire du droit Français.* Paris, 1898.
Calisse, C. *History of Italian Law.* London, 1914.
Chrimes, S. B. 'Richard II's Questions to the Judges, 1387'. *Law Quarterly Review*, LXXII. 1956.
Clarke, M. V. *Fourteenth Century Studies.* Ed. L. S. Sutherland and M. McKisack. Oxford, 1937.
Dumont, C. E. *Justice Criminelle des Duchés de Lorraine et de Bar, du Bassigny et des Trois Évêchés.* Nancy, 1848.
Esmein, A. *History of Continental Criminal Procedure.* London, 1914.
Flaherty, W. E. 'The Great Rebellion in Kent of 1381 illustrated from the Public Records'. *Archaeologia Cantiana*, III. 1860.
Gairdner, J. *The Life and Reign of Richard III.* Cambridge, 1898.
Harcourt, L. W. Vernon. *His Grace the Steward and the Trial of Peers.* London, 1907.
'The Baga de Secretis'. *Eng. Hist. Rev.*, XXIII. 1908.
Harriss, G. L. 'The Commons' Petitions of 1340'. *Eng. Hist. Rev.*, 1963.
Haskins, G. L. 'Executive Justice and the Rule of Law'. *Speculum*, XXX. 1955.
Henderson, E. F. *Historical Documents of the Middle Ages.* London, 1896.
Holdsworth, W. S. *History of English Law.* 3rd edition, London, 1923.
Holmes, G. A. 'Judgment on the Younger Despenser'. *Eng. Hist. Rev.*, LXX. 1955.
Jolliffe, J. E. A. *Angevin Kingship.* London, 1955.
Keen, M. H. 'Treason Trials under the Law of Arms'. *Trans. Roy. Hist. Soc.* 5th ser. XII. 1962.
The Laws of War in the Late Middle Ages. London, 1965.
Kern, F. *Kingship and Law in the Middle Ages.* Oxford, 1939.
Lander, J. R. 'Attainder and Forfeiture, 1453 to 1509'. *Historical Journal*, IV. 1961.
Lear, F. S. *Treason in Roman and Germanic Law.* Austin, 1965.
Lyon, B. *A Constitutional and Legal History of Medieval England.* New York, 1960.
Lyte, H. C. M. *The Great Seal.* London, 1926.
McFarlane, K. B. 'Had Edward I a policy toward the Earls?'. *History*, L. 1965.
McKisack, M. *The Fourteenth Century.* Oxford, 1959.

Maitland, F. W. *Bracton and Azo*. Seld. Soc., 1895.
Constitutional History of England. Cambridge, 1908.
Myers, A. R. 'The Captivity of a Royal Witch'. *Bulletin of the John Rylands Library*, XXIV. 1940.
Paston Letters. Ed. J. Gairdner. Edinburgh, 1910.
Pickthorn, K. W. M. *Early Tudor Government: Henry VII*. Cambridge, 1934.
Plucknett, T. F. T. 'The Relations between Roman Law and English Common Law down to the Sixteenth Century'. *University of Toronto Law Journal*, III. 1939.
'The Origin of Impeachment'. *Trans. Roy. Hist. Soc.*, 4th ser. XXIV. 1942.
'The Impeachments of 1376'. *Trans. Roy. Hist. Soc.*, 5th ser. I. 1951.
'State Trials under Richard II'. *Trans. Roy. Hist. Soc.*, 5th ser. II. 1952.
'Impeachment and Attainder'. *Trans. Roy. Hist. Soc.*, 5th ser. III. 1953.
A Concise History of the Common Law. 5th edition. London, 1956.
Pollock, F. and Maitland, F. W. *The History of English Law before the time of Edward I*. Cambridge, 1895.
Post, G. 'Two notes on Nationalism in the Middle Ages'. *Traditio*, IX. 1953.
Powell, E. *The Rising in East Anglia*. Cambridge, 1896.
Powicke, F. M. *The Thirteenth Century*. Oxford, 1953.
Putnam, B. H. *Proceedings before the Justices of the Peace in the Fourteenth and Fifteenth Centuries, Edward III to Richard III*. London, 1938.
The Place in Legal History of Sir William Shareshull. Cambridge, 1950.
Réville, A. *Le Soulèvement des Travailleurs d'Angleterre en 1381*. Paris, 1898.
Rezneck, S. 'The Early History of the Parliamentary Declaration of Treason'. *Eng. Hist. Rev.*, XLII. 1927.
'Constructive treason by words in the fifteenth century'. *American Historical Review*, XXXIII. 1927–8.
Richardson, H. G. *Bracton. The Problem of his Text*. Seld. Soc., 1965.
'John Oldcastle in Hiding, August–October 1417'. *Eng. Hist. Rev.*, LV. 1940.
Richardson, H. G. and Sayles, G. O. *Law and Legislation from Aethelberht to Magna Carta*. Edinburgh, 1966.
Robertson, A. J. (ed.) *The Laws of the Kings of England from Edmund to Henry I*. Cambridge, 1925.

Roskell, J. S. 'Sir William Oldhall, Speaker in the Parliament of 1450–1'. *Nottingham Medieval Studies*, v. 1961.

Ross, C. D. 'Forfeiture for Treason in the reign of Richard II'. *Eng. Hist. Rev.*, LXXI. 1956.

Schultz, F. 'Bracton on Kingship'. *Eng. Hist. Rev.* LX. 1945.

Scofield, C. L. *The Life and Reign of Edward IV*. London, 1923.

Somerville, R. *History of the Duchy of Lancaster*. Vol. I. London, 1953.

State Trials. Ed. T. B. Howell. London, 1816.

Stephen, J. F. *A History of the Criminal Law of England*. London, 1883.

Stones, E. L. G. 'The Folvilles of Ashby-Folville, Leicestershire, and their associates in crime, 1326–41'. *Trans. Roy. Hist. Soc.*, 5th ser. VII. 1957.

Stubbs, W. *The Constitutional History of England*. Oxford. The edition of 1874–8 is used unless stated otherwise.

Studies in Medieval History presented to F. M. Powicke. Ed. R. W. Hunt, W. A. Pantin and R. W. Southern. Oxford, 1948.

Thornley, I. D. 'Treason by words in the Fifteenth Century'. *Eng. Hist. Rev.*, XXXII. 1917.

'The Act of Treasons of 1352'. *History*, VI. 1921.

Timbal, P. C. 'La Confiscation dans le Droit Français des XIIIe et XIVe siècles'. *Revue Historique de Droit Français*, XIX–XXI. 1940–2.

Tout, T. F. *Chapters in the Administrative History of Medieval England*. Manchester, 1920–33.

Ullmann, W. 'The Development of the Medieval Idea of Sovereignty'. *Eng. Hist. Rev.*, LXIV. 1949.

The Principles of Government and Politics in the Middle Ages. London, 1961.

Van Caeneghem, R. C. (ed.) *Royal Writs in England from the Conquest to Glanvill*. Seld. Soc., 1959.

Von Bar, C. L. *A History of Continental Criminal Law*. London, 1916.

Wilkinson, B. *Constitutional History of Medieval England, 1216–1399*. London, 1952.

RECORD SERIES

Oxford City Documents. Ed. J. E. Thorold Rogers. Oxford Historical Society, 1891.

Virgoe, R. 'Some Ancient Indictments in the King's Bench referring to Kent, 1450–2'. *Kent Records*, XVIII. 1964.

INDEX

INDEX

247

attainder by act of parliament (*contd.*)
  particular acts: of 1400, 183; of
    1403, 185, 194; of 1406, 188; of
    1410, 188; of 1424, 195; of 1450,
    97, 186–7, 192; of 1451, 187, 192;
    of 1453, 186, 187 n.1, 196; of 1459,
    97, 177, 187, 194, 199, 203; of
    1478, 212; of 1484, 202; of 1495,
    196–7
  posthumously, 124, 183, 184, 186,
    187
  record of the king as basis of, 165
  setting degree of forfeiture by, *see*
    forfeiture
  supplementing common law judge-
    ments by, 137, 195, 204
  supplementing outlawry by, 203
  suspended, 126
  touching lands of dead traitors, 137,
    184
attainted provably of open fact by
  men of own condition, 89, 109,
    132
atteindre, 177
attired in manner of war, 62
Audley, Hugh, the younger, 49
Audley, John, lord, 199, 202
Aylesbury, Franciscan convent of,
  117, 164

Ba, William de, 42n.
Bagot, Henry, 99
Baker, Geoffrey le, 74
Baker, William, 73
Bakere, John, 142
Baldock, 116
Ball, John, 139
Balliol, John, king of Scots, 27, 29 n.3,
  31, 32, 36, 37, 206
Balsshalf, William, 145
banners, displaying of, 35, 36, 37, 47,
  48, 49, 51, 62, 67, 71 n.2, 75 n.2,
  95, 104, 199, 200, 201, 202
Bardolf, Thomas, lord, 159, 170 n.1,
  180, 182, 183, 188, 192, 202
Barnet, battle of, 193
Barons' wars (1264–7), 27, 28, 32, 34
Barton, Elizabeth, *see* Nun of Kent
Basset, Sir Ralph, 52
Bath and Wells, Robert Stillington,
  bishop of, 119
battle, trial by, *see* trial
Baynard, John, 118

Baysio, Guido de, 10
Bealknap, Sir Robert, C. J. C. P., 138,
  167, 233
Beams, 69, 91
Beauchamp, Sir John, 221
Beauchamp, William, 68
Baumont, Henry de, 47
Beaumont, Louis de, bishop of
  Durham, 47
Beche, Margery de la, 69–71, 87, 91
Beche, Sir Nicholas de la, 69
Becherel, 110
Bedemansone, John, 235
Bedford, John, duke of, 159, 172
Belmyn, William, 121
Belsham, John, 146
benefit of clergy, *see* clergy
Benningholme (Yorks.), 106
Bermondsey, 120
Bernard, John, 145
Berners, Sir John, 221
Bernewell, Peter, 235
Berwick, 45, 159
Betewang, Thomas, 235
Biller, Master William, king's pro-
  moter of all causes before judges
  of the constableship and admir-
  alty, 162
Billing, Thomas, 197
Birmingham, Richard de, 51 n.3
Black Death, 86
Blackheath, 140, 175
Blake, Thomas, 127
Blanot, Jean de, 11
blood feuds, 60
Bloreheath, battle of, 97, 124, 187,
  198, 199, 202, 204
Blount, Sir Thomas, 156, 164, 192 n.1
Blount, Sir William, 81
Bocking, John, 197 n.3
Bodrugan, Henry, 164
Bolingbroke, Roger, 126, 127, 128,
  149, 153, 154, 236
Bologna, 3
Boniface VIII, pope, 31, 48, 57, 206
Boroughbridge, battle of, 49, 60
Boston, 68
Boteler, David, 235
Boteler, Isabel, 125, 133, 189 n.2
Botelisford, William de, 62
Botharm, William de, 42
Boughton (Kent), 103
Bourchier, Sir William, 150